SILENT REBELS

SILENT REBELS

THE TRUE STORY OF THE RAID ON
THE TWENTIETH TRAIN TO AUSCHWITZ

Marion Schreiber

With a foreword by Paul Spiegel
Translated by Shaun Whiteside

Atlantic Books
London

First published in Great Britain
in 2003 by Atlantic Books,
an imprint of Grove Atlantic Ltd
Originally published in Germany in
2000 by Aufbau-Verlag as *Stille Rebellen*

Copyright © Marion Schreiber 2000
Foreword copyright © Paul Spiegel 2000
Translation copyright © Shaun
Whiteside 2003

Text design by Lindsay Nash.

1 3 5 7 9 8 6 4 2

A CIP catalogue record for this book is
available from the British Library.

1 903809 89 4

Printed in Great Britain by
CPD, Ebbw Vale, Wales

Atlantic Books
An imprint of Grove Atlantic Ltd
Ormond House
26 –27 Boswell Street
London WC1N 3JZ

To my sons Till, Benjamin and Jonas

CONTENTS

LIST OF ILLUSTRATIONS

Picture credits are shown in brackets.

1. Youra Livchitz
2. Robert Maistriau
3. Jean 'Pamplemousse' Franklemon
4. Youra with Marcel Hastir and Henriette Vander Hecht at summer camp, 1937
5. Youra and Minnie Minet
6. 'Free University' of Brussels (*Felix Engel*)
7. The Jospa family, 1945
8. Jean Franklemon's sister on her wedding day, 1942
9. Rachel Livchitz after the war, with the son of Lily Allègre
10. Alexandre 'Choura' Livchitz's farewell letter to his mother (*Fort Breendonk Archive*)
11. Robert Maistriau at the spot where the raid took place (*Felix Engel*)
12. Mendelis and Henda Goldsteinas on Avenue Louise
13. Memorial at former Gestapo Headquarters, 453 Avenue Louise (*Felix Engel*)
14. Claire Prowizur and her husband Philippe, 1951
15. Labour Deployment Order (*Service des Victimes de la Guerre*)
16. Ita Gronowski
17. Simon Gronowski with his parents
18. Detail from the list of deportees (*Service des Victimes de la Guerre*)
19. Régine Krochmal, 1944
20. Philippe Franklemon, Jacques Grauwels, Régine Krochmal, Marion Schreiber, Robert Maistriau, Simon Gronowski (*Wim van Cappellen*)

'Anyone who saves one human life,
saves an entire people.'

If I survived the Holocaust, it was only thanks to those Belgian citizens who were brave enough to take in a little Jewish boy and hide him from the Nazis. My mother, too, escaped being deported because during the German occupation she lived with a Brussels family who not only sheltered her but repeatedly helped her to escape the persecution of the SS.

Belgium is Germany's unknown neighbour. And that is particularly true as regards the chapter of resistance and civil disobedience against the Nazi regime in Belgium. Four thousand children like myself survived the Holocaust living under false identities with families, in boarding schools, monasteries and children's homes. Sixty per cent of the sixty thousand Jews living in Belgium at the time were not deported because they were able to escape the clutches of the German racial fanatics with the help of neighbours, friends and strangers. These Belgians risked imprisonment or even transportation to a concentration camp because they were infringing the laws passed by the German military administration, according to which any help for the persecuted Jews was to be considered a serious crime.

I was two years old when my father, Hugo Spiegel, set off for Belgium to find a safe haven for his family. During the anti-Jewish pogroms in 1938, as a respected cattle-dealer in Warendorf, he had been beaten up by the Nazis. His licence, and thus our basic standard of living, were taken away. For my parents that was the signal to leave Germany, with a view to moving back to the region around Münster once the Nazi horrors had passed. In 1939 my father found lodgings for the four of us in St Gilles, in the home of the butcher Blomme. Shortly after the German invasion of Belgium, my father was arrested in the street and brought to the French internment camp of Gurs, from which he was later deported to Buchenwald, then to Auschwitz and finally to Dachau. He miraculously survived the concentration camps. My mother, whose first name was Ruth, was 'Madame Régine' to her Belgian neighbours. She earned her livelihood by cleaning for Jewish families who at first had been spared deportation because of their Belgian nationality.

My sister Rosa was nine years older than me, and very independent. Our mother had drummed it into her that if she was addressed by a uniformed man she was under no circumstances to say that she was a Jew. One day she went with a friend of my mother's to a place where food cards were distributed. A man in civilian clothes asked the thirteen-year-old girl if she was a Jew. My sister guilelessly replied that she was. Rosa was arrested, and we never heard anything from her again. According to the deportation lists of Mechelen transit camp, she was, along with 130 other children on 24 October 1942, on the fourteenth transport to Auschwitz.

Now my mother looked for a hiding place for me. After a brief stay in a house in Uccle, where about ten children were living in wretched and unhygienic conditions, an organization gave my mother the address of a farmer in Chapelle-lez-Herlaimont, who was prepared to take in a Jewish child. So at the age of five I went to stay with this elderly couple with an adult son, who pretended I was their nephew from Germany. Only the priest in the village, whose services I regularly attended with my Catholic family, knew my true identity. To give me even greater protection against the Nazis, my host parents suggested that I be baptized. But the priest refused. He was not one of those who would use the opportunity to evangelize Jewish children.

I spent three and a half years with those kind farmers. I still clearly remember the American soldiers marching into our little provincial town. My mother had prepared me for that great moment by teaching me the English phrase, 'I am a German Jew'. Now, when I stood at the edge of the street amongst the flag-waving, cheering villagers, a huge tank suddenly stopped, and a black soldier looked down at me. I shouted out my English sentence to him, he bent down to me and lifted me up, kissed me and gave me sweets. I can still remember how terrified I was, and how glad I was when he put me back down on the street.

'He who saves one human life, saves an entire people.' Many Belgian citizens acted according to this saying from the Talmud during the German occupation. I most devoutly hope that their courage and helpfulness will now be made known through Marion Schreiber's book, even beyond Belgium's borders.

Paul Spiegel
President, Central Council of
the Jews in Germany

1 20 January 1943

There was an unusually euphoric atmosphere on Avenue Louise. As if obeying some secret command, people streamed down the wide street to number 453. That cold winter day, they came from all parts of Brussels to witness the unexpected humiliation of the occupying German forces, which was etched in the pale sandstone façade of the apartment building near the city forest. The front of the building was riddled with more than a dozen bullet-holes.

The incredible had happened. On that January morning in 1943, an RAF pilot had dared to fly into Belgian air space. Keeping low in the sky, he thundered across the wide boulevards of Brussels to the Belgian branch of the Reich Security Office or Sicherheitsamt, sprayed the building with shells and gunfire, banked rapidly away and vanished.

His aim was good. None of the neighbouring civilian houses was touched. Only the cream-coloured frontage of this notorious apartment block had been devastated. Windows were shattered, metal frames twisted and the balcony railings had been torn apart. Empty black window frames gaped on the upper storeys.

The crowd drifted slowly past the building. None of them dared to stop, and none of them dared to express their delight. Only the people driving past in the over-crowded tram waved triumphantly to the hordes of strollers. They thought they were safe from attack from the grim, grey-uniformed German policemen who stood in a semi-circle, cordoning off the building. Their whistles and shouted commands, as they tried to make the curious onlookers disperse, were all that disturbed the calm atmosphere.

Youra Livchitz couldn't take his eyes off the ruined façade. He hadn't felt such a feeling of victory for a long time now. The young Jewish physician knew the building's terrible secrets. Friends of his, Resistance fighters, had been tortured and interrogated in that building before they disappeared into prison or labour camps. In the cellar, Jewish men, women and children – arrested in the raids carried out by Hitler's SS lackeys in the Security Police and the Security Service – waited to be transferred to the transit camp at Mechelen. The higher up the building you went, the crueller were the methods employed for the capture and destruction of human beings. It was on the two top floors that the Secret Police – the Geheime Staatspolizei, or Gestapo – had their offices.

That afternoon Livchitz had left work earlier than usual. In the offices and laboratories of Pharmacobel – where he worked as a laboratory manager, since the occupying Germans had forbidden him to practise the medical profession for which he was qualified – the air-raid was the sole topic of conversation. Was this a sign that Nazi rule was coming to an end? For the first time the Germans had shown themselves to be vulnerable. Was it not possible that the concerted power of the Allies might soon achieve what this daring pilot had managed to do all on his own? Even the evening newspaper, *Le Soir*, forced ideologically into line by the Nazis, could no longer conceal the desperate state of the German army in the snow and freezing cold on the Eastern Front. The Wehrmacht units, the newspaper reported, were 'isolated' at Stalingrad, and the target of 'ruthless attacks from the Russians'.

But Youra also heard pessimistic voices. They feared that the humiliated Nazis would react even more violently and intensify their searches and raids to regain their authority of terror. But one thing was certain: the Germans would do anything within their power to ensure that nothing would be written about the pilot's attack on their headquarters.

The young doctor wanted to see first-hand evidence of the defeat of the hated occupying forces; he wanted to hear what the people in the street were saying, even if he had to take risks to do so, since the Germans were sure to tighten up their checks on individuals. If he proved not to be wearing a yellow star, the remainder of his journey was predetermined: he himself would end up in the cellar of this building, the Nazi headquarters, and from there he would be transported to Mechelen transit camp, where the trains set off for Poland. But as always, Youra relied on the fact that he bore not the slightest resemblance to the hook-nosed Nazi caricature of a Jew displayed in the posters for the anti-Bolshevik Exhibition, *Voici les Soviets*, at the Cinquantenaire. Livchitz was tall, athletic and blue-eyed – a type that was very popular with the ladies.

The people here in Avenue Louise, it seemed to the young doctor, were walking taller today than they usually did; they had a calmer, more optimistic look in their eyes. The stiffness of fear had left them. From the excited conversations going on around him, the young doctor learned that the attack must have been carried out by a Belgian pilot, clearly a patriot who knew the area. His precise target had been number 453. And as he flew over Brussels he had dropped the Belgian national flag – banned by the Nazis – over the house of a well-known aristocratic family. The hated German police had clearly suffered casualties. The people living in the neighbouring buildings reported that fire engines and ambulances had been driving back and forth all morning.

Only later was it known throughout Belgium that the raid had been carried out by the thirty-two-year-old Jean de Sélys Longchamp. The Belgian pilot had left his squadron on an RAF reconnaissance mission, to fire on the Gestapo building.

Suddenly Youra flinched. Someone had clapped him on the shoulder. It was Robert Maistriau, his old friend from school. The two young men hadn't seen each other for weeks. Robert had also made the pilgrimage here to witness the disgrace of the German occupiers. Robert, four years younger than his friend, and with wavy blond hair, was unlikely to attract suspicion to Youra as they wandered through the crowd. They were both excited and speculated that this visible defeat of the Germans might be followed by others. And attacks by underground fighters were on the increase. Wasn't the mood of the cold and hungry population becoming increasingly hostile to the occupying forces? Robert had impulsively decided to join one of the Resistance movements. He was bored with his desk job with the metals company Fonofer, where he had started working after abandoning his medical studies. He was dying to find some way of doing damage to the Germans. It wasn't just that everything the Belgians had saved by careful husbandry – food, fabrics or coal – was going to Germany. Now young people were going to be forced to work in German factories to keep the wheels of Hitler's arms industry in motion. Around this time, Robert often found himself thinking about his father. A military doctor, and originally an ardent admirer of German culture, with its poets, musicians and philosophers, he had lost all his respect for the German nation in the First World War, at the Front at Yser. He considered it particularly barbaric that during their invasion in 1914 the Germans had set fire to the precious university library in Leuven with all its irreplaceable books and manuscripts. 'In one way and another,' Maistriau recalls, 'we young people were opposed to the Germans even before the Second World War.'

Robert's great friend Youra, whom he had admired so much in grammar school, was ahead of him now as well. He was active in the Resistance, he told Maistriau, working as a courier. Because he knew his way around some of the hospitals, he had even, along with some young underground fighters, helped to smuggle a hospitalized victim of the Gestapo out of the clinic, while dressed in a doctor's white coat. But unlike his elder brother Alexandre, a convinced Communist who was a member of the armed partisans, Youra still hadn't joined up with any particular group. As an intellectual free spirit he abhorred all forms of compulsion, and didn't want to be tied down by any one organization or ideology.

All of a sudden German policemen forced their way into the crowd, some of them with Alsatians straining on their leashes. They had clearly received instructions to break up the gathering. They grabbed a few curious onlookers and marched them off. High time for Youra to get away. The two school-friends still lived in the same district, near their former grammar school in Uccle. So they took the twenty-minute walk back together.

From the third floor of number 453 Avenue Louise, Judenreferent Kurt Asche watched the crowd slowly dispersing. Over the course of the day the Nazi official had come to the window several times to peer out through the shattered panes and down upon the activity below. The sight of such cheerful people sent him into a fury. To avoid being seen, the little man with the pinched expression stayed back in the darkness of his office, which had, by some miracle, been unharmed.

Asche was Adolf Eichmann's representative in Belgium. And as a 'Referent' – an expert in Jewish matters – and an SS Obersturmführer he enjoyed the privilege of an office on this magnificent boulevard, with a view of the park of the Abbaye de la Cambre. That morning, when the plane came roaring down towards the building, several of his other colleagues had gone running to the window to find out where the deafening noise was coming from. Some of them had paid for their curiosity by being seriously injured or even killed.

At around midday a telegram had been sent to Berlin. It informed the Reichssicherheitshauptamt – Reich Security Headquarters, or RSHA – of the attack by 'a low-flying English plane on the Chancellery building'. They reported five serious injuries and four fatalities. One of Asche's good friends had been hit. This was unfortunate for the Judenreferent, because he had got on very well with this colleague from division IVc. Every now and again they had, for a fee, struck affluent Jews off the list of deportees and sold them French passports. Who would fill that post now? the Obersturmführer wondered. He couldn't possibly afford his extravagant night-life, his trips to the brothels of Brussels and his alcoholic evenings in the low dives of the city on his salary alone. Asche's greed exceeded even his anti-Semitism.

He was left cold by the fact that the head of the Security Service, Alfred Thomas, had been fatally injured by a shell while sitting at his mahogany desk. Thomas's widow in Stettin and his children would now receive the highest compensation from the dependents' fund in the Party coffers. Asche could not have known that the following day his superior's widow would bring a third son into the world, Günther Alfred, born on 21 January 1943.

There was a possibility that the SS Sturmbannführer's death would give Asche, his subordinate, the chance of the promotion that he so longed for. His ambition was aroused. After all, he had already deputized for Thomas at important discussions in the capital of the Reich, as for example in June 1942 at a discussion with Adolf Eichmann, the architect of the 'Final Solution'. At that time he and his colleagues from Paris and The Hague had received an order for 'large numbers of Jews from the occupied Western zones to be transferred to Auschwitz concentration camp for use as labour'.

Since then Asche had put his shoulder to the wheel. Nineteen transports and around 16,000 deportees had already left Belgium by now, the most recent train leaving on 15 January. It was as though the 'evacuees', as they were referred to in the jargon of the Nazi bureaucrats, had vanished from the face of the earth. Now Kurt Asche, stepping into Thomas's shoes, would have to organize the next transport, the twentieth convoy.

Down in the cellar of the elegant building, with its ruined façade, sat a dainty young woman in a nurse's uniform. The previous night lovely Régine Krochmal had fallen into the net of the '*voleurs de la vie*', as she called Kurt Asche's manhunters. The twenty-two-year-old was a member of the 'Austrian Liberation Front', a group of Jewish Resistance fighters who distributed flyers in an attempt to inform Wehrmacht soldiers in Belgium about Hitler's true intentions. 'Fairly primitive agitation material,' according to Régine's then fellow fighter Hans Mayer, who became famous as a writer after the war under the name of Jean Améry: 'I have reason to suppose that the grey-uniformed soldiers immediately picked up our duplicated writings, which they found in front of their barracks, and passed them on to their superiors with a click of their heels; and that they in turn, with the same dutiful promptness, passed them on to the security authorities.'

During the night of 20 January, Régine and her Austrian friends had run off the copies of their newspaper *Truth*. As always, she was wearing her nurse's uniform with its blue bonnet. 'That was my best disguise,' she explains, decades after these experiences. 'It got me through all the checks, and I wasn't subjected to any curfews.' At about midnight the young people became aware of a car parked on the other side of the street from their house. That was unusual in this neighbourhood, especially since the Germans had commandeered almost all Belgian cars. It was true that Bobby, the tenant of the apartment, had an Argentinian passport. But if the SS police found their little printing operation, they faced torture and possibly execution.

They hastily hid the precious duplicating machine, their paper and their matrices. Then the two friends escaped through the window facing the garden. Régine went to bed. When the knock came she answered the door as though she had been woken from sleep. A man had brought her to the flat, she explained to the two men in their long leather coats, and left her here alone so that she would have a roof over her head for this night at least. Régine identified herself as a Jew. And the men, happy to have found such easy prey, neglected to search the flat for anything else.

By the early hours of the morning the door of the cellar of number 453 Avenue Louise was opened over and over again to receive other depressed and despairing new arrivals. It was past midnight – when their victims, woken from their deep sleep, no longer had a chance to escape – that the ruthless hunters came into their own.

Shortly after nine o'clock in the morning the noise of gunfire stopped, and Régine heard the guards running and shouting in the corridor. For a moment she considered escaping. More than fifty years later she is still wondering whether she did the right thing. 'I thought, there's no point, they're nearby and they're furious, they'll kill you.' She stayed put.

Before the Nazis' racial laws put Régine out of work in the summer of 1942, she had finished her training as a nurse and midwife. She loved her job. She couldn't imagine anything finer than standing by the mothers-to-be and helping babies into the world. And she remembered a night in the hospital at Etterbeek when she, the apprentice nurse, helped to deliver a child along with a young assistant physician. The handsome, dark-haired doctor had made a lasting impression on her. 'A man you could have fallen in love with,' she remembers. He was Youra Livchitz.

2 Youra Livchitz

The little flat was soon filled with dense smoke and heated discussions, as it was every Saturday evening. The bohemians of Brussels crammed their way into Minnie Minet's drawing room: artists, intellectuals and pretty young girls in short pleated skirts and long, tight-fitting jackets, in the style of the 'zazous', the swing-loving youth of the capital. This regular date at the home of the exotic pianist was for many people the only gleam of light in an otherwise grim week. The walls of the flat were papered with photographs of works by Minnie's artist friends. And the musical interludes of the guests were anything but amateur. Some of the soloists, like the violinist Arthur Grumiaux, would later become world famous.

Here, in the Rue Van Goidtsnoven, they were among like-minded people. They came together to make music, to listen to music and above all to talk. After all, talking openly with one another – the longer the German occupying forces made the whole country hold its breath – was even more important even than their beloved music.

Somehow one of the habitués always managed to get hold of some wine or even coffee. Minnie's Javanese preparation of the precious beans was a sensation. They were ground with a mill, and then, in a procedure that seemed to last for hours, Minnie poured tiny quantities of water on to the coffee powder. The filtered result was black and thick, and could only be enjoyed with a great deal of milk. The soup that stood in a big pot so that the guests could serve themselves was made communally by everyone. Everyone brought what they had: rice, vegetables or potatoes, perhaps even a piece of meat that someone had managed to get hold of. From one wartime month to the next the soup grew thinner and thinner.

Their plump and shapely little hostess, with her high cheekbones and slanted cat's eyes – the daughter of an Indonesian woman and a Dutchman – was a rather unusual phenomenon in hidebound, bourgeois Brussels. She was bubbly, spontaneous and sexy. She insisted that the kiss she was given as a greeting was placed on each of her deep dimples. Was she thirty-five or forty-five? Impossible to tell. She was separated from her much older husband, a professor at the Conservatoire. But he supported her nonetheless. Minnie wasn't just an artist, she was a big-hearted character.

She had no time for narrow-minded conformists. She found the occupying Germans absolutely intolerable, with their burnished, high-sided boots, trying to force their goose-steps and marching music on the country. Increasingly, Minnie's musical soirées were becoming a pretext for her intellectual and artist friends from the Resistance to exchange information or even to discuss their next coups. The painter and music-lover Marcel Hastir, who enlivened many of these Saturday evenings at Minnie's with his sparkling wit, shakes his white head in 1999 as he remembers those times: 'Some of those people were pretty reckless in those days, they were actually out for an adventure. And many of them talked too much.'

Youra Livchitz was among Minnie's favourite guests. He was spirited, well-read and interested in politics. A brilliant mind with a great future in store, according to his teachers and professors. And when, at one of these parties, Youra came across someone he could talk to as an equal, he would talk about God and the world, or philosophize at great length about the 'ideal man'. The ideal type for Youra was not the socialist hero, or the brilliant artist or the scientist. Youra rejected the very notion of commitment to a doctrine, of being restricted to one specialist area. 'The perfect human being,' he asserted, 'is someone who has been rained on in many different fields, who doesn't plan out his life in a straight line running along a narrow set of tracks, but who allows himself to be defined by the most diverse range of interests.'

Youra's brother Alexandre, his elder by six years, also made regular appearances in this colourful company. He seemed more reserved and serious than his eloquent brother. They were both tall and athletic, and very attractive to women. Because of their age difference they didn't step on each other's toes. Alexandre had taken up with Wilhelmine Cohen-Baudoux, who was the same age as himself. The voluptuous blonde, who dressed to make the best of her figure, was separated from her husband, and wildly flirtatious. 'Willy had loads of affairs,' Marcel Hastir remembers. A woman painter who was a frequent guest at Minnie Minet's soirées, puts it more harshly: 'Willy was a minx.'

When the trams had stopped running or the curfew was in force, the guests could find refuge at Minnie's until Sunday morning. Sleeping bags and blankets were rolled out on the floor, and there was room for someone to sleep in the empty bath-tub. And in the winter Minnie improvised hot-water bottles for everyone out of old yoghurt jars.

Minnie and Youra must have been very close. A snapshot shows the two of them sitting side by side, enjoying the view of the Meuse near Namur. The Minets owned a little summer house in nearby Profondeville.

Like everyone who knew Youra from those times, Evelyn Coulon-Allègre raved about the young medic. Lily, as she was known in those days, was a pretty young teenager when she met Livchitz in 1938. Her parents and Youra's mother were members of the Theosophical community in Brussels. And at the concerts and lectures that she attended with her parents, the girl with the gleaming blonde hair was very struck by the good-looking medical student. He was her first love. It was all entirely platonic because Youra, six years older than Lily, was very fond of her but saw her as a little sister more than anything else. For a while Youra gave his young friend extra maths lessons. But Lily learned practically nothing. 'I simply couldn't think straight, I was so in love with him.'

These were politically volatile times, and Youra brought Lily along to the Université Libre de Bruxelles when protests were held against the Franco regime in Spain or the Japanese invasion of China. She also joined him in his protests against Léon Degrelle and his 'Rexists', Belgians on the far right who supported Hitler and were trying to gain political ground. In Brussels, Degrelle led mass demonstrations, where he was marched in by a group of matrons in green hunting-skirts, high-heeled boots and little hunting hats, their arms outstretched in a Hitler salute.

'There were no social barriers where Youra was concerned, all doors were open to him,' Lily Allègre recalls. She was seventeen years old when she was allowed to accompany him to a fellow student's birthday party, a garden party, in accordance with the fashions of the day, in the elegant villa district of Rhode-Saint-Genese. As the two young people approached the finely dressed guests in the lantern-lit garden, Youra leaned down to his intimidated friend: 'Sorry for exposing you to the haute-bourgeoisie.' After all, Youra had always presented himself to her as a vehement advocate of socialism, of hostility to all things bourgeois.

There was another reason why Lily has never forgotten that evening. Their young host later became her husband. He had taken an interest in Youra's shy companion at that very same birthday party.

Since 1928 Youra had lived with his mother and his older brother Alexandre in Brussels, Jewish immigrants from Eastern Europe, it would have seemed, fleeing from economic misery. But in fact Youra's mother Rachel Livchitz came from one of the wealthiest families in the then Russian province of Bessarabia.

Rachel Livchitz, as everyone who met her immediately noticed, was an extraordinary person. She didn't come from the simple, restricted conditions of the '*stetl*'. This tall woman with the striking features and radiant blue eyes, which she had passed on to her son Youra, was a member of the Jewish aristocracy. She spoke fluent English, French, German and Russian. 'She belonged to the haute-bourgeoisie, not because of her circumstances, but because of the way she acted. She had class,' remembers Yvonne Jospa. Yvonne and her husband Hertz

Jospa had come to Belgium from Bessarabia at about the same time as the Livchitz family, to study. The sociologist and her husband were part of the same circle of left-wing intellectuals as Youra and his brother Alexandre, and played a crucial part in the Jewish Resistance.

Anyone with an eye could have discovered in the modest but tastefully decorated flat of the Livchitz family some clues to their affluent origins. A few old woodcuts, a magnificent samovar and some very fine silver. The teaspoons, decorated with art nouveau ornaments, engraved with the initials R.L., are now treasured by Russian friends as a cherished souvenir of that *grande dame* – although it should also be borne in mind that Rachel was sometimes capable of snobbery.

The Mitchniks, Youra's maternal grandparents, were among the richest families in Kishiniev, the capital of Bessarabia. Rachel's father was a member of the noble tsarist guild of businessmen, and owned vast estates, vineyards and a stud in which horses were bred for the Russian army. Rachel's parents were observant Jews, and brought up their thirteen children in open-minded and unorthodox fashion. Rachel, the youngest, was looked after by a French governess, who was the only source of annoyance in that childhood paradise, a large family blessed with all manner of worldly goods. Their father, the enlightened businessman, ensured that his daughters also enjoyed the best possible education. Rachel, born in 1889, informally attended lectures at St Petersburg university, and studied for two terms at the Sorbonne, where one of her older sisters was also enrolled. Study tours to England and Switzerland completed the young Russian lady's demanding training programme.

Laughing, and by now some way into her eighties, she told her friends in Brussels of an unforgettable evening at her sister's in Paris. One day Rachel had been assured that she was going to have an interesting companion at dinner that same evening. It wasn't a false promise. Her compatriot with the high forehead and glowing eyes greatly impressed the student. It was Vladimir Ilyich Lenin. And it is even possible that the revolutionary and his charming young companion were related, given that Rachel's mother and Lenin's shared the maiden name of Blank.

On that occasion Rachel might have told her dining companion how, as a schoolgirl in 1905, she had marched on one of the many mass demonstrations against the Tsar's regime. Whenever she thought there was a danger that she, the girl from the well-to-do family, might be recognized amongst the demonstrators, she pulled the black apron of her school uniform over her face. Rachel Livchitz would never entirely lose her sympathy for socialist revolutionaries. And Yvonne Jospa, for many years a member of the Belgian Communist Party, remembers that however haut-bourgeois Madame Livchitz might have appeared, she never made a secret of her sympathy for the left.

On the other hand Rachel Livchitz seldom spoke of her husband, who, like herself, came from Kishiniev. Salomon (or Shlema) Livchitz was a childhood sweetheart who had been in the same grammar school class as one of her elder brothers. But the marriage was not a particularly happy one. They married young, before the young husband had finished his medical studies. As the Russian universities forbade Jews access to universities on the basis of a quota system, Youra's father was forced to study abroad.

There is a reference to the young couple in the files of the register of Munich residents. On 1 December 1910, twenty-four-year-old Shlema Livchitz, born in Meshirov, arrived in Munich with his wife Rachel, née Mitchnik. He was a Russian national studying medicine. On 20 April 1911, their son Alexandre was born. In 1913, 'Schlema Liwschiz' – to give him his German spelling – graduated as an MD from Munich University. Then the First World War broke out, and the newly qualified physician was called up as a military doctor. It was probably the turmoil of war that drove the family to Kiev, where Youra was born on 30 September 1917.

At some point Rachel Livchitz could no longer bear the fact that her husband was deceiving her with other women. She was thirty-eight when she separated from him and filed for divorce. In the same year, 1927, she came to live in Brussels with her two sons. Brussels was considered particularly hospitable and liberal. Rachel's home town of Kishiniev was ceded to Romania in 1918 along with the whole province of Bessarabia. Consequently her Belgian identity card and those of her sons give their nationality as 'Romanian'.

Separating from one's affluent extended family and going abroad with one's children was not only an extraordinary act for the times. It testifies to the great independence and confidence of Rachel Livchitz, who was known to everyone as 'Saps', after the name that Youra had given his mother when he was just starting to talk. Photographs from the happy years in Brussels show a slender woman with pronounced features that suggest a great inner strength. Her heavy, piled-up hair falls softly into her face. She is described as extremely cultivated and warm-hearted. Yvonne Jospa, now almost ninety, remembers her compatriot with great respect: 'She was always most helpful, and terrific at finding solutions for difficult problems.'

As a young woman Rachel Livchitz had come into contact with Theosophy, the doctrine of the 'supersensible' knowledge of the world. This philosophy, with its mystical and esoteric elements, and strongly influenced in German-speaking parts of the world by the anthroposophist Rudolf Steiner, was very widespread both in Russia and in Germany. Upon her arrival in Brussels, Rachel approached a physician by the name of Dr Nyssen. It was probably well known in the international Theosophical community that a group of members in Brussels had come together in a progressive experiment in communal living.

The artists and intellectuals around the white-haired and white-bearded Dr Nyssen had knocked together two spacious turn-of-the-century town-houses. They lived there in a kind of Theosophical commune, and after work – the members earned their livelihoods as architects, teachers, musicians and writers – they devoted themselves to the study of Theosophy. The walls were covered with treatises and mottoes of the higher calling and life beyond earthly existence. As in a commune, class boundaries and social differences were to be overcome, the wages or salaries of the working members went to the 'Monada', as the community was called, and all adults took care of the communal housekeeping. As there was also a small boarding school attached to the commune, Youra's mother was kept very busy. Twelve little girls slept in two dormitories. They had to be cooked for and have their homework supervised. As the patron of the house, Dr Nyssen, was also the chairman of the Belgian Vegetarian Society, much emphasis was placed on organic fare.

The children all took part in the housework, says Henriette Vander Hecht, who was one of the first little boarders in the 'Monada'. Her parents were members of the Theosophical Society. And since a difficult pregnancy had left her mother unable to look after little 'Riquet' (so-called after the Perrault fairy-tale character because of her black tuft of hair), Henriette moved temporarily into the art nouveau house in the Avenue de Floréal: 'It was paradise for me.' She has never forgotten how, at the age of nine, she was assigned to washing-up duty in the kitchen with thirteen-year-old Youra. 'Youra struck me as very grown-up, he was very chatty and liked philoso-phizing.' That evening, tea-towel in hand, he slipped into the role of Socrates. He put one question after another to little Riquet, expecting a serious reply. Later on Henriette learned at her lycée that Socrates had used the very method that Youra was trying out with her, in order to stimulate his interlocutors to 'think about existence itself'.

Youra's elder brother Alexandre, known to everyone as Choura, only came to the 'Monada' in the holidays and at weekends. As Rachel Livchitz was supported with a small monthly allowance from her family in Bessarabia, she was able to finance her oldest son's engineer-ing studies in Ghent. Choura, although practical by temperament, was not particularly hard-working. He enjoyed his casual student lifestyle to the full.

When a love affair between Alexandre and a young Montessori teacher began in the 'Monada', Dr Nyssen intervened. He demanded that the Livchitz family leave the commune. The white-bearded patri-arch and his strict, bony wife also disliked the way the young girls in the boarding school idolized the young Youra.

Nearby, in the Avenue Brugmann, Rachel Livchitz found a flat on the third floor of a corner-house. She furnished the bright rooms very cheaply. Brightly coloured decorative cloths concealed the shabbiness of some of the furniture that she had bought in second-hand shops.

From here Youra had only a fifteen-minute walk to the Athénée in Uccle. The liberal socialist majority of the local community had only founded this city grammar school in 1930, when the rural resort for the affluent citizens of Brussels had become a thriving suburb. Whole terraces were built for the bourgeoisie and the petite-bourgeoisie making their way from the city to the green open spaces. The wealthier refugees from the city built modern Bauhaus-style villas on huge tracts of land.

The new city grammar school was the expression of this new spirit. It was the left-liberal riposte to the classic Catholic college. And it was the first mixed grammar school for boys and girls. Religion did not feature on the timetable of this free-spirited institution, to which all the citizens who would later be a thorn in the flesh of the occupying Germans sent their children: socialists, freemasons, Jews. Even Communists were tolerated as teachers.

The headmaster, on the other hand, was a man who placed the strongest emphasis on discipline and order. He insisted on absolute punctuality, correctness of speech and smart clothes for his pupils. After break-time, Youra and his schoolmates had to wait strictly in pairs in the courtyard before they were allowed into the building in single file after roll-call. The philologist Albert Peters, who was to be the first headmaster of the European School in Brussels, was a declared opponent of Rousseau's principles of freedom and laissez-faire. But as a supporter of a humanist ideal of education he was tolerant enough to give his hand-picked staff all the freedom they required, so long as the education of the pupils benefited from it.

One of the most outstanding teachers at the Athénée d'Uccle was the history teacher Léon Moulin. This convinced socialist inspired whole generations of pupils for his subject with his unconventional teaching methods. Youra was one of his favourite pupils. And he stayed in constant contact with him even after he left the school, so keen was he on the boy whose character combined a radiant love of life, a hunger for knowledge and a reflective disposition.

Such a climate of discipline and intellectual openness produced large numbers of spirited and independent-minded young people.

This little local institution sacrificed more people than any other grammar school in Brussels in the struggle against the Nazis. Three teachers and fourteen pupils died fighting for the Resistance, and eight of those former pupils of the Athénée d'Uccle were executed by the Germans.

In 1931 Youra began his studies at the grammar school, which at the time contained only one hundred pupils and twelve teachers. He was fourteen years old, and was placed in the fourth secondary class. When he walked through the school gate each morning, he found himself in a verdant idyll. In the enchanted park of Wolvendael there was a castle, the school building. The city fathers had lodged their new grammar school in the old building, which was not particularly suited to pedagogical purposes. But both pupils and teachers loved their temporary romantic surroundings behind the wall on Avenue De Fré. On hot summer days, lessons were held in the shade of an old beech tree.

For his fellow pupils, Youra Livchitz was something of a star. 'He was seen as a philosopher, an idealist, he was very highly regarded among us – even if we didn't always understand what he said,' remembers Robert Maistriau, who was four years younger than Youra.

The clown in Youra's class was Jean Franklemon. The boy with the reddish-brown hair and the mischievous expression was known as 'Pamplemousse' – 'Grapefruit' – presumably because he was rather podgy as a child. He was a gifted mathematician and had tremendous artistic talent, drawing and playing music. He shared Youra's love of sweets and his enthusiasm for the theatre. The son of an engineer and a teacher, he found the strict discipline in the Athénée d'Uccle hard to cope with. After two years he transferred to the lycée of St Gilles, but his classmates didn't lose touch with him.

Robert Leclercq, Youra's closest friend, was a very different kettle of fish. An excellent pupil, solid and serious, he shared Youra's interest in philosophy, literature and the theatre, and the two boys competed for the best marks in the class. They passed their leaving exam with flying colours. It was because of Robert that Youra chose Latin as his main subject, and passed the Greek exam required for medical studies. Robert crammed him full of grammar and vocabulary.

This young intellectual duo had a very charismatic effect on the rest of the pupils. Both of them made fun of the empty-headed posers who desperately followed the fashionable trends of the day. According to an observation of Youra's that Leclercq later liked to quote to illustrate his friend's character, some of them were only as popular as they were 'because the author lets certain people present themselves as intelligent by pretending they have understood his work'.

In his memoir *Une mère russe*, which was awarded the Grand Prix of the Académie Française in 1978, the French writer Alain Bosquet recalls his youth in Brussels. Bosquet was also a son of Russian Jewish emigrants, and the only school friends that he mentions from that period are Leclercq and Livchitz. Livchitz impressed the younger boy by being so well-read. According to Bosquet, he devoured Kierkegaard, Spinoza and Bergson. And discussions with his friends Leclercq and Livchitz about the freedom of the individual, the need to overcome fear, to break away from the role of the obedient son and strike out on one's own path, clearly had a great influence on the young writer. 'I was far from unresponsive to their crusades.'

People in such a small community of pupils knew each other, even if they were three classes lower down. And since Robert Maistriau lived almost around the corner from Youra, he was able to get to know his fellow pupil better. Robert was able to organize his timetable so that the two boys walked to and from school as often as possible. He loved his conversations with Livchitz, who fascinated the younger boy without intimidating him.

The two schoolmates were in similar family relationships. Their fathers had been military physicians, one in the Belgian, the other in the Russian army. And since her husband's death, Maistriau's mother also lived alone with two sons. The similarities went further than that. Like Youra, Robert had a brother six years older than himself. Claude was the son from his mother's first marriage to a Jewish biscuit manufacturer from Strasbourg, who had died as a reserve officer in the First World War. That made Claude half-Jewish. And Claude's

Strasbourg grandmother was also Robert's beloved 'Grandma'. Perhaps that was why he had such an understanding of the situation of his Jewish fellow pupils, some of whom did not arrive in Brussels with their parents until their teenage years. 'I felt sorry for them,' Robert Maistriau said in retrospect; despite their hard work and intelligence they were held back a class in the lycée because their French wasn't good enough.

That could not have been said of Youra, who was among the best in his class from the start, both in French essays and in the sciences. In their free time the young people met to play croquet – an English fashion that was very popular at the time – in the garden of Roos the pharmacist. And as they sent the wooden balls flying with their mallets, the schoolboys and students swapped the most recent adventures of Tim and Struppi, the popular comic heroes created by the Belgian artist Hergé.

They keenly discussed the most recent films from Hollywood, Paris and Berlin. Every district of Brussels had its enticing picture palaces and little neighbourhood cinemas. Families queued outside their box offices on Sunday afternoons. Although dramas were the most popular entertainment of the day, to Youra's critical eye all that mattered was a very few art films and documentaries. Otherwise the film industry only produced illusory worlds and cheap 'ersatz', he said, using the German word, because he knew that language too.

In an article for the student journal *Les Cahiers du Libre Examen*, young Livchitz attempted to initiate a discussion of the modern entertainment industry. 'In the cinema we can experience the strongest emotions with certainty of physical "safety". We can wage war without being mutilated, we can murder without fear of punishment, we can love the most beautiful women without thinking of our future mothers-in-law...' But above all the cinema was dangerous because it satisfied 'the deep need to escape ourselves'. It was the perfect 'drug for everyone'.

Four years later the occupying forces were to flood the country with German films. Heinz Rühmann was amusing in *Quax der Bruchpilot*, Zarah Leander's dark voice was fascinating in *Die Grosse*

Liebe. During the war years, this form of escapism brought 1.4 million Belgian viewers into the cinemas every week. And audiences sank into the comfortable, warm seats, allowing themselves to be enraptured by the shameless effects of skilfully-made propaganda films. The Belgian public murmured their applause as the greedy and lecherous Jew Süss was hauled up in a cage with a trapdoor at the end, until all that could be seen were his dangling feet.

3 Brussels 'Free University'

Perhaps one would have to come from far-off China, like Youra's fellow medic Han Suyin, to find the Université Libre de Bruxelles (ULB) wonderful from very the first day. 'I began to understand,' the daughter of a Chinese engineer and a Belgian mother writes in her memoirs, 'the meaning of democracy.' The institution, in the style of an American campus university, with generous sports grounds, bright auditoria, seminar rooms and laboratories, was considered to be one of the most advanced universities in Europe.

The functional architecture of the new buildings on the Avenue des Nations followed the principles of 'libre examen' – the free, unprejudiced and independent examination of all problems – to which its founders were devoted. The university was the response of liberals and freemasons to the conservative Catholic University in Leuven. At this 'Free University', science and theory were not to be impeded by ideological or religious constraints.

For many of its three thousand students, the ULB was also the backdrop for constant debates about abstract art, music and politics. The most diverse groups rubbed shoulders at the university; dyed-in-the-wool Catholics, liberals, Trotskyists and Communists, but also the reactionary sons of the bourgeoisie who were close to the Belgian fascists, the Rexists. They engaged in wars of words that were sometimes backed up with fisticuffs.

Not a weekday passed without protests, demonstrations or debates; meetings against Mussolini's invasion of Abyssinia, collections for the victims of the Franco regime in Spain, seminars on Soviet Communism. Concerts and conferences were held. 'Groups were devoted to all kinds of things. Some defended the rights of bald people,' said Han Suyin, 'others fought for votes for women in the Congo.'

Like Han Suyin, Youra began his medical studies in October 1935. He plunged enthusiastically into this new, unknown life with the battle cry: 'Down with the slavery of the lycée! Long live freedom!' Youra's expectations were high. Too high. In an article for *Les Cahiers du Libre Examen*, he described how he had initially suffered from 'beginner's disappointment', how he had been paralysed by false expectations.

The lectures seemed to have hardly any more depth than the lessons he had had in the lycée. And there was practically no contact with the professors. Like automata, these gentlemen delivered their lectures for sixty minutes precisely, wearing wing collars and high-buttoned waistcoats, before vanishing without so much as a goodbye. Often they assumed knowledge that the school-leavers lacked. And the famous student parties offered nothing but stupid jokes and pranks, or at best perhaps the latest football results...

Youra's advice to freshers in this article is very revealing about his philosophy of life:

> Just do what interests you, make your personal choice.
> Gradually you'll work out that the university is more than
> a school preparing you for a job, it's more than an evening
> school that happens to take place in the morning. In the
> meetings you'll find an enthusiasm that you had lost, and
> comrades who share your longings. And you'll discover
> that life doesn't consist in arriving at your goal, but in the
> journey there.

Youra's initial scepticism towards the anonymous world of the university soon left him. The medical student immersed himself in the hectic life of the campus and enjoyed the many possibilities of student life. Along with some fellow students he founded a basketball department in the ULB's sports association, and became a passionate player of the game. For a time he sought people who would help him realize his idea of erecting basketball nets for the children of the city on quiet side streets or squares. It wasn't just a sporting initiative, it was also a social one. What he had in mind was a way of keeping street-boys from going astray through boredom. He became a committed member of the university's 'Youth Theatre', and wrote poems and articles for the student newspaper.

Along with his school-friend Robert Leclercq, a student of philology, Youra was one of the organizers of the 'Cercle Libre-Examen'. Its 1937 manifesto reveals a solid belief in progress and human rights in the midst of a world of 'isms', Fascism and Communism: 'We are ready to bond together, beyond all ideological barriers, to fight against all those who wish to silence the idea of humanity and hinder progress. We all have the same hope: a rich and inclusive life in peace and brotherhood.'

This debating society, which involved both teachers and students, influenced the atmosphere of the 'Free University' more than any other political grouping. And the same circle of students, which also included Richard Altenhoff, Henri Neuman and Jean Burgers, produced one of the most hard-hitting resistance organizations in occupied Belgium, 'Groupe G'. Its members trusted each other implicitly. Years later the lives of the student friends Altenhoff and Livchitz were to be linked once again, although this time in a tragic context.

Youra's older classmate Jean Franklemon had also enrolled at the ULB. The cheerful bon viveur was studying mathematics. But Jean was seldom seen at lectures. Like many intellectuals and artists of that time he saw Communism as the panacea for society, and the tried and trusted antidote to Fascism. When 'Pamplemousse' had had enough of theoretical debates, he turned his back on the university for a few months and joined the Red Brigades. He was one of several ULB students who actively committed themselves to the Spanish Civil War against the Franco regime.

At university, Jean's heart was with a little theatre group that he had founded with his friend Jacques Huysman. During the warmer months of the year, Huysman and Franklemon travelled the country with a street theatre company called the 'Comédiens Routiers'. The repertoire of the little troupe of thespians included Molière and Shakespeare, but also contemporary plays.

Youra was well disciplined as a student. Despite all his distractions, he found studying easy, and from the beginning he was one of those at the top of his year. His brother Alexandre, on the other hand, had abandoned his engineering studies in Ghent, and now worked as an electrician. He no longer wished to be dependent on his mother. But Youra earned his own money as well. The stepfather of his little girl-friend Lily Allègre, a good acquaintance of Rachel Livchitz from the Theosophical community, gave him a job. Youra was able to share the work. He became a sales representative for the pharmaceuticals company Pharmacobel.

The 'Société Théosophique' had become something like an extended family for Rachel Livchitz. Most of her wide circle of acquaintances in Brussels were devotees of this international society, which at the time had about fifty thousand members around the world. The goal of the Theosophists – to learn about all the world's great religions, compare them with one another and merge them all into a single philosophy – attracted many artists and intellectuals, and also many members of the liberal bourgeoisie. The movement's co-founder, Helena Blavatsky, born in Russia in 1832, brought strong mystical and occult elements to Theosophy, enriching it with Hindu theories of Karma and rebirth.

'Some reflections on mysticism,' was the heading that Youra gave to an essay in *Les Cahiers du Libre Examen* in May 1939, which reveals the powerful influence of Theosophical teachings. 'The mystical exists. Each of us feels an irrational and fanatical connection to some doctrine or other … A political conviction, if it is not dictated by a personal or a class interest, is in essence nothing other than a religious conviction.' The author is deliberately provoking his contemporaries who are convinced of the scientific truth of Marxist theory, materialism.

A Communist, Livchitz writes, is just as much of a mystic as the follower of any religion:

> One believes in God, the other in the happiness of mankind as the product of dialectical materialism. The liberal believes in neo-liberalism, the Socialist in struggle and class solidarity. The scientific basis is absent in every case. The predictions of Marx have precisely the same value as the prophecies of the Apocalypse... We are mystics and we don't know it; a large proportion of our sufferings and discussions derives from this latent conflict between reason, which seeks power, and emotion, which seeks its justification. In the current chaos of opinions and facts there is no point in denying the value of the mystical. One does not prove a moral, one believes it. One can also reject it. That, for me, is the task of youth today.

There were always some affluent Theosophists who generously supported Rachel Livchitz and her two sons. Thus Youra, with his brother and his mother, was able to spend three whole summer holidays at the Theosophical summer camp in Ommen, where up to three thousand devotees from all parts of the world assembled, including prominent figures such as Aldous Huxley.

Even sixty years on, the painter Marcel Hastir still raves about those 'incredibly wonderful' weeks: 'It was pure happiness, mutual understanding, although we all came from very different countries and cultures. In the evening we assembled in a big tent and listened to the most exciting lectures.' In those days the main speaker was the Indian philosopher Krishnamurti, the movement's great guru.

A photograph from the summer of 1937 shows Youra and Marcel Hastir in a Dutch port, sitting on a ship's railing, with Henriette Vander Hecht – little Riquet from the 'Monada' – now a teenager, standing between them in a white summer dress. The three young people had hitch-hiked to nearby Ommen. Marcel Hastir was one of the people in charge of the running of the camp, and under his direction the young people helped to erect the wooden huts and tents that held audiences of more than a thousand. The last camp was held in 1938. As Hastir put it: 'When the Germans occupied Poland, that was the end.'

The young people were particularly taken with the charismatic Krishnamurti, who was then about forty years old. The Indian had grown up around the headquarters of the Theosophical Society in Adyar on the Madras coast, and such was the enthusiasm of the society's members for the handsome, intelligent boy that he had assumed the role of a religious superstar within the movement. Eventually he felt this role to be a burden, and rejected it. The 'World Teacher' reluctantly preached to his audience in Ommen that everyone must find his own way to the truth, rather than depending upon some external authority for help with his quest: 'Truth is a pathless land, and you cannot approach it by any path whatsoever, by any religion, by any sect... Truth, being limitless, unconditional, unapproachable by any path whatsoever, cannot be organized.'

Youra Livchitz was also greatly impressed by the Indian philosopher. The fact that the young doctor did not later join any ideologically motivated resistance group, that he remained a wanderer between the worlds of the Resistance, may well have something to do with the beliefs that Krishnamurti conveyed to his audience each evening as he addressed them in the massive tent in Ommen: 'Whether they be Western or Eastern gurus, doubt what they say... The spirit must be free of all authority – no devotees, no disciples, no stereotypes'.

Medical studies at the 'Free University' were demanding and very difficult. In the third year of his studies Youra not only took practicals in biochemistry, physiology and histology as well as attending a philosophy lecture, but he also had to spend five mornings in the anatomy room. One of the other trainee medics laying bare the nerves, veins, muscles and arteries of a corpse on the dissecting table was Han Suyin. Youra and the young Chinese girl were considered the stars of their year in the medical faculty. 'For two years,' Han Suyin writes in her memoirs, 'we were elbow to elbow, the young Jew Livchitz and I.'

The other female presence in their six-member anatomy group was a Jewish girl who had fled from Germany, as Han Suyin recounts. Quietly spoken, almost apologetic in manner, she told her fellow students about the terrible time she had endured at the hands of the SS. Her boyfriend had been tortured with red-hot irons, and was still severely psychologically disturbed. None of the young people could imagine – in 1938 – that Hitler's troops would invade Belgium two years later, and bury their university's spirit of freedom and humanity beneath their jackboots.

4 The Coming of the Germans

As the general approached Brussels, the first thing that struck him was the massive dome of the Palais de Justice. The enormous hemisphere of the neo-classical building stood out against the sky. 'Take that as a symbol,' said Alexander von Falkenhausen to his companions in the military limousine. 'Law, justice and humanity stand over everything.' He had acted according to these maxims throughout the whole of his life, and he would continue to be guided by them in his new duties.

Baron von Falkenhausen, a picture-book Prussian aristocrat, tall and gaunt, arrived in Belgium on 30 May 1940 as military governor. Two days after King Leopold III had capitulated to the superior forces of the German army, the energetic sixty-two-year-old general took over the government of the country. On 10 May Hitler had attacked Belgium on threadbare pretexts. German soldiers had invaded their neighbour for the second time in twenty-five years.

About two weeks later a stocky, moustachioed man in a long military coat emerged from a black Mercedes in front of the Palais de Justice in Brussels. With his head thrown back, the Führer studied the colossal nineteenth-century building from beneath his peaked cap. The eighty-foot porticoed vestibule was even larger than that of St Peter's in Rome.

The imperial architecture clearly impressed Adolf Hitler. He lingered for several minutes in front of the Palais de Justice, occasionally making appreciative noises. Only later did his military commander Falkenhausen learn of his flying visit. The Chancellor had been chauffeured incognito into Brussels on his way to Paris, having just conquered the French capital. Hitler wanted to avoid a meeting with Falkenhausen because he mistrusted the baron. It ran contrary to his convictions that a military man should be in charge of occupied Belgium rather than a prominent Nazi Party member. It was a sop from the Chancellor to the army. He had promised to put military governments in the occupied zones as a way of breaking the resistance of the officers to his planned Western offensive.

The generals wanted to ensure that what had happened in occupied Poland would not take place in Western Europe. In Poland, the Nazi policy of occupation had led to bloody excesses and economic disasters. A purely military administration, Major General Eugen Müller had said in 1939, should 'combine soldierly leadership with expert knowledge in military discipline'.

Falkenhausen was Commander-in-Chief von Brauchitsch's first choice for the job. After a long period in China as a military adviser, he had been appointed deputy commander of the military district of Dresden. It was an open secret among Germany's generals that the wiry Prussian, prudent and elitist, held Hitler and his Party comrades in profound contempt. Nonetheless, at some point he decided against an early retreat. He stayed for the sake of the Fatherland. 'My country right or wrong,' was the patriotic explanation for his decision, which he recorded in his memoirs. 'We were clear that the war would not be waged against Hitler and the regime, but against the German people as a whole.' He joined in to protect the Germans against their enemies. An argument straight out of Goebbels's propaganda drawer.

The Belgian population were terrified of the 'Boches', as their unloved neighbours were known, because the havoc wrought by the German soldiers in the First World War was still a living memory. During their 1914 invasion, the army had, in revenge for resistance, laid waste to villages, and murdered women and children. The military governor who had assumed responsibility for those terrible acts of cruelty was Ludwig, Baron von Falkenhausen, an uncle of the new commander. The fact that the new man bore the same name and title as the earlier baron made it a heavy burden for Belgium to bear.

His nephew wanted to do things better, and differently. He wanted to administer the occupied country after the fashion of Alexander the Great. 'He allowed the subject people to keep not only their customs, but also their civilian laws, and often even their kings and governors. He respected old traditions, he conquered in order to preserve.' Falkenhausen wanted to resist Hitler's brutal policy of subjection in the spirit of that conqueror, and to prevent the Nazis and their brutal troops of police from having their say in Belgium.

By the time Falkenhausen arrived in Brussels, an endless trail of refugees was drifting to the north and west. One million of the eight million Belgian population tried to escape the Germans. Anyone with enough money or a car tried to flee to France. They hoped to be safe from the Germans on the other side of the border.

In his autobiography the writer Alain Bosquet describes meeting his two school-friends Robert Leclercq and Youra Livchitz in a café on the Chaussée de Waterloo. They hadn't seen each other for a year. But now Bosquet hoped his two admired fellow pupils from the lycée in Uccle might be able to give him an assessment of the situation, and perhaps even advise him on what to do next. 'I had hoped that my two old friends would react similarly to the situation, which would have forced me to copy them. But a few words were enough, and my illusions fled. Livchitz had decided to fight the barbarians, come what may; Leclercq, for his part, was more cautious… We would have to wait for a while.'

Alain Bosquet's family fled to unoccupied southern France and then to America. Robert Leclercq also moved to France, as did the family of his classmate Jean Franklemon. A few months later they all returned to Belgium. Youra Livchitz didn't join the exodus. The young man saw his future in Brussels. Wasn't he most of the way to fulfilling the dream of his professional life? After his first state exam he had had work experience as a physician in a Brussels hospital, being recognized by the established doctors and adored by the patients. His plan was to train as a neurologist. Was he to give all that up?

Mayors and councillors fled, sometimes taking the council coffers with them. The whole government, including the defence minister, had fled to England. The National Bank had closed. Only King Leopold III had stayed. As Hitler's most prominent prisoner of war, under the supervision of a German guard of honour, he spent the war under house arrest in the Laeken Castle.

The Goldsteinas family, originally from Lithuania, and their little daughter Abela, took up with an affluent Belgian couple who owned a car. On the back seat of this car, they got as far as Marseilles, in greater comfort than most refugees. The trained chemist Mendelis Goldsteinas, who had held a senior post in the Graeff sugar factory in Brussels, hoped to travel on from there to America. Relatives in the USA planned to send him an affidavit, which would enable him and his small family to cross the Atlantic. In the end, though, the money ran out. They had to go back to Belgium.

At first, life there seemed to be much as it was before. Their flat and all their belongings were untouched. Mendelis Goldsteinas returned to his job in the sugar refinery as though nothing had happened. Later, their lives would be dramatically influenced by Youra Livchitz.

The Gronowski family had also fled the Germans. All four of them – two parents, two children – had also set off on the refugee trail westwards, heading for France. Léon Gronowski was reluctant to leave his house and his leather goods shop in Brussels. He was proud of what he had accomplished as a poor Polish emigrant. As a young man he had slogged away under wretched conditions in the coal-mines of Liège. Then he had travelled the country as a salesman of leather goods. And now he owned a house and a shop, and was even able to send his family to the seaside at Ostende in the summer holidays.

When he strolled along between the chestnut trees that lined the broad Avenue Louise on Sunday with his wife Chana, his daughter Ita and his little son Simon, in his dark three-piece suit and black hat, carrying a copy of Le Soir in one hand and an inevitable cigarillo in the other, Léon Gronowski was the epitome of the Brussels bourgeois. He had not stayed in St Gilles, where many Jewish immigrants from

Eastern Europe lived, but had built himself a modest house in Etterbeek, on the Chaussée de Wavre. He wanted his children to grow up outside the Jewish ghetto, and, unlike himself, to enjoy a free, non-religious education.

Léon Gronowski and his family got as far as Panne, a popular resort near the French border, before the German bombers caught up with them. For eight-year-old Simon, the night of the air-raid was an unforgettable experience. The family had fled from the house where they had found refuge, and escaped into a nearby forest. From there, clinging to his parents, Simon watched the impacts and explosions.

The following morning, as Simon walked along the promenade with his father, he finally understood what war meant. Dark smoke still rose from the ruins. Almost all the houses were burnt out and destroyed. The heavy bombing of Dunkirk boomed out in the distance. The German army had already advanced into northern France. There seemed little point in fleeing any further. So Léon Gronowski, like many others, decided to return to Brussels. On the way back, Simon saw the first of the dead. Along the side of the road lay the corpses of British and Belgian soldiers, who had tried in vain to defend the country against the onslaught of Hitler's army.

The German commander Falkenhausen attempted to use his troops to establish calm and order. He ordered his soldiers to be helpful and correct in their dealings with the population. The dreaded barbarians were courteous and friendly. The returning Belgians could hardly believe their eyes when German military vehicles stopped to bring them home. The army even helped those travelling in cars by giving them petrol. And in Brussels the German soldiers welcomed the home-comers with soup from their field canteens.

Falkenhausen had his quarters in the Place Royale, a square above the old city, built in the symmetrical style of Louis XVI. It was from here that he gave out orders to the 456 employees of the military administration and the 708 workers in the new military and general administrative headquarters of the Belgian provinces. And it was from here that the instructions and orders for the Belgian administration were issued, and their execution strictly overseen by the Germans.

The words 'Ministère des Colonies' still stood in big letters over the general's headquarters. German guards stamped back and forth in front of the main entrance of the colonial ministry. The rear wing of the stylish palace abutted the royal city castle. An appropriate location, then, for a governor general.

In line with Falkenhausen's role as general, countless military maps lined the back wall of his office. And from his desk the commander looked out over an equestrian statue in the Place Royale. It represented the crusader Godfrey of Bouillon, who had declared himself the first King of Jerusalem in 1099. Diagonally across from it, still within the general's field of vision, was 'Old England', the finest department store in Brussels, with its elaborate and decorative art nouveau façade.

During Falkenhausen's governorship, the trade in luxury goods moved from the elegant department stores of the city to the proletarian Rue des Radis. Anyone who couldn't stock up with extra groceries on the black market went hungry. The people of Belgium, a nation of gourmands and gourmets, were allotted a total of just 1,350 calories on their daily grocery list.

During the week Falkenhausen stayed in the Hotel Plaza on Boulevard Max. There the early riser was able to have his first discussions with his colleagues at dawn over a cup of tea. Or read the London *Times*, which the commander obtained a few days late from Lisbon. He had had to apply for a special permit for the privilege.

His head of administration was Eggert Reeder, a lawyer loyally devoted to the general, a pragmatist, a Party member, but neither an anti-Semite nor a blood-and-soil fanatic. Formerly a company director in Cologne, he was good at anticipating conflicts with party heads in Berlin, and often placed himself protectively in front of his boss, who had a tendency to stick his head above the parapet. 'I certainly didn't make life easy for him,' Falkenhausen later wrote in his memoirs. 'The weight of the administration rested on his shoulders.'

The general thought the Belgians were 'an awkward people'; their state was merely an 'artificial formation, held together by religion, administration and monarchy, governed by money, priests and lawyers'. In Flemings and Walloons, for all their differences, the governor observed a 'strong sense of personal liberty'. In fact Falkenhausen found it difficult to become used to these people, who clearly lacked the Prussian virtues that the baron held in such esteem. A people that had learned, over the centuries and under different occupying forces, to keep a low profile. Falkenhausen's head of administration, Reeder, also discovered that the Belgian authorities were not complying as enthusiastically as they might have done with the orders of their new masters. They were effectively working to rule.

Falkenhausen had been given only one useful piece of advice by Berlin: to favour the Germanic Flemings and keep the French-speaking Walloons on a short leash, advice that the Francophile aristocrat chose to ignore. During his four years in office he avoided all close contact with the Belgian supporters of the SS, the nationalist Flemish VNV movement and the followers of the fascist New Order. Even Léon Degrelle, the Wallonian Rexist, was not welcome in the general's office. Falkenhausen argued that the far right constituted a minority of less than ten per cent of voters: 'I considered it very important to establish contact with the Belgian nationals who constituted nine-tenths of the population.'

In actual fact, however, Alexander von Falkenhausen effectively socialized only with the upper ten thousand of the country: the Belgian aristocracy, the industrialists and the wealthy bourgeoisie, who shared his love of vintage burgundy, champagne and fine French cuisine. The ascetic-looking general with the narrow, bald head and the glittering spectacles was actually a bon viveur and a great lover of parties. He led the life of a merry bachelor. Only his closest associates knew that he had left his wife behind in Dresden.

On a visit to an old battlefield, the baron, accompanied by his long-haired dachshund Striezel, had discovered the baroque palace of Seneffe to the south of Brussels. The eighteenth-century building behind its weather-beaten walls struck him as looking 'like something out of a fairy-tale'. It was built in the baroque style, and surrounded by a park with huge birch and oak trees, an old tulip tree and two gingkos that reminded him of his happy years in China. The uninhabited castle seemed like an ideal weekend residence. Both romantic and stylish, it was the perfect location for private moments and formal dinners worthy of a governor general.

The property belonged to the family of the Jewish banker Philipson, which had emigrated abroad. According to the rules of the German occupying forces, it was an abandoned, non-Aryan property. Falkenhausen claimed it as a national monument. The palace was restored and rendered habitable. Every weekend Falkenhausen travelled to Seneffe to enjoy 'some truly wonderful time far from all the disturbance and evil of a world that had lost its bearings'.

At parties in the castle the same attractive lady was always by the host's side. Every now and again the vivacious blonde would also turn up in his office, leaving a trail of expensive French perfume in her wake. She preferred to wear softly falling, flower-printed dresses that set off her exquisite figure. The general was clearly head over heels in love with Princess Elisabeth Ruspoli, who was a good twenty years younger than he was. Officially he had engaged the aristocratic beauty as his agent for public relations. The widow of an Italian pilot, she was a member of the Belgian aristocracy, and had excellent connections to the upper circles of society. 'Elisa' became an indispensable part of the general's life.

In his 1943 diary a meeting with 'Elisa' is recorded almost every day, including 20 January 1943, the day that the British plane fired at Gestapo headquarters. According to his diary, the commander, who was sitting at his desk in the Place Royale at the time, was holding a number of discussions with, amongst others, Reeder and Albert de Ligne, a Belgian aristocrat. At about half past seven he went to dinner with Elisa and stayed with her until half past one in the morning. The air attack is not mentioned.

The liaison between the governor and the princess was a source of gossip. Above all, the general's worst enemies, the Party members in Brussels police headquarters, tried very hard to bring the relationship to the attention of those in the highest positions in Berlin. It was even rumoured that Falkenhausen had married his lover in Antwerp

Cathedral. Small wonder, it was said, that the commander showed such forbearance in his treatment of the Belgians.

Certainly the military administration was the lesser evil for the Belgians. 'It is whispered among the refugees,' Jean Améry wrote, 'that the general in Brussels isn't all that bad.'

The Nazis in Berlin were angry with the commander, who was trying to be fair in his rule of the occupied country. Hitler's head of general staff Keitel accused Falkenhausen of not being harsh enough. And Josef Goebbels noted in his diary that the governor 'was not quite up to his task', and that what was needed in Belgium was an 'energetic National Socialist'. But the 'military and political situation', Goebbels lamented, did not allow the National Socialist leadership to transform the military administration into a civilian commissariat as it had in the Netherlands. Hitler was dependent on the infantry generals, and had no intention of annoying them.

Despite the fact that Falkenhausen – rather to his own surprise – was able to remain in his post for four years, he had lost the power struggle with the Reich Security Headquarters (RSHA) over the presence of German police after only a few weeks. He and Reeder only managed to keep the Security Service (Sicherheitsdienst or SD) and the Security Police (Sicherheitspolizei or Sipo) out of Belgium for a short time. At first the Field Police assumed all police duties. Then the RSHA sent its first delegations as personal reinforcements to Brussels. Finally, in October 1940, Berlin decided that Himmler's security forces should no longer be subordinate to the Field Police. From now on they received their instructions directly from Heydrich, leader of the SS and head of the Security Service, completely bypassing the military administration.

On 20 October of the first year of the occupation, the SS opened the fort of Breendonk as a concentration camp for so-called Schutzhäftlinge, or 'protective prisoners'. In the dark fort between Brussels and Antwerp, hundreds of arrested Resistance fighters would die of hunger and weakness or of the consequences of brutal mistreatment.

Ernst Landau, an Austrian journalist, was one of the first to be interned in this inhospitable fortress. On his striped prisoner's jacket he wore the number 31. This young Jew, who had fled from Vienna, had translated flysheets for the Belgian Resistance, aimed at the German soldiers, to inform them about the cruelties of the Hitler regime. When the Gestapo in Brussels unearthed a printing-press, he was arrested. With his fellow prisoners, whether Resistance fighters, freemasons or Communists, he had to carry sandbags and stones for twelve hours each day, under the lash of the sadistic warders, to build the concentration camp. Only after twenty-eight months was Ernst Landau released from that 'hell on earth', as he still calls it. He went to Mechelen transit camp, and from there, on 19 April, on to the twentieth deportation train to Auschwitz.

Governor General von Falkenhausen tried in vain to raise objections when he heard of the terrible conditions in the punishment and labour camp. The fort, he predicted, would 'go down in Belgian history as the hell of Breendonk'. But even in those early months the SS had stopped taking orders from the general. Their task in occupied Belgium was clearly outlined by the government in Berlin: 'the detection and surveillance of efforts directed against the Reich: 1. Jews 2. emigrants 3. [Masonic] Lodges 4. Communists 5. Churches.' The witch-hunt had begun.

5 The Jews in Belgium

Never before had Régine Krochmal reflected on what it actually meant to be a Jew. Was it her black curly hair that distinguished her from her Catholic schoolmates? Jewish traditions played no part in her non-religious parental home. Petite Régine was born in the Netherlands in 1920, daughter of a German mother and a Polish-Austrian family. In Belgium, where she grew up, religious affiliation was not even mentioned on IDs.

She remembered the director of the school of midwifery looking up with astonishment when the trainee nurse Régine pointed out to her that she wasn't Catholic but Jewish. 'I have no idea what that means,' said the director, 'but I'm going to keep an eye on you.'

The Nazis had barely found their feet in Belgium when they tried to teach the ignorant people of the country what an inferior and dangerous race the 'hébreux' were. Their propaganda did not fall on fertile ground. There was no pronounced anti-Semitism in Belgium, but there was more of a lack of knowledge, as revealed by Régine's head of training. Jews with Belgian nationality, who had been living in the country for generations, were often respected citizens and dignitaries.

The biggest wave of emigrants reached Belgium in the 1920s: Eastern Europeans fleeing economic hardship and social ostracism. Many of them had actually planned to travel overseas from Antwerp. But because they were unable to get visas, they stayed in the benignly indifferent country. They settled in Brussels, or in the Flemish port of Antwerp, where the diamond trade was traditionally in Jewish hands.

There were also young people from the Eastern European countries who were eager for education, and who could not hope for a university place at home because of anti-Semitic quotas. In Liège, an affluent Jewish jeweller from the Russian province of Bessarabia looked after these fellow countrymen, who had set off for Belgium with little money but a great thirst for knowledge. One such man was Hertz Jospa. At the age of seventeen, the pharmacist's son came to Liège and trained successfully as a mining engineer. His wife Hava, who later changed her name to Yvonne, was from the same small town as Hertz and studied sociology in the then flourishing Wallonian industrial city. She earned her livelihood as a children's nurse. When she sat her exam in the early 1930s, she was among the first graduates in this new discipline. The couple moved to Brussels where their paths soon crossed with the Livchitz family.

The Goldsteinas family had a similar story. As a young man Mendelis Goldsteinas had left his homeland of Lithuania to study chemistry in Brussels. Today, his son Jacques wonders how his father managed to complete his studies at all under the conditions of the time. At first Mendelis spoke barely a word of French, and on the little money that his parents scrimped together he was just able to afford the rent for a cold attic and his meagre evening meal, a herring. His wife Henda followed him to Brussels a year later from Mariampole in Lithuania – together they managed to survive. His wife studied sociology for two years and then found a post as a secretary. Mendelis graduated in chemistry in 1930 and was given his job as a chemist with the Graeff sugar company.

The second great influx of Jews reached Belgium in 1935, this time from Germany and Austria. At first the Jews were fleeing the effects of Nazi racial policy. Later they were coming to save their lives. Rachel Livchitz, who spoke fluent German after living in Munich, helped to find money and lodgings for the exiles. She worked on the Refugee Committee of the Israeli Community, an organization that Judenreferent Asche tried in vain to incorporate within the Jewish

Council that he himself had set up. Some of the inmates of the twentieth transport to Auschwitz had – like Rudolf Schmitz from Cologne, who came to Brussels with his family in 1939 – been looked after by Youra's mother. Madame Livchitz, Yvonne Jospa remembers with admiration, was not only helpful, she was also full of ideas. Thanks to her roots in the Theosophical Society she had also had close contacts with the Belgian establishment. Yvonne Jospa remembers: 'If things got very difficult, people were sent to Rachel Livchitz. She always sorted things out.'

In Germany's little neighbour the emigrants were not exactly welcomed with open arms, 'but a blind eye was turned to illegal immigration', as a 'Special Report on the Jews in Belgium', published by the National Socialist Security Service in 1941, complains. According to this report, of the 90,000 'religious Jews' in Belgium about 60,000 were illegal immigrants. By 1939 the influx had reached an estimated 116,000 Jews, many of whom fled yet again when the Germans invaded Belgium.

The German Security Service's report on the Jews characterizes the attitude of the Belgian government towards the refugees as 'benevolent'. Typical of their 'loyal attitude' is the 'case of the SS *St Louis*'. The passenger ship had set off from Hamburg in 1939, with nine hundred German Jews on board. They were bound for Havana. The Jewish passengers considered themselves lucky to be in possession of expensive Cuban visas, and were thus able to escape the Nazi terror. But the government in Havana withdrew its agreement to receive the refugees, and the passengers were not allowed to land. For weeks the *St Louis* wandered the seas of the world, since its human cargo was undesirable everywhere, until the ship finally came into Antwerp harbour. Belgium was the first European country to declare itself willing to take two hundred of the desperate passengers. France, England and Holland followed Belgium's example, and gave asylum to the remaining refugees. For 75 per cent of the passengers of the *St Louis* who found asylum in Belgium, it was merely a postponement. They were later deported, and died in the concentration camps.

According to their analysis, the Nazis held the Catholic Church and 'freemasonic liberalism' responsible for Belgium's positive attitude towards the Jews. These two powerful groups in the Belgian state, the Nazis argued, had 'opened wide the gates to the spread and encouragement of Jewry'. Twelve copies of the Security Service report went to the RSHA in Berlin.

The tragedy of the *St Louis* also illustrates the response of the rest of the world as regards National Socialist policy towards the Jews. They closed their eyes to the hardship of the Jewish victims of Nazi policy and allowed Hitler to get on with it. In July 1938, representatives of thirty-two nations had assembled in the French spa resort of Evian-les-Bains to negotiate the reception of the Jews expelled by the Nazis. The Americans were not willing to liberalize their immigration policy. With their veto they also paved the way for the other states. None of the countries raised its reception quotas.

'*Juden unerwünscht*', 'Jews unwelcome', the phrase that excluded the Jews in Germany, now also applied to the international community of states. Of course, at the time no one could have guessed that the decision in Evian meant the certain death of untold thousands, and that Hitler's policy of expulsion would turn into a policy of extermination.

In Belgium, in the first year of the German occupation, the manhunters went quietly about their work. The first thing to do was to register the Jews, because in the residents' offices, and on identification cards, the category of religion was not mentioned. In addition, the Belgian administration resisted the separate registration of a faith community. A register of Jews contravened the Belgian constitution, which forbade discrimination on the basis of race or religion.

General von Falkenhausen's military administration passed its doubts on to Berlin. But the Nazis were ruthless, and they applied pressure. Soon the Brussels office of Heydrich's Reich Security Headquarters on Avenue Louise was able to boast that 'through the constant active work of this branch' – meaning constant pressure from SS headquarters – the first anti-Jewish regulations were passed. Forty-two thousand Jews over the age of fifteen obeyed the order and were given ID cards marked conspicuously in red with the words 'Juif

– Jood'. Only a minority of those who registered, four thousand in all, had Belgian nationality.

The communities were obliged to send a duplicate of their file to the headquarters of the Brussels Gestapo. At the headquarters of the Security Police on Avenue Louise the wooden filing boxes containing the addresses that would lead the murderers to their victims took up six square metres of office space.

Eighteen-year-old Claire Prowizur was one of those who registered. And why not? After all, you only had a right to food cards if you were properly registered. There wasn't yet any cause to be suspicious of the order to register. During the first year of the war, she writes in her autobiography, there was hardly a sign of 'the anti-Semitism imported from Germany'. The synagogues and Jewish schools were still open, weddings according to traditional Jewish rites were permitted, and Jewish children were still allowed to attend Belgian schools.

'For a time our parents, who had experienced pogroms, believed that things were relaxing. No, they thought, we're not the only victims; the Germans are occupying the whole of Europe, and we'll suffer the same fate as those other nice people.'

Claire was the eldest of four children. Her parents – her father came from Poland, her mother from Leipzig – had met in Germany. The couple moved to Belgium without a penny, a fate they shared with thousands of new arrivals. In a small flat in a Brussels suburb Claire's mother saw that her four children made it through. She had had better days. At any rate, in Leipzig she had passed her leaving exams and been interested in German literature. Now, by the dim light of a paraffin lamp, she washed and ironed for strangers. Often the electricity was turned off because the bills weren't paid.

Claire's father was more of a burden than a help to his family. Like so many emigrants he had no resident's or work permit. Men like him worked for starvation wages as tailors, furriers or cutters in basements and backyards. He took to drink, got into trouble with the police, and on a number of occasions was sent back over the border to Germany.

Claire suffered from the conflict at home. When she was fifteen she had written a letter to Queen Elisabeth of Belgium asking for help.

She described her family's unfortunate situation and requested an intervention on her father's behalf. Elisabeth, the mother of Leopold III, was venerated by the people because of her generosity and kindness. And the queen actually helped. Claire's father received a work permit on bail equal to the young girl's annual income, working for Herr Libermann, the manager of a German chain of stores. Claire had started there as an office worker a year earlier, although she would much rather have been at school; as the eldest she felt obliged to contribute to the family income.

The Nazis, shocked by the peaceful cohabitation of Jews and non-Jews in Belgium, adapted their strategy to the situation. No conspicuous 'major actions', which meant no assaults on Jewish businesses, no broken shop windows, no brutal attacks on schools or synagogues. In small, finely graded doses, the National Socialist policy was administered in such a way that the Belgians would slowly get used to it.

The victims were lulled into a false sense of security. In October 1940, Léon Gronowski had to register his leather goods shop with the German authorities, and hang a sign with the inscription '*Joodse Onderneming – Enterprise Juive*' on the door. But for the time being he received no further trouble. The German soldiers from nearby Etterbeek barracks proved to be good customers. The men in the grey uniforms didn't haggle over prices, they paid in cash, every penny. And they turned out to be grateful for being served in German by the proprietor.

The Jewish community recognized the insidiousness of the Nazi tactics too late. As Claire Prowizur remarks today: 'To deceive us, the monster had hidden its claws, and had put on velvet gloves.'

6 Eichmann's Lackey

Kurt Asche was an inconspicuous man in his early thirties, easily overlooked. He was short, his face rather bloated from drinking, his eyes hidden by thick glasses. When the SS man boarded the tram at the Abbaye stop just before nine o'clock in the morning, he might have been taken for a grouchy accountant or office worker on his way to a miserable office somewhere.

But at the time Asche was a powerful man in Belgium. As Judenreferent at Gestapo headquarters in Brussels he was able to decide a person's life or death. He ensured that the trains to Auschwitz were filled with men and women, children, young people and the elderly. And he was the one deciding who was to be crossed from the list of those to be deported. He was the prototype of the respectable-looking National Socialist lackey, who enjoyed the enormous power he had over people intellectually and physically superior to him. His eyes began to sparkle behind his thick glasses, his voice grew thick with eagerness when he was able to throw down the gauntlet to a well-educated or affluent member of the race ostracized by the Nazis.

Kurt Asche's Nazi party file identifies him as a man without particular qualities, as a Party member of little importance. His 'overall racial picture' is judged to be 'predominantly Nordic', his personal attitude 'correct', his 'appearance and behaviour' 'disciplined', his 'financial and family relations orderly', his 'strength of will and personal toughness' was said to be 'purposeful'. Kurt Asche, born in 1909 in Hamburg, son of a cabinet-maker, was 5ft 7in tall and a holder of the bronze SA sports award. He had finished his primary school education, attended business school for two years and completed a three-year apprenticeship as a chemist, including an examination in poisons.

The twenty-two-year-old chemist's assistant had joined the Party in 1931, and four years later he applied to the Party's Security Service in Berlin. Acquaintances had recommended this secure job. The fellow-traveller became a perpetrator. Asche was at first a warder, and then, because he had typing and shorthand, he was employed as a clerk. On internal training courses he was taught the theory and practice of National Socialist racial teachings, until the young Nazi was so ideologically consolidated that in 1936 he became a Hilfsreferent, or assistant expert, in the Jewish Department. From more than twenty offices in Berlin he now gathered information from spies and informers about Jewish organizations and individuals. In Brussels, too, the SS man would later construct a network of informers who helped him to eradicate the Jews.

His workplace in Berlin at the time was called Office IIB of the Security Service. In organizational terms, it was the predecessor of that office that, from 1941, under the direction of Adolf Eichmann, organized the deportation of European Jews to the extermination camps. And, as they would later do in Brussels, Asche and his colleagues in the capital assembled information about 'enemy of state number one', providing 'the relevant state authorities with useful information and suggestions for the progressive fight against the Jews', as Theodor Dannecker, a close colleague of Eichmann's, defined the task of the department.

In November 1938, when the synagogues burned on 'Kristallnacht', when SA and SS troops smashed the windows of Jewish shops, wrecking businesses, when the terror-commandos forced their way into apartments, manhandling the Jews and smashing their furniture to pieces, Kurt Asche was also doing his part in Berlin. He would later boast of his involvement in the arson attack on the big Berlin synagogue on Oranienburger Strasse.

A year later, as Untersturmführer, or Second Lieutenant, he was transferred to the office of the Security Service in Ljublin. He had only heard of the mass-shootings of the murderous task forces in that area of Poland, he explained forty years later at his trial in the courtroom in Kiel, 'by word of mouth'. On 20 April 1941, the Führer's birthday, the assistant expert was promoted to Obersturmführer, or First Lieutenant. SS Untersturmführer Asche, it says in explanation, had 'always shown great industry and eagerness', and his accomplishments were 'entirely satisfactory'.

In November 1941 Asche started work in the Belgian branch of the SS sub-district in Berlin. His Berlin colleague Theodor Dannecker, by now the Judenreferent in Paris, introduced Asche to Brussels. Because of his vigour and his talent for organization, he was particularly highly thought of among his superiors. On 27 November, the two Nazi functionaries called the senior rabbi Salomon Ullmann to SS headquarters in Brussels. This first contact with Ullmann was the prelude to the foundation of a Jewish Council (Judenrat) in Belgium. The most senior head of the Security Police, Reinhard Heydrich, had ruled as early as 1939 that a council of Jewish elders should be set up in every Jewish community. This committee would be responsible for the 'precise and punctual execution of all instructions that either have been made or remain to be made'.

The Jewish community feared that the Nazis themselves might assume control of the administration of the Jews. For that reason the foundation of a self-administered Jewish Council was accepted throughout the whole of the occupied territories. In Brussels, too, respected members of the Jewish community made themselves available for this office, thinking that by doing so they were preventing something worse from happening. However respectable their motives may have been, the members of the Jewish Councils were primarily helping the Nazi thugs to accomplish their goals.

In Belgium the Jewish Council was called the 'Association Juive en Belgique' (AJB). This Jewish Council had an important part to play within the National Socialist strategy of extermination. The Jews themselves were to help to deprive their co-religionists of their rights, and to assist with their deportation. Officially, the purpose of this legal public body, set up in November 1941, was to 'bring together the Jews as Jews, and encourage them in their needs, particularly in the areas of emigration, schooling and attentive care'.

The chairmen of the Jewish Council, academics and affluent bourgeois businesspeople, were to have repeated dealings with Kurt Asche at their weekly meetings in the headquarters of the SS police. The trained pharmaceutical assistant, now in the pay of the Security Service, might have been only a small cog in the extermination machine, but so far as they were concerned, he still represented the power of the system. And Asche stressed his own importance. 'He gives us to understand,' the minutes of the AJB record, 'that he is aware of the intention of the occupying power to accomplish a general settlement of the Jewish question.' He had also, they said, 'to implement all the intentions of the military commanders concerning the Jews'.

Their experience of the SS man was as a pitiless negotiator when it came to freeing sick people, children or the elderly from deportation. Maurice Benedictus, who was a member of this compulsory Jewish Council until he fled for Lisbon in 1943, called Asche a 'Nazi criminal par excellence... moody, coarse, hurtful, sadistic, a drinker'.

The SS man was feared in the cellars on Avenue Louise. William Smordynia, who was given the task of bringing daily rations to the people imprisoned there on behalf of the Jewish Council, went on record after the war as saying that from some cells in the cellars he would regularly hear the cries of people being maltreated. He saw people being led away with their faces beaten bloody. And he saw handfuls of hair pulled out on the floor. He had not been able to identify the perpetrators behind the closed doors. But he had established that under Asche's supervision 'the measures were even more relentless and brutal than usual'. Asche, according to Smordynia, 'was beyond a doubt the most violent of them all'.

After work, the bachelor showed a quite different side to his character. Then the rigid SS functionary became the jolly drinking companion. Asche spent many evenings with Unterstürmführer Karl

Mainzhausen and Hauptsturmführer Fritz Erdmann in pubs and brothels, and always in civilian clothes, so as not to be too conspicuous. One popular destination for their nocturnal wanderings was an establishment at number 33 Rue Berger. This was a secret place, because from outside the club was not recognizable as a bar, and the door opened only for regulars. Here ladies of the night offered more than drinks to their exclusively male guests. Kurt Asche had his eye on a waitress called Ellen. At the time, the black-haired young woman was on the register of prostitutes in the commune of Ixelles, and, like all women practising her trade, was obliged to undergo regular health checks. Ellen was a Jew who had fled from Germany, and who made her living as a waitress and a prostitute. Although it meant infringing the National Socialist racial laws, Asche began a relationship with her. Ellen was even smaller than Asche, she spoke German and, as a Jew, she was dependent on his goodwill. When he tired of her, he would be able to get rid of her whenever he felt like it.

The liaison between the anti-Semite and the Jewish serving-girl was short-lived. In September 1942 Ellen was deported from Mechelen transit camp to Auschwitz. Her powerful 'friend Kurt', as she called Asche to the other guests, did not save her.

In his work as a Judenreferent, Asche's apprentice years in Berlin proved useful. He had to ensure that the anti-Jewish measures were adhered to, and that infringements of the regulations did not go unpunished. In the capital of the Reich, he had been one of the countless little SS functionaries who, with the help of secret messengers and spies, checked that the Jews were being progressively excluded from economic and cultural life. The Nazis also put their programme of racial discrimination into action in Belgium, although at rather greater speed.

From October 1940 until September 1942, the military administration passed a total of eighteen anti-Jewish regulations. First, all Jews over the age of fifteen had to register with the residents' office, then all Jews were dismissed from public service, their properties were sequestered, their radios confiscated, they were permitted only to live in the cities of Antwerp, Brussels, Charleroi and Liège, and they were forbidden to leave their apartments between eight o'clock in the evening and seven o'clock in the morning. They were forbidden to attend non-Jewish schools or to visit swimming-pools or cinemas.

The military administration might officially have been responsible for the issuing of orders, but fundamentally it was only acting on instructions from the RSHA in Berlin. In fact all the threads of anti-Jewish policy came together in Gestapo headquarters. And on Avenue Louise, Obersturmführer Kurt Asche ensured that no gaps appeared in the net, which then drew tighter and tighter around the Jews. Whenever he discovered holes in the system of persecution, he threatened the representatives of the Jewish Council with serious reprisals. When he found out that nearly 1,500 Jews had failed to register in Antwerp, he threatened the chairmen of the Jewish Council with severe punitive measures, unless they performed their duty and took care that the German regulations were followed by everyone.

A perfidious strategy, which, for Maxime Steinberg, the historian of the Holocaust in Belgium, was aimed at making the Jew 'ripe for compulsory deportation': 'He is identified, marked, kept to his apartment, he belongs to a compulsory community that is responsible for his administration, he is isolated from the rest of the population, robbed of his goods and his economic and professional activities... He is ready for the Final Solution.'

Cleverness and an enterprising spirit helped the persecuted Jews to survive. Those who recognized the deadly threat or even only sensed it, sought hiding places, ways of escaping the trap. Claire Prowizur can no longer remember the date when she was summoned to see her boss, Herr Liberman. No, he told her, when she sat down in front of his enormous desk and got out her notepad, she didn't need to take shorthand, he had nothing to dictate to her. He handed her a piece of paper from the military administration. All employers who have personnel of Jewish origin, it said, must now fire them without compensation. Only the employers themselves, the shop-owners, the Jewish craftsmen and the self-employed, were allowed to remain in their jobs.

The businessman looked sadly at his employee, who had begun working for him four years previously as a young teenager. 'The wheels of the infernal machine were set in motion,' Claire wrote in her memoirs. 'We Jews were the common denominator. He probably knew that it would be his turn tomorrow.' Despite the prohibition, Liberman paid her a generous settlement. And along with Philippe, whom she would marry shortly afterwards, she sought the chance of survival in those increasingly difficult conditions.

For almost two years Claire had led a double life. By day the industrious and conscientious secretary, out of office hours she was the militant member of a Trotskyist cell. She had followed Philippe, whom she had met in the 'Bund', the socialist Jewish youth organization, into the Trotskyists. They both became out-of-hours revolutionaries. The young Ernest Mandel, later a well-known economist, was a member, as was Abraham Wainstock, one of the leaders of the Fourth International.

They wrote their newspaper, *The Workers' Struggle*, which they distributed to the letter-boxes of the 'proletariat' at night. They debated, swotted up on Marxism and analysed the errors of Stalinism. Claire says in retrospect:

> We lived in the wonderful world of the young, who believed that their ideals held the solution for a change in society. We were convinced that we were fulfilling an important role; we lived intensely, in an almost overwhelming way, we were serious, honest, happy, we loved life, but were also prepared to give it up. We came home late at night and counted the minutes until the next meeting the following day.

But what would they live on, if the German occupying forces took away their livelihoods? 'With each new law introduced by the Germans we had to take a bigger step than they did,' Claire wrote later, 'we had to be ahead of them. We were well aware that we were just throwing sand in their eyes, and that they would catch us sooner or later. We were prepared for anything, but we were juggling, it was our only way out.' Had it not said, on that piece of paper from the military administration, that Jews who worked at their own expense could keep their jobs? Claire decided to learn tailoring, and to learn it quickly. Within a short time the eighteen-year-old had acquired her diploma. Philippe also set himself up as a self-employed tailor. They opened up their 'shop' in a corner of the little apartment they shared. Life went on.

But Asche and his colleagues were exerting more and more influence on the policies of the occupation. Step by step, the economic situation of the Jews was deteriorating. Thus the leather goods seller Léon Gronowski received a letter from the military administration in November 1941, requiring him to provide an inventory of his assets and supply a German auditor from the Brussels Trusteeship Company with 'any information they might request' about the business, as well as 'a look at his accounts'. For the auditor's visit he had to pay an additional 3,100 francs to the Brussels Trusteeship Company.

In April 1942 the military administration then told Gronowski that 'on the basis of the third Jewish law', one Karl Schneider had been appointed as the administrator of his business. He would learn the 'administrative costs and expenses' from a 'separate regulation'. So Gronowski had to pay for his own expropriation. In July 1942 he received a receipt for a typewriter that was 'taken as a loan'; on 13 August he learned that 'all of his assets were to be removed'. The Jewish businessman was no longer permitted to have a bank account.

His son Simon learned nothing of his parents' worries. Since the beginning of 1941 the nine-year-old had proudly worn a scout's uniform. With his friends from the neighbourhood he was a member of the '*louveteaux*', the cubs, the 145th section of the Belgian boy scouts. A new world was opening up for him. They met every Saturday, went on expeditions through the Forêt de Soignes on Sundays and every day, as befits a good scout, they performed a good deed. For two summers Simon had an uncomplicated, happy time in scout camp. He learned Morse code, how to tie complicated seamen's knots, how to find his way alone in a forest and how to take his bearings from the stars; skills that were later to be very useful to him.

Ita, Simon's sister, was eight years older and had left the lycée at the end of December 1941. According to a new regulation, 'all Jewish pupils had to leave non-Jewish educational institutions and courses'. After the Christmas holidays the vivacious girl with the lively black eyes and the dark mane of hair visited the Jewish Ecole Moyenne Cymring, which, on the instructions of the Jewish Council, and with the agreement of the military administration, was to train teachers for the Jewish children who had been expelled from Belgian schools. Unexpectedly, Ita enjoyed the new class, perhaps in part because she was the only girl. In her diary she wrote:

> I'm moody, very up-and-down, overbearing, an ambitious thing, very proud. I'm good-hearted, I'm just as quick to make someone happy as I am to disappoint him again two minutes later. I may be intelligent, but I'm not really a very good pupil, above all because of my bad memory.
> I love music, Liszt, Chopin, Bizet, Rossini, Verdi, Puccini.
> I love romantic literature, Balzac, Musset, Goethe, but not Voltaire, Chateaubriand, Mérimée.
> I love flowers, birds and my little kitten, Minou.

Little Simon loved and admired his big sister. Ita didn't only play piano, she also started to write a novel, entitled *Kurt*. She wrote poems and long love-letters when she fell in love yet again. She owned a record-player, and almost every Sunday evening she browsed in the pre-war stock of the record shop 'La Maison Bleue' in Brussels city-centre in search of jazz and blues recordings by Louis Armstrong, Ella Fitzgerald or Duke Ellington. Then she brought her discoveries tri-umphantly home. An enthusiasm for American music banned by the Nazis was a form of resistance among the young people of the city.

Simon Gronowski has an old photograph showing his sister Ita with five of her classmates from the Ecole Cymring, hiking in the Ardennes. It is May 1942. Only two months later the law enforcing the wearing of the yellow Jewish star would come into effect. In the picture, the boys wear knee-high socks and short trousers, as people did in the summer in those days. Ita, in solid shoes and white socks, is wearing a short dark skirt with a light blouse, her long hair held back by a headscarf. Jacques Angielzyk is there too. The slim young man, standing behind Ita in the picture, is a good head taller than she is.

Many years later Jacques would remember that class outing. Ita's 'little' brother Simon, wanting to find out more about his sister, would ask him about it. And Jacques, the doctor from Ostende, would tell Simon, the Brussels lawyer, about those last carefree days in the open air.

Each night they slept in a different youth hostel, and they wanted to see as much as they could of the blossoming landscape and the picturesque villages before they returned to Brussels. By the time they got back, their city had changed. It was now dominated by the grey uniforms of the German soldiers, the marching music and the victory announcements that boomed from the loudspeakers in the city centre. The young people were aware that their happiness would not be long-lived.

Just a year later two of them, Jacques and Ita, met again, in Mechelen transit camp, from where the trains travelled to Auschwitz.

7 The Deportations Begin

Official trips to Berlin made a pleasant change for Kurt Asche. Berlin's night-life had lost none of its attractions. And thanks to the extra pay he earned for living abroad, the not particularly handsome bachelor was now able to live a quite different life from the one that he had led before the war. But the best thing was that everyone spoke German. In Belgium, the SS officer was deeply disturbed by the fact that the inhabitants simply refused to understand him. Only the Jews with whom he had the bulk of his dealings in his Brussels post made an effort to speak German to him.

The meeting on 4 March 1942, at 116 Kurfürstenstrasse, was arranged for ten o'clock. The suits of the two friends, Asche and Dannecker, still smelled of a long night in the pub when they arrived, along with their colleague Willy Zöpf from The Hague, in Adolf Eichmann's office. He had fresh instructions for them. On 20 January, under the direction of Reinhard Heydrich, the 'Final Solution of the Jewish question' had been decided at the Wannsee Conference. The systematic mass-murder of European Jews was to be implemented 'in an appropriate way in the East'. The branches of the Reich Security Office in the occupied western territories were given a key role in this. They were to organize the deportation of the

Jews to the concentration camps as inconspicuously as possible.

A quarter of a century later the camp administrator Kurt Asche, who had initially gone into hiding under a false name after the end of the war, delivered his own version of this crucial meeting to the public prosecutor in Hamburg.

> In about the spring of 1942, Thomas, my superior, revealed to me that I was to go to a discussion in the Judenreferat [Jewish Office] of the RSHA ... The meeting was led by Eichmann, and must have been held in Eichmann's room. Eichmann told us that on the basis of an order from the Führer the Jews were to be deported from occupied Western Europe (France, Belgium and the Netherlands) to the East, to Auschwitz concentration camp. Large petroleum and Buna rubber factories had been set up in Auschwitz, and the Jews were to work there. Eichmann gave more detailed technical instructions for the equipment of the transports, as well as the kinds of Jews who were to be deported. I also seem to remember that he mentioned a bounty, in connection with the deportation of the Jews from Slovakia, which was to be paid for the Jews from somewhere or other. Eichmann also mentioned the numbers of the Jews who were to be deported from the three countries. Belgium was to deport a good ten thousand people. As far as I remember, children, women and old people were also supposed to be included on the transports. But not Jewish members of mixed marriages or Jewish half-breeds, so long as they were not 'Geltungsjuden' ['Jews by definition']. However, Jews of Belgian nationality were not initially to be deported, but only stateless Jews and Jews with the nationality of certain European countries.

But the first thing to do was to stigmatize the Jews. The Jewish star, Eichmann ordered, was to be introduced immediately in France, Belgium and the Netherlands. Because only then could the mass deportation to the East begin. A first test run was to be started from

France. The Paris Judenreferent Dannecker was in charge of the preparations for the deportation of five thousand Jews from France. The gas chambers were already in operation in Auschwitz concentration camp.

The Final Solution was now on the agenda for Kurt Asche in Belgium. Just two weeks later he met Dannecker in Paris to coordinate the introduction of the Star of David for the occupied western territories. It bore a bilingual inscription in Belgium and was to be introduced simultaneously in the three countries. An explanation of this measure in the national regulations, 'rather in the form of a preamble', was superfluous, it says in the files. Because the duty of marking must be seen 'in the context of the Final Solution of the European Jewish question'. Marking for the purpose of annihilation – the Nazis didn't want to put it quite as clearly as that.

In Paris, Dannecker was concerned with organizing transport for the first deportation. He found a ready, indeed an enthusiastic helper in General Lieutenant Kohl, the head of the Rail Transport Division. Dannecker wrote in a note: 'I was able to establish that he is an uncompromising opponent of the Jews, and agrees one hundred per cent to a Final Solution of the Jewish question with the aim of the total annihilation of the enemy.'

Once again, the only place where problems arose was in Belgium. The mayors of the Brussels communities refused to comply with the law of 27 May 1942 for the marking of the Jews, and to distribute the fabric stars to the 'Israelites'. The new law, they explained, was unacceptable to them because it 'directly injured the dignity of humanity, whoever the people concerned might be'. For two days High Field Command took over the distribution, and then the Jewish Council had to distribute the Stars of David.

Léon Gronowski collected the yellow stars for his family. His wife sewed them on to coats and jackets, as the Germans had decreed, visibly on the left-hand side, where the heart beats. Ita described how terrible it was to be publicly branded in that way. In a letter to a classmate she complains 'about being stared at like a rare animal, they assess you, they weigh you up. I force myself to laugh, but deep inside

I'm filled with bitterness.' The little cub scout Simon didn't have to wear a star. His life seemed to be just as carefree as before.

At his regular meetings with the representatives of the Jewish Council, Obersturmführer Kurt Asche repeatedly referred to the decree that the Star of David must be worn in public. Anyone caught without a star 'would receive a single punishment: Breendonk concentration camp'. In June 1942 the transit camp at Mechelen, from which the road led to certain death, did not yet exist.

Early in June 1942, the military administration forbade the Jews to practise the medical profession. Youra Livchitz had to relinquish his job as an assistant physician at the hospital of St Pierre. It was a sad farewell. Régine Krochmal, the trainee nurse and budding midwife, was not allowed to continue her training as a nurse either. Régine was terribly disappointed. So close to the end of her course, she was thrown out and excluded from further instruction. But when she said her tearful goodbye to her head of training, he said, 'I am banking on you sitting your finals.' And so Régine, who prepared even more intensely for the examination, did receive her midwife's diploma, after passing her exam in great style.

Régine had befriended Marianne, a refugee from Germany. From her she learned of the terrible deeds of the National Socialists. Marianne had a handicapped brother who lived in a home. One day he and all his friends were collected from the home. Later her parents received the news that their eighteen-year-old son had died. Being disabled, he had fallen victim to the Nazis' euthanasia programme.

Marianne and Régine refused to comply with the 'degrading order of the Nazis' and wear the Jewish star. The friends found work in the soup kitchen of the Jewish community. There, at 'Soupe Populaire' in the Rue Ruysbroeck, the emigrants who had fled the Nazis met in the lunchtime food-queue, along with veterans of the Spanish Civil War, students and workers. Many of them spoke German. The two young women, who had mastered the language of the enemy, made friends with some Austrians who had founded a resistance group.

They joined the 'Austrian Liberation Front', and immersed themselves enthusiastically in their conspiratorial tasks. Their plan was to inform the German soldiers about the criminal nature of the regime they were serving, and induce them to desert with their flysheets and newspapers run off on a roneo machine. To Marianne and Régine fell the task of talking to the men in their army uniforms on the street or in cafés. 'We asked them the time,' Régine recalls, 'and the soldiers were usually very happy to hear their mother tongue.' They then involved them in conversation, turning the subject towards the war, which affected them all. As soon as Régine became aware that the man she was talking to might possibly be receptive to critical information, she arranged a date for a further meeting. This time she would bring with her the flysheets they had produced themselves, believing, in her youthful naivety, that the soldiers would need only to read them to become convinced opponents of the war.

Like Claire Prowizur in her Trotskyist group, Régine Krochmal was profoundly convinced that she 'was doing something useful and meaningful'. She also found a feeling of community, friendship and helpfulness in the twenty-strong group. Never again in her life had she been so happy, she confirmed decades later. The deadly danger into which she and her friends were headed was something she was already aware of. 'I was already condemned as a Jew. So what risk was I taking in working against the Germans?'

In June 1942, the military administration was able to state, in its quarterly report to Berlin, that regulations had been put into effect. By excluding the Jews from the medical profession and marking them with the Star of David, they had concluded the legislative part of the Jewish persecution in Belgium. The Jews had 'only extremely limited life opportunities'. Now – under the euphemistic slogan 'evacuation' – the next phase of the extermination policy could begin. The deportation of the Jews, or 'their evacuation from Belgium', must from now on 'be carried out in the wake of the general planning by the responsible Reich authorities'.

This went into effect immediately. On 20 June, Theodor Dannecker and Kurt Asche met early in the morning at the Gare du Midi in Brussels, to travel together to Berlin. SS Obersturmbannführer Adolf Eichmann had invited the Judenreferenten from Paris, Brussels and

The Hague to his office at 116 Kurfürstenstrasse. They needed to find a replacement for the Jews who had been deported from Germany so far, and who could not be deported to the East 'for military reasons during the summer', and they needed to find them as soon as possible. Deportation trains from Germany had been affected by a transport blockade on East–West connections because of the preparations for the German summer offensive in Russia. The resulting shortfall in supplies of Jews for the extermination camps was, according to Eichmann, to be made up by Jews from Holland, Belgium and France. In the bureaucratic language of the desk-bound director of operations: 'Larger quantities from the occupied western territories are being transferred to Auschwitz concentration camp for use as labour.' Fifteen thousand were to be deported from the Netherlands, ten thousand from Belgium and one hundred thousand from France. The deportees 'of both sexes' were to be between the ages of sixteen and fifty. Ten per cent of the transports were also permitted to consist of 'Jews unfit for work'. A hidden reference to the fact that it wasn't only labour that awaited the Jews when they reached their destination.

'Because of the nature of the transport material,' the same note states, contact would be established with Lieutenant General Kohl in Paris. 'At the same time the question of the ten transport trains required for Belgium also needs to be answered.' The RSHA had set his goals high: 'the transports – about three each week – were to begin' from mid-July.

When the military administration learned of the plan, General von Falkenhausen sent his head of administration, Reeder, to Reich Security Headquarters. The honorary SS general was to intervene on behalf of the Belgian Jews. In a telegram, the military administration in Brussels once again voiced their doubts about a general deportation: Jews of Belgian nationality were 'seen as Belgians' among the population 'where the understanding of the Jewish question is not yet very widespread'. For that reason the measures could be seen as 'the start of a general compulsory deportation'. As the Jews were 'to a large extent involved in the contemporary economic process', shortages might be experienced in the labour market. 'Practical difficulties' could also be expected. Because as the deportations from France and Holland started to become common knowledge 'a certain unease has arisen among the Jews here'. The Israelites were trying 'to escape our clutches'.

At the same time, on 7 July 1942, the representatives of the Jewish Council received their first indirect reference to the impending deportation. At one of the regular meetings in his office, Kurt Asche referred these notables to the association's obligation to ensure that it kept its staff at their present level. The organization would have to be capable of accomplishing the great tasks that would shortly be coming its way.

Six days later, the representatives of all organizations involved in the deportation met for a discussion. Among those present was Sturmbannführer Alfred Thomas from police headquarters in Brussels, who would lose his life six months later in the air attack by the Belgian pilot Jean de Sélys Longchamp. The meeting also included a representative of the Brussels Trusteeship Company, to which all Jews had to hand over their possessions, an official from the military administration and a captain of the Brussels housing office. The object of their discussion was the division of the expected spoils. 'The 10,000 or so Jews of the first transport are registered as having 2,500 Jewish apartments,' reads the file entry, 'which will first be sealed by the security service', before then being examined for interesting material. The subsequent procedure by which the Nazis would appropriate the possessions of the Jews is recorded in great detail: 'Keys to the flats are packed in paper bags and sent, instance by instance, to the housing office in Brussels, and placed at our disposal by that office... We may expect to clear the apartments only in the second half of August, or more precisely towards the end of August 1942.' The representative of the military administration tried in vain to insist that for the furniture seized by the SS police 'a receipt with an estimated value' should be supplied by a neutral expert and handed to the military commander. This check by the military administration was strictly rejected by Sturmbannführer Thomas and his colleagues.

While the first trains to Auschwitz were setting off from France and Holland in July 1942, in Belgium preparations for deportation were going ahead rather slowly. The Brussels military administration didn't want to involve the Belgian police in these controversial actions fearing that conflicts might arise. The RSHA had another tried and tested idea for how such a case might be handled. In order to make up for the lack of local police forces, the Jews themselves were involved in the organization of the deportation. The same thing would happen in Belgium.

When the chairmen of the Jewish Council were called to Gestapo Headquarters in June 1942, Asche was not alone in his office. This time a beefy SS officer from Berlin was boasting about his accomplishments. The RSHA had sent Anton Burger to Brussels. The task of the SS Hauptsturmführer was to get his colleagues in Avenue Louise on the move to ensure that the 'Abschub' from Belgium finally got under way. Burger brought the relevant experience to the job. Along with Eichmann he had already made Vienna 'Jew-free'. The 'Butcher of Vienna' stayed only a few weeks in the Belgian capital, but left a lasting impression. Maurice Benedictus of the Jewish Council insisted that he 'far exceeded in brutality and sadism' his colleagues in the Brussels SS.

By way of greeting, Anton Burger first made the envoys of the Jewish Council stand to attention, before, his voice breaking, threatening them with deportation: 'The time is past when the Jews needed only to think about their businesses or lounge about as thousands of German soldiers sacrifice themselves for Europe.' Ten thousand of them were immediately engaged for labour service outside Belgium. And the Jewish Council would be responsible for ensuring that this measure was put into effect in an orderly manner. 'Where are they being taken to?' asked one of the chairmen. 'Inside the old borders of the German Reich,' replied Burger evasively. The forced labourers would be treated 'humanely', they would be paid for their work and they would be allowed to write letters and receive packages. But the representatives of the Jewish Council remained suspicious. 'I am worried,' Salomon Vanden Berg subsequently wrote in his war diary, 'that this is a mass deportation to Poland. I hope I am wrong, but I fear the worst.'

Nonetheless, Vanden Berg and some of his fellow chairmen allowed themselves to be turned into lackeys of the Nazis. The wealthy, educated gentlemen on the committee of the Belgian Jewish Council believed they would be able to prevent worse things from happening by being willing and compliant. No one suspected that what awaited the deportees would far exceed any cruelties known hitherto. They were banking on the idea that the Germans were a civilized nation.

So the Jewish Council agreed to prepare a file of the names and addresses of all the Jews living in Belgium. Burger had threatened the Jewish notables: 'If you refuse to produce the list we require, and thus prevent the orderly enforcement of the deportation to forced labour, the German police will arrest Jews in the street at random, regardless of age or health.'

The Jewish Council complied, and set up another office at number 56 Boulevard du Midi, acquiring additional typewriters and employing office workers. On 17 July the new assistants, using the communal register and their own lists, began to produce the list of addresses, in triplicate, of all the Jews living in Belgium.

Three days later, Asche and Burger unexpectedly arrived in the afternoon. They wanted to find out how the work was going. By that point three thousand file-cards had been written. Not nearly enough, thought the controllers from Avenue Louise, threatening 'unpleasant consequences' if the whole register were not completed within the next five days. Even the excuse that the hired clerks could only work by day because there was no electricity at night fell on deaf ears so far as the two SS Obersturmführers were concerned. They didn't care how they accomplished the task. 'For these gentlemen,' the office supervisor said in the report he wrote for the committee of the Jewish Council, 'it is clearly of crucial importance that the work should be completed in time.'

The threatening gestures had their effect. Punctually, on 25 July, the Nazis had a comprehensive file of about 56,000 people ready to be dispatched to their death. The first conscriptions for forced labour could be sent out. Robert Holzinger from the Jewish Council was responsible for that. Together with colleagues from the 'Judenrat' he selected those people on the Jewish register who would receive a letter to that effect. The letters would be dispatched by messengers from the Jewish Council.

The labour deployment order was authorized by the military commander, and bore the signature of the head of the Brussels SS Chancellery in Avenue Louise, the lawyer Ernst Ehlers. From this letter the unfortunate recipient also learned that he would be part of the labour deployment 'with immediate effect', and that on the morning of a particular given day he would have to report to Mechelen transit camp. In the event of refusal, recipients were threatened with the very same consequences that would await them if they complied with the order:

> You are expressly forbidden to revolt against this order by
> contacting any German or Belgian authorities or individuals.
> Any objections can be raised at the transit camp. Failure to
> report to the transit camp at the assigned time will lead to
> arrest and deportation to a concentration camp in Germany,
> and the sequestration of all of your property.

The Nazis had chosen the picturesque little town of Mechelen in Flanders as the starting-point for their transports to Auschwitz. The ancient Episcopal seat proved to be ideal for their purposes. Mechelen – Malines in French – lies directly between Brussels and Antwerp, the cities where most Jews lived at the time. On the edge of the medieval town centre was the infantry barracks named after General Dossin, built in 1756 on the orders of Maria Theresa of Austria. This barracks had room for a thousand people and its own railway connection; a 'dienstspoor' (service railway line) that connected the barracks with the network of the Belgian railway service meant that the deportation could be accomplished discreetly.

Offices for the German guards were set up at great speed, and dormitories were built in wooden sheds that had been roughly knocked together for the prisoners. Three members of the Brussels police department moved to Mechelen: the SS officer Philipp Schmitt became the director of the transit camp, SS Hauptscharführer Max Boden was his deputy, and Asche's drinking companion from the 'Diana' bar, SS Untersturmführer Karl Mainzhausen, was responsible for baggage inspection, a lucrative position from which his friend Kurt would also profit.

On 27 July the first Jews arrived in Mechelen. They had obeyed the demand of the military administration, and stowed in their suitcases and bags everything that seemed to be required for their stay in a labour camp. Along with the labour deployment order, they had been sent a list of the 'equipment' that they would need to bring with them:

1. Foodstuffs for 14 days (only non-perishable goods such as pulses, pearl barley, oats, flour, preserves, etc.).

2. 1 pair stout working boots, 2 pairs socks, 2 shirts, 2 pairs underpants, 1 work-suit or dress, 2 woollen blankets, 2 sets of bed-linen, bowl, beaker, 1 spoon, 1 pullover.

3. Food and clothing cards, identity card and other forms of identification.

The camouflage was almost perfect. Wasn't it obvious that the Germans required a workforce in their factories? After all, in the First World War, 200,000 Belgians had been in labour service in Germany. Many obeyed the order because they feared reprisals on themselves or their families.

Several pupils at the Ecole Cymring were among the first to receive the innocuous-sounding 'labour deployment order' and report obediently to the transit camp. When the headmaster of the school, Charles Cymring, heard about it, he tried to negotiate the liberation of the adolescents with the responsible parties in Mechelen. After all, his pupils belonged to an institution that the Jewish Council had set up on the instructions of the occupying Germans for the training of Jewish teachers. But Cymring's words fell on deaf ears in the barracks. The Nazis there had only one thing in mind: to fill the first transport to Auschwitz, scheduled for 4 August. If the headmaster was not deported to Auschwitz along with his pupils, it was only because he had Belgian nationality.

The Nazis were disappointed. Their clever idea of a quiet and peaceful deportation from Belgium, masked as labour deployment, didn't seem to be working. Far fewer Jews complied with the demand than had been expected. If things went on like that, barely half of the planned quota of 10,000 would be effectively deported to Poland.

In the Brussels SS headquarters, Asche and Burger gave the representatives of the Jewish Council a good talking-to. They were kindly requested to ensure that the deportation went ahead smoothly, or else in future the SS would use other, more brutal methods. Perhaps the gentlemen knew what had happened in Poland? This time, again, the notables set to work. After they had delivered the file of Jewish addresses and distributed the fatal conscription orders, they declared themselves willing to urge their co-religionists to comply with the labour-deployment order.

From now on, each demand by the military administration was sent out with a letter from the Jewish Council, guaranteeing that 'this was simply a labour deployment and not a deportation measure'. In addition, the Jewish notables appealed to the recipients' sense of responsibility. 'The regrettable events of the last few days oblige us to bring it to your attention that non-compliance with the labour deployment order would have very grave consequences for you, as well as for the members of your family and the Jewish population as a whole.'

Edith, Claire Prowizur's younger sister, was one of those who believed that her family could only be protected from further unpleasantness if she obeyed the call to Mechelen. None of her relations were able to persuade the girl otherwise. Not even her boyfriend, whom Claire quickly rang up and called over to their flat. Jean loved Edith, and wanted to bring her to safety. He had the chance to do so; he had the money, and he was a 'goy', a non-Jew. Her parents and brothers and sisters would also hide from their persecutors, and thus be safe from the threatened reprisals. But Edith had made her mind up. She reported punctually in Mechelen for the labour deployment.

Her two sisters had insisted, as she left, that Edith should try to write to them at the address of a friend who was not suspected of anything by the Nazis. 'If you're having a hard time,' Claire said, 'then slant your handwriting to the side.' Weeks later they received a postcard from Mechelen. Edith's handwriting slanted strongly sideways. They never heard from her again.

On 4 August the first transport set off for the East. From the first convoy to Auschwitz onwards, the claim that the inmates of the eastbound trains were being transported to a labour camp was revealed to be a barefaced lie. From the very start, the people deported were not only those who were capable of work. The transports also included children and old people. More than half of those deported to 'forced labour' were older than forty and younger than sixteen.

On 15 September, in its quarterly report, the military administration summed up the 'anti-Jewish measures' as follows:

> In accordance with an instruction from the SS Reichsführer, the deportation of the Jews to the East has begun. At first it was carried out as a labour-deployment measure, and therefore applied principally to Jews who were capable of working. Only on the basis of later instructions from the RSHA has it acquired the character of a general evacuation of the Jews, so that recently, Jews who are not completely capable of complying with labour deployment are also being transported. Nationals of the British Empire, America and neutral states such as Italy are – along with the 4,000 or so Belgian Jews – exempted from these measures. So far a total of 10,000 Jews have been transported to the East.
>
> Among the Jews this action naturally produced a considerable panic. Many people have tried to escape to unoccupied France, but most of them were arrested by border guards and the French police authorities...
>
> Among the Belgian people, the action did not cause

much of a stir, as the Jews were relatively unimportant here, and nine-tenths of them were emigrants and other foreigners. Representatives of the Belgian Ministry of Justice and other Belgian offices repeatedly stressed that they would only intervene on behalf of Belgian Jews.

The report by the head of the military administration reproduces, in contorted form, the dramatic turn that the persecution of the Jews had taken in Belgium. 'Gentle' deportation via the 'labour deployment order' was a failure. Of the expected 10,000 conscriptees, only 4,000 had reported in Mechelen. In order to fill their trains to Auschwitz, the SS had taken to arresting the Jews on nightly raids and bringing them to Dossin barracks. Field Police, Flemish SS men and Wehrmacht soldiers were involved in these raids. On the nights of 15 and 28 August, in the ghetto near the diamond market in Antwerp, on 3 and 11 September in Brussels, as well as in the immigrant communities of St Gilles and Anderlecht, Jews were rounded up and transported away on lorries. The SS officers usually followed the same pattern. Late at night, military vehicles circled the areas where the Jews lived. Then German Field Policemen and German and Flemish SS members would search one house, one flat, one room after another. Still half-asleep and caught unawares, the Jews had only a few minutes to get dressed and pack a bag. Then, to the sound of loud commands, they were driven to the trucks; young and old men, weeping children, young girls, mothers with their crying babies in their arms, a little boy supporting his grandmother.

Behind their curtains, their Belgian neighbours looked out into the street, illuminated by the headlights of the waiting trucks. And the cries of 'Faster, faster, keep on walking!' rang out far into the night. The next day the atmosphere in the area was leaden; there were no children's cries, no shouting, no chattering on the pavement. People stayed in their houses. They were frightened.

Samuel Perl reads from his diary in a halting voice. Fifty-seven years after the raid on 15 August in Antwerp, the memories of that night still bring tears to his eyes. And the observant Jew can no longer understand why, as a young diamond-grinder, he wrote his diary in German, the language of the occupiers and executioners. As an eight-year-old he had come to Belgium from Hungary with his parents; at home they spoke Yiddish, at work Dutch or French. Perhaps, he guesses, it was the influence of the *Brüsseler Zeitung*, the paper produced in German by the Nazis, which he read every day.

Samuel Perl had spent the night at the house of a friend who was to join the labour deployment of the Todt Organization the following day. The two boys wanted to spend the last few hours before his departure talking to each other – regardless of the curfew. Long after midnight they finally went to sleep. Perl wrote in his diary:

> I suddenly woke up. Cars and trucks were driving past
> down below. I heard hammering on the door of a neighbour's
> house, someone shouting. Then we heard the cries of the
> inhabitants, women and children. We quickly understood
> that this had to be the Gestapo. At first we thought they were
> looking for young people who hadn't complied with the
> conscription. We got dressed and stood in the dark room and
> followed all the tiniest movements of the Gestapo. We heard
> them shouting 'Shut your windows' and 'you bastards',
> accompanied by the sound of gunfire. A car was started,
> turned into our street and lit up our house with its
> headlights. 'Number 53', we heard a rough voice saying. 'No,
> we want number 35,' replied another murderer's voice, and
> the car drove past our house. Down below we heard cries,
> laments and crying for a long time. 'If I don't go mad now, I
> never will,' I said to my friend. I was overwhelmed with grief,
> without really knowing why. We comforted one another. Now
> there was no question of going to sleep.

When Sam ran to his parents' house in the early morning, he discovered the Gestapo seal on the front door. His parents and brothers and sisters had been taken away. He would never see them again.

8 The 'Unsuspecting'

The military commander of Belgium might have been expected to be a man with access to all sources of information. Although it always arrived a few days late, Alexander von Falkenhausen liked to read his London newspaper. As the most senior military official in the country, he was familiar with the findings of the Field Police. He studied transcripts of recordings of foreign radio broadcasts, and all the reports of the intelligence services were shown to him. Nonetheless the general – who was in charge of Belgium from May 1940 until July 1944 – writes in his unpublished memoirs that he knew nothing about the concentration camps and the extermination policy of the Nazi regime.

His fairy-tale castle in Seneffe was not only a meeting place for the Belgian aristocracy and the moneyed classes. Friends, acquaintances and relations from Germany also visited the baron, who was considered as an opponent of Hitler, in his remote idyll:

> My friends came to Brussels and Seneffe in ever greater
> numbers: Ambassador von Hassel, Counsellor von Trott
> zu Solz, Professor Jessen, my cousin Gotthard von
> Falkenhausen, a bank commissioner in Paris, Minister
> Popitz, General Fellgiebel, Count von Moltke, from whom
> I heard of the planned and unsuccessful attacks on Hitler's

life. We had long been opposed to an attempted assassination, but now even he could see no other way out. The 'Kreisau circle' had drawn up plans which I discussed with Moltke and Trott. Goerdeler, too, had worked everything out in writing, and was tirelessly active. But I asked him not to visit me, since it struck me as too dangerous for us both… When I last met Moltke in Seneffe, in summer 1943, he was very depressed, and said, 'I think the German people must descend into the abyss before it can rise again.' Sadly he was right. At about the same time Planck came for the last time. He asked me, on behalf of a number of groups, whether I would be willing, in the event of the Führer's being toppled, to assume the role of leader. I declared myself willing, on condition that I myself could be in charge of withdrawal from Belgium… But I was later surprised that I had learned nothing, from the countless visitors that I had in the course of those years, about the horrors in the East and the concentration camps and extermination camps. Even men like Planck, Moltke, Hassel and others living in Germany never talked about them to me. But they must have known nothing about them either. The SS Reich was hermetically sealed.

But the commander did receive instructions from the 'hermetically sealed' SS Reich which could have left him in no doubt about the true intentions of the anti-Semitic measures. After all, the military administration was applying the policy of Hitler's regime in Belgium. It authorized the commands of the RSHA in official orders and announcements. And it passed on the briefings of the SS leadership in Berlin internally to its own Field Police. Thus, towards the end of October 1942, a secret letter from the military commander in Belgium and northern France reached all administrative and military headquarters, alerting the Field Police to the difference between 'deportation to the East and the bringing of prisoners to a concentration camp in the Reich' in order to 'avoid misunderstandings'. According to this letter, a protective detention order from the RSHA was required for 'protective' prisoners, who were mostly political and always non-Jewish. Deportations, on the other hand, for which the National Socialist Security Police and the Security Service had sole responsibility, were to be kept secret. 'Deportation to the East is a different and more severe measure than simply being sent to a concentration camp.' What measures could the general in whose name this briefing was issued have considered 'more severe' than a period in a concentration camp?

Governor General von Falkenhausen did not deal with the representative of the German Foreign Office in Brussels solely in an official capacity. The diplomat Werner von Bargen and his wife were also welcome guests at the illustrious dinners in Seneffe castle. The Foreign Office officials regularly reported on the progress of the deportations to Assistant Secretary of State Luther, who was responsible for the 'evacuation' of the Jews in the Foreign Ministry in Berlin. Von Bargen drew his attention to 'illegal emigrations' to France and Switzerland, and reported 'rumours of the slaughter of the Jews etc.' because of which the labour deployment order was no longer being obeyed. Now the Jews would have to be arrested in raids and individual operations. Is it really possible that Bargen and Falkenhausen would never have discussed those rumours?

If even the most senior commander in the country declared that he had heard nothing of the Holocaust, how could the Jews in Belgium have known of the true destination of the transports to the East? In June 1942 the BBC, alluding to the Polish government in exile, had reported the extermination of the Jews in the East for the first time. Two months later, when the first deportation trains had left Belgium for Auschwitz, a single Belgian underground newspaper, the Flemish *De Vrijschutter*, picked up this revelation: 'They are being killed in groups by gas, and others are killed by salvos of machine-gun fire.'

Or did they not want to hear, as Claire Prowizur, a deportee on the twentieth convoy, suspects in her memoirs? In October 1942 a French comrade turned up in her Trotskyist group in Brussels, tall, blue-eyed and blond, quite the Aryan type. He had managed to escape from a camp in Upper Silesia and made his way across Germany. He had worked in a mine in Silesia, and a warder whom he had befriended had helped him escape. His plan was to alert the comrades in Brussels and, with their help, draw the attention of the world to the monstrosities that were being carried out in Poland. He had seen the Nazi death factories with his own eyes.

In her book, Claire Prowizur describes how happy and proud they were to have spread the report to British radio:

> Via illegal channels we managed to get the BBC to broadcast the news on one of its programmes. It reached people in the free nations and those people in occupied countries who were secretly listening to forbidden stations. The gas ovens were made official. On radio, through the voice of an eyewitness!

And finally the bitter acknowledgement: 'But the oven chimneys did not stop smoking until after liberation. A few bombs could have destroyed the incinerators. Instead of bombs, the news was followed by silence. Now we know the reason: we weren't worth any bombs.'

The Resistance had heard of mass-shootings, starvation and inhuman working conditions. And those Communists who, like Hertz Jospa, had already encountered the dark side of Hitler's Germany before the war, believed the Nazis capable of the worst atrocities that anyone could imagine. 'Their cruelty, their methods, were only waiting for an opportunity to come into their own,' Jospa said after the war in an interview for the London-based historical institute, the Wiener Library. 'As far as I was concerned there was no doubt that the Jewish population in particular was in great danger.' But the true extent of the organized extermination was not yet known even to this Communist in autumn 1942.

Through the Belgian umbrella resistance organization, the Front de l'Indépendance, Jospa learned of an economist at the university of Leuven, Victor Martin, who was planning to travel to Poland on research matters. Under this cover, there was a possibility that he might be able to use that disguise to convey information to the

Belgian Resistance. For the 'Comité de Défense des Juifs' (Jewish Defence Committee or CDJ) co-founded by Hertz Jospa in 1941, here, at last, was an opportunity to learn more about the fate of the deportees. Jospa explains:

> For some time gloomy but imprecise rumours had been reaching our ears from Germany, concerning the extermination of the deported Jews and the existence of an extermination camp with incinerators near Auschwitz. We were accused of purveying the incredible rumour that soap was being made of human fat there. The Nazis had already committed such loathsome crimes that there would have been no point in adding incredible stories which would have tended to damage the credibility of our propaganda. We wanted to have a clear conscience. It was a matter of finding out, whatever the cost, what was actually happening to the transports of the Jews.

The lecturer Victor Martin declared himself willing to take the risk and undertake research into where the Belgian Jews had ended up. In 1938, while studying for his doctorate, he had established contact with various German universities, and now, in the autumn of 1942, Cologne University supported him in his desire to continue his academic research into the 'deployment of workers in Belgium and abroad' in Poland. In Wroclaw he planned, in order to finance his stay, to teach French at the Berlitz School.

Early in 1943, Martin arrived in the region of Auschwitz. Once he was there, he questioned French forced labourers working in the factories, and then set about gathering information in the cafés and pubs of Katowice. In the ghetto of Sosnowitz he met deportees from Belgium working in the Auschwitz detachments. Of the women, children and old people who had left Belgium in the autumn of 1942 he found not a trace. He saw the huge incinerators of Auschwitz, which were far too big for a normal crematorium, and learned that those Jews who were unfit for work were being burned there. But he had aroused suspicions with his curious questions. In February he was arrested in Katowice, but at the end of March he was transferred from prison to a labour camp from which he managed to escape. He did not reach Brussels until May. In a packed meeting of the Jewish Defence Committee he reported on the children, women and old people who had vanished without trace, the huge incinerators in the concentration camp, and what was being said about the fate of the deported Jews in Poland. 'But even then,' he said in his interview for the Wiener Library, 'some of my listeners could not believe that these highly civilized Germans had moved on to genocide.'

In the columns of the Nazi press, above all in the French-language gazette *L'Ami du Peuple*, rumours about the extermination camps that were trickling into Belgium were dismissed as 'Bolshevik horror stories'. Even some Jews suspected that the rumours might be nothing but Communist propaganda. Time and again, members of the Resistance who went to Jewish families to persuade them to hide their children found doors slammed in their faces, as people accused them of being vile Bolsheviks.

By mid-October thirteen trains had left the transit camp in Mechelen for Auschwitz. There were still no concrete references to the actual fates of the deportees. But the rumour that many of them were killed in the East was a persistent one. For that reason *L'Ami du Peuple* considered itself obliged to respond and present the information as wicked gossip. 'The Jew is spreading rumours to the effect that the evacuees are being badly treated.' By this point, 8,849 of the total of 12,454 deportees were dead. They were gassed immediately upon their arrival in Auschwitz.

During those autumn days of 1942, SS functionary Asche had one of his regular meetings with the representatives of the Jewish Council. The notables humbly asked permission to set up eight to ten benches in the Gestapo cellar. In the course of the conversation the SS Obersturmführer made a remark that would come back to haunt him decades later in a Nazi trial before the regional court in Kiel. In the minutes of the meeting held on 23 October 1942 Asche is quoted as coming out with the following sentence: 'The evacuation applies to all the Jews in Belgium, and none of them will return to this country.'

Kurt Asche must have been aware of the destination and purpose of the deportation. A secretary from Gestapo headquarters later stated before the regional court in Kiel that each time the departure date for a further transport from Belgium to Auschwitz was revealed, Asche had cynically commented: 'The German Reich needs soap again.'

At his trial, Asche claimed not to be able to remember any such comments. He declared:

> I didn't know that most of the Jews in the East were being murdered. Neither did I fear that the deported Jews were systematically being killed. However, with the passing of time, I had a disagreeable feeling about the deportation of the Jews in general. I did not actually begin to have doubts about the true fate of the Jews. But it was clear to me that when children and old people were deported some of them would lose their lives. Because like anyone else I knew that life in the concentration camp was hard and involved many privations, and that weak people would not always survive it. Rumours about the murder of Jews never reached me in Brussels. I remained unaware of the overall extent of the extermination of the Jews that had actually taken place.

The doctor Youra Livchitz, according to Yvonne Jospa, 'was one of the few who had an idea what was happening to the Jews in the East'. Youra added to his knowledge about the crimes of the Nazi regime from all imaginable sources. As he could speak not only French and Romanian, but also English, Russian and German, he was able to follow the news broadcasts of the BBC, Radio Moscow and the German-language press. He was also a friend of Hertz Jospa, his Bessarabian compatriot, who was twelve years older than him and without a doubt one of the best-informed members of the Resistance. His closest friends from school and university belonged to the Resistance organization 'War Office', and through his brother he had close contacts with the armed partisans.

Along with other left-wing intellectuals, Youra translated the news broadcasts of the so-called enemy stations into French, and they were then distributed in the underground newspaper *Radio Moscou*. At the end of December this information sheet, under the heading 'The total extermination of the Jewish population in Europe', printed an article describing the murderous extermination policy of the Nazis:

> In line with this criminal plan four million Jews are to be concentrated in Europe, particularly in Poland, with the sole aim of their extermination. According to data from the Jewish congress in America and information from the Polish government, several hundred thousand Jews have been brought together in Poland. They are shot in large groups, exterminated with gas and, in the concentration camps, with prussic acid. The Nazis are practising all imaginable excesses, and encouraging individual massacres. The terrible crimes are carried out in a state approaching frenzy. These people are killing Jewish children who are not yet twelve years old, they are ordering sick people to be eliminated, by whatever means. Only the few qualified and strong men who are useful and usable in the war factories are temporarily exempted, before finally, weakened by the exhausting work and the extreme privations, being sent to their deaths. According to official figures, the Warsaw ghetto, which numbered a total of 400,000 Jews in 1939, and which had received thousands and countless thousands of Jews since the German occupation, now numbers only 40,000 inhabitants. The result of methodical extermination, carried out at a crazed rate.

9 The Resistance

Marcel Hastir is a '*débrouillard*', someone with the very Belgian quality of being able to get himself out of situations, however difficult, using only his wits and his cunning. The bright eyes in the ninety-three-year-old's mischievous face light up when he talks about the deceptions the Belgians used to practise on the Germans in those days. 'They were hard times, but so exciting that after liberation we asked ourselves: now what are we going to do?'

The painter and musician still lives in the former centre of the Theosophical Society at number 51 Rue du Commerce, which Youra, Alexandre and Rachel Livchitz used to frequent. On the first floor of the whitewashed town house is the little room where members, friends and interested people used to go for the demanding cultural programme of the Theosophists. He has organized two thousand concerts in these spaces in the course of his long life, Hastir proudly announces, 'and the most celebrated musicians were among them'. Despite his venerable age, the old man, with his white shock of hair, and despite the fact that he suffers from serious rheumatism, has lost none of his vivacity. And he has an excellent memory.

He followed the careers of Youra Livchitz and his brother Alexandre to the very end. 'They were two unusual boys,' he says, 'particularly the younger one, Youra, he had a very powerful charisma.'

The painter Hastir already had a studio in the Theosophists' house in the 1930s. And as a chairman of the 'Jeunes Théosophiques' he hosted weekly discussions and lectures on religion and philosophy, which were particularly well received by young people. Youra often brought his friends from university along. Among them were Robert Leclercq, the Russian Ilya Prigogin, who was awarded the Nobel Prize for Chemistry after the war, and Szmul Rzepkowicz, who was to be deported in April 1943 as number 1405 on the twentieth convoy to Auschwitz.

Like many of his compatriots, Hastir had gone to the South of France when the Germans invaded Brussels. Theosophy, as everyone knew, was banned by the Nazis. They would persecute the devotees of this international group of esoterics and free-thinkers as they had already done with great brutality in Germany. As his money ran out after a few months, and no alarming news came from Belgium, in 1941 Hastir decided to go back. When he arrived from the station at the Rue du Commerce, he saw the Gestapo stuffing the community's whole library into boxes. The books were to be brought to Germany. 'We never saw them again,' Hastir recalls.

What was to be done? The Theosophical Society was closed, the centre faced being requisitioned by the occupying forces. A painting school for young people struck Hastir as the right solution. After all, he already had his studio in the building. Thanks to his many contacts, he was able to get hold of papers with the necessary stamps, confirming that he had already run a small art school at number 51 Rue du Commerce before the war. The German military administration officially approved the school. For all members of the institution – about thirty pupils and their teachers – this had the invaluable advantage of meaning that they were, for the time being, exempt from being deported to Germany for labour deployment.

Under the direction of the enterprising Hastir, the Theosophist centre, having been cleared out by the Nazis, turned back in the blink of an eye into a great attraction for both young and old. It became an unofficial cultural institute in Brussels. As it was said among the artistic elite that young men and women were constantly sitting as models for the painting school, painters such as Paul Delvaux and René

Magritte would from time to time turn up with their sketch pads in the big studio at the back of number 51 Rue du Commerce.

In the evening, the students pushed aside their easels and carried the chairs out of the conference room of the Theosophists and up to the big studio, which was thus transformed into a concert hall. And at least once a week a colourful, cheerful troupe occupied the little hall on the upper floor. Marcel Hastir had allowed the 'Comédiens Routiers' of Jacques Huysman and Youra's school-friend Jean Franklemon to rehearse there. The Livchitz brothers occasionally sat as models to earn some extra money, and often dropped in on their friend Marcel. If the busy man had no time to chat, they would take a little chess game out of their pockets. Hastir recalls, 'Chess was a passion of theirs; they and their friends were gripped by a real chess-fever. They'd barely sat down, and off they would go.'

The painting school, called 'Les Ateliers', became an indispensable meeting point for young members of the Resistance. For the school had one precious thing: in one of the graphic studios – shoved inconspicuously into a dark corner – was a machine with which fly-sheets could be printed. Here the transcripts of the news from the BBC and Radio Moscow were duplicated. Sometimes Youra also took part in the conspiratorial distribution of information sheets or flyers, which tried to counter the lies and cover-ups of the Germans with a bit of truth. It was all done effectively under the nose of Goebbels's propaganda apparatus: just a few yards away from the art school, at 38 Rue du Commerce, was the Brussels branch of the Department of Propaganda, which had the task of bringing the Belgian media into line, spreading anti-Semitism and putting the population in the picture about the successes of Hitler's war.

'I realize how much I've been drifting, how little I've thought about what was going on around me,' Youra wrote in his diary in 1942. Drifting? He had just passed his finals with flying colours after seven years' medical studies. He had to pass an exam set by a 'Central Examination Commission' consisting of professors from all the Belgian universities, as the Université Libre de Bruxelles had closed its doors in November 1941. The ULB authorities had refused to follow the orders of the German commissioner and appoint Flemish nationalists as a substitute for the fired university teachers.

Since then, professors and students of the ULB had taught and studied underground. They met in private homes, schools and cafés, to discuss their material and their tasks. In the laboratories of industrial concerns, hospitals and state research institutions, the students were able to get the work experience they required in order to pass the examination. Youra had got involved as well, and gave introductory courses for freshmen in the '*université clandestine*'. To avoid rousing suspicions they met in different places each week.

At the very beginning, a spark had passed between Jacqueline Mondo, the first-year student, and her tutor. When Youra, the charmer, directed his bright blue eyes at a girl, she was conquered. In the little group taught by the young medic, Jacqueline was certainly the prettiest. To the annoyance of her parents, the young student had, in line with the fashions of the time, lightened her chestnut hair with peroxide. Young Jacqueline made a big impression on the painter Hastir: 'She had a classical profile, she was really quite special.'

But times were hard for young couples in love, particularly if one of them was Jewish. There could have been no question of meeting in a café in the evening or going to a dance. The risk would simply have been too great. The curfew from eight o'clock in the evening until seven in the morning, which applied only to Jews, was strictly enforced by the German security forces. So Youra and Jacqueline met in the Bois de la Cambre to go for walks. Or sometimes they would use Rachel Livchitz's absence to drink tea undisturbed in the flat.

Youra had used a quote from Antoine de Saint-Exupéry as an epigraph to the diary that he began to write in that crucial year of 1942: 'What gives life a meaning, gives death a meaning.' All that remains of his diary entries are a few fragments of such thoughts, which his mother selected for a little Festschrift three decades later. Throughout her lifetime, she kept the letters and documents of her two sons in a crammed drawer in her desk. They can no longer be found.

Youra was not happy. How could he have been? He clearly felt the need to shed some light on his situation by writing. 'The changes in my life have been dictated by circumstances. And how have I reacted to the inevitable? What have I done to ensure that events don't get too much for me? In the face of these new conditions, I can't just wait like some primitive mollusc and see what happens next.'

After his philological studies at the ULB, Youra's friend Robert Leclercq had moved to the village of Morlanwelz, where he had found a job as a grammar school teacher. He fled to Brussels from the boring little provincial place as often as he could, and would always visit Youra's family on Avenue Brugmann. Young people were always very keen to engage in conversation with Rachel Livchitz, who was by now over fifty. Robert once called her 'my spiritual mother' in one of his letters addressed to 'Chère Sapinska'. Since the occupation of Bessarabia by Soviet troops Rachel Livchitz had been 'a poor woman', as she told her friends. The regular consignments of money from her homeland had dried up because the Communists had expropriated her wealthy family.

What was to be done? The question didn't just bother Youra. German rule was becoming increasingly violent, and the Germans had long since dropped their mask as '*bons occupants*'. And what had become of the people who had boarded the train in Mechelen, confidently believing that it would take them to a labour camp?

By now Youra's student friends from the 'Free University' had, like Robert Leclercq, found their place in society. Jean Burgers, who had come up with the concept of the 'minus-type' – a listless, apathetic character – in the 'Libre Examen' debating circle, was married, and employed as an engineer in an electricity company in La Louvière. Henri Neuman was working as a lawyer in a barristers' chambers, and Richard Altenhoff, who had also been active in the student group in the past, was employed by a large construction company.

The young Anglophile academics were particularly taken with the British Intelligence Service. They were convinced that this powerful organization would, with its wide network of information, help to decide the outcome of the war. In his book, *Avant Qu'il Soit Trop Tard*, Henry Neuman relates how Youra's friends, the 'War Office', at first supplied information to the British secret service via a former ULB professor. Above all, Richard Altenhoff, who was in charge of carrying out public commissions for his construction company, proved to be a valuable informant. He supplied the Allies with the precise plans for the extensions of the country's airports.

But soon the young people were impelled into action. They formed a Resistance group committed to the principles of 'Libre Examen' – freedom, democracy and human rights. In the first months of 1943 this auxiliary unit to the British Intelligence Service developed into a professional organization, which sought to sabotage the economic exploitation of the occupied country by the Germans. They finally built up a network of more than ten divisions in all areas of business and in various regions of the country, with around four thousand highly specialized and highly motivated members. After the initial letter of the code-name 'Gérard' taken by their leader Jean Burgers, they called themselves 'Groupe G'. With a generous portion of self-irony the lawyer Henri Neuman, one of the leading thinkers in 'Groupe G', describes the first sabotage action that he undertook with Richard Altenhoff and Walter de Sélys Longchamp in the autumn of 1942. Walter was a cousin of the pilot Jean de Sélys Longchamp who, some months later, on 20 January 1943, was to fly the raid on Gestapo headquarters.

The young people planned to set fire to a Wehrmacht tyre depot kept in a barn outside Brussels. Being keen readers of the adventures of Tim and Struppi, they had drawn their inspiration for their baptism of fire into the Resistance movement from the popular Belgian cartoon. They disguised themselves as secret agents. As in Hergé's comic-strip, they wore long raincoats and dark hats. 'We looked like members of the Gestapo,' Henri Neuman later wrote in his book, describing the course of the action in such detail to some extent because the episode tells us much about the Resistance fighters and how carefree they were at the start:

> Since the barn lay behind a house where people lived, the
> first important thing was to 'neutralize' the inhabitants.
> At nightfall we rang them up from a telephone box and didn't

put the receiver down, so that the line was blocked. Shortly after that we rang on the front door. An elderly woman, rather flirtatious despite her age, with a grey-haired, but cheerful and curious husband in her wake, opened the door to us. A delicious aroma reached us from the kitchen. Clearly they were making their dinner. Richard, who spoke good German, gave them the order: 'Gestapo, stay calm, stand with your face to the wall. Do everything we say and nothing will happen to you.' I translated that into French and drew my gun. Trembling, the couple obeyed, and while one of us kept an eye on them, the others cautiously approached the barn, guns in their hands and protected by the darkness. We planned to intimidate the guards and knock them down with our coshes so that we could get on with scattering the fuel that Richard had made himself. But unfortunately the barn was empty. When we got back to the house we learned that the tyres had been collected the same day. We left the baffled couple behind and disappeared, gravely disappointed by our failed undertaking.

But the unsuccessful operation, says Henri Neuman in his book, 'brought us even closer together as friends and reinforced our decision to undertake new actions'.

Youra's elder brother had also decided in favour of the action. Alexandre joined the armed partisans. This underground organization had been set up in Belgium in 1941 by veterans from Spain. In the Civil War against the Franco regime, many young Jewish immigrants had joined up to fight against fascism. They now formed the core of the partisan army, which was rigidly constructed on military principles. The divisions, or units, operated at grass-roots level, four of them forming a company. In turn, four companies formed a battalion, and at the top was head office, which was ultimately responsible for decision-making.

It was not only a deep ideological gulf that separated the Jewish underground fighters of this left-oriented partisan army from the

The 'bande des amis':
1. Youra Livchitz   2. Robert Maistriau
3. Jean 'Pamplemousse' Franklemon

4. Youra (right) with Marcel Hastir and
   Henriette Vander Hecht at summer camp
   near Ommen, 1937
5. Youra with Minnie Minet, on holiday in
   Namur.

6. The 'Free University' of Brussels, where Youra
   and his friends studied, became the unofficial
   centre of resistance during the war.

7. Hertz and Yvonne Jospa with their son Paul, 1945.
8. Marguerite, Jean Franklemon's sister, on her wedding day, November 1942. Jean is fourth from right; his parents first and third from right.
9. Rachel Livchitz after the war, with the son of Lily Allègre.

10. Alexandre 'Choura' Livchitz's farewell
    letter: 'for two hours now I have
    known for certain that I will be
    executed tomorrow morning.'

11. Sixty years on: Robert Maistriau
    in April 2003, at the spot near
    Boortmeerbeek where the raid
    took place.

Belgian Jewish Council, which had been founded by the military administration and received its instructions from Gestapo head-quarters in Brussels. There was also a class difference between the members of the Jewish, often Communist partisans, who, as recent emigrants, had little to lose, and the affluent Jews with Belgian nationality who sat on the committee of this association of dignitaries. Most members of the Jewish Council saw armed resistance as being primarily the long arm of Soviet Communism. In their opinion the actions of the Resistance were useless and superfluous, they only gave the occupying Germans fresh pretexts for further repressions. In his diary entry for 4 September 1942, committee member of the Jewish Council, Salomon Vanden Berg, voiced his fury about the 'stupid anti-German attacks' by the Resistance fighters: 'Those who deliver the blow don't even have the courage to be arrested for it, so that innocent people have to pay for the broken china.'

In the sights of the '*partisans armés*' who got hold of their weapons in attacks on military depots and police stations, were the Belgian collaborators. The Field Police reported on 4 August 1942: 'Numerous attacks on the lodgings and dwellings of Belgians who sympathize with the Germans are the order of the day. Fortunately few human lives have been lost. Most of those responsible are presumed to be recruited from members of the Belgian Communist Party.'

The fact that the Communists called the tunes in this Resistance organization did not put Alexandre off. He was not a Party member, but he did have Marxist sympathies. 'Choura' was also a man of action, less philosophically-minded than his younger brother. And there was not as much at stake for him after he had dropped out of his engineering studies.

David Lachman gave him his military training as a partisan. Red-haired David, the son of Polish emigrants, who had grown up in the Socialist youth movement, had joined the Resistance fighters as a seventeen-year-old. He never lived in the same place for long, and drew a monthly income of 1,200 Belgian francs from Resistance headquarters. Since, as an illegal immigrant, he had no food cards, he bought food on the black market with the money. Now seventy-five, David

Lachman is one of the few living witnesses of the Jewish partisan struggle in which so many young men died, and in which even more were executed as terrorists on the orders of the military governor.

The young underground fighter had learned that 'Courage is not a quality that you simply possess. Courage means overcoming your fear again each time.' Only when fear, his constant companion, left him, was David ice-cold and prudent, as his dangerous and sometimes deadly actions required him to be. By the age of eighteen, he was already an '*instructeur*'. He didn't only teach the use of guns to schoolboys in knickerbockers, who joined the Resistance full of enthusiasm and thirsty for action. He also taught the much older Alexandre. The former partisan remembers Alexandre as a quiet person, very intelligent and courageous, 'a good, dependable comrade', but ever the gentleman as well. David Lachman remembers Alexandre's enigmatic, almost English sense of humour, and the fact that the tall, slim man always wore a hat – even when drawing a gun on collaborators.

Soon the Resistance fighter with the air of an English gentleman had risen to the rank of commander. His code-name was 'Jean', a straightforwardly Belgian name. With his small unit, 'Commander Jean' broke into the council offices in Molenbeek and stole 62,000 food cards. His little troop got away with twenty-four revolvers in an attack on a police station.

'The finest of all struggles,' Youra noted in his diary at the time, 'is the struggle against human beings, against what they are and for what they should be.' Nonetheless, he did not join the partisan organization. He didn't want to be constrained by its ideological straitjacket and military hierarchy. And he didn't want to go underground like his brother and leave his mother alone on the Avenue Brugmann. Youra, the brothers had agreed, would stay at home with Saps. After all, he was also doing a decently paid and demanding job as a laboratory director with Pharmacobel.

But when his brother's comrades needed him, he helped them with his knowledge and experience. In the book *Partisans Armés Juifs*, a surviving fighter tells of an attack from the beginnings of the

Resistance in late autumn 1942, in which Youra was also involved: 'Aside from the successful missions, a number of failures revealed our inexperience. At first we were only amateurs in guerrilla warfare. Our will to fight and our courage in the face of the enemy distinguished us. But there were also many weaknesses.'

A Belgian fascist, who was wounded after an assassination attempt, lay in the intensive care ward of the St Pierre hospital. The partisans wanted to liquidate him there in the maze-like reddish-brown brick building. Youra, who knew the hospital from his time as an assistant doctor, had offered to guide the audacious underground fighters to the collaborator's sickbed. But when they turned up at the hospital only Youra was wearing a white doctor's coat. The rest were wearing their normal street clothes. When they asked a ward nurse the way to the Belgian collaborator's room, she clearly didn't take the young people all that seriously. She claimed, the ex-partisan relates, 'that the guy wasn't being treated in the hospital any more. So we cleared off again. The nurse probably got suspicious and lied to us.'

Among the members of the Jewish Council, Robert Holzinger had attracted the particular hatred of the fighting Jewish partisans. They saw him as a vile Nazi collaborator who was responsible for the enforcement of labour deployment orders. Certainly, the senior members of the Jewish Council believed they were acting in accordance with their consciences when they put all the more youthful and resilient and the unattached on the list for the presumably heavy workload in the labour camp. For in July and August 1942 nothing had yet seeped through about the Nazis' extermination machinery. People still believed the fairy-tale about labour deployment in the East.

Holzinger had signed up a number of young people, whom he sent out each morning from his office on the Boulevard du Midi to bring the recipients their conscription notice in person. Régine Krochmal, who was working in the soup kitchen of a Jewish aid organization, had been one of those put forward as a messenger for the AJB. A special ID would have protected her against deportation. But the young nurse furiously rejected the offer: 'I'd have felt like a traitor.'

The bringers of this bad news encountered suspicion and hostility among their fellow Jews, but many of them still complied in order to protect their families.

It was never entirely clear which unit it was that lay in wait for the Jew Robert Holzinger on 27 August outside his apartment in Anderlecht. He was felled by four bullets. He died of his injuries in hospital a day later.

Kurt Asche had just learned of Holzinger's murder when he turned up in the office of the Jewish Council, snorting with rage. Committee member Salomon Vanden Berg recorded the SS officer's violent arrival in his diary. His voice breaking with anger, Asche yelled at the terrified Jewish representatives: 'If Holzinger's murderers are not found within twenty-four hours, you'll see what's what! Everything you've known in the past will be child's play in comparison.'

For Belgian historian Maxime Steinberg, Holzinger's death marks an important turning point in the Nazi deportation policy. The transportation of the Jews still bore the official stamp of 'forced labour', but from now on Asche's department on Avenue Louise began to use different methods in assembling the deportation trains. It was from now on that the big raids began. Jewish resistance became more militant, and many of those being hunted began to understand that they had to evade Nazi imprisonment whatever the cost.

10 Hide Where You Can

Most Belgians rejected the brutal methods that the German occupying forces used against the Jews. Especially in Brussels and Wallonia, the population proved to be largely immune to the poison of National Socialist racial hatred. In vain the Nazi weekly newspaper, *L'Ami du Peuple*, appealed to the 'duty of the good Belgian' not to show 'any false pity' for the Jews. For many, it was an act of resistance to help the people slandered and ostracized by the Germans. Claire Prowizur, who has lived in Israel since 1969, has never forgotten the Belgian people's helpful and humane treatment of the immigrant foreigners. It was thanks to their help that the young Trotskyist, with her husband Philippe, was able to escape the deadly clutches of the Nazis time and again. 'They held out their hands to us even though they didn't know us,' she wrote in her autobiography.

On 1 August 1942, when the preparations for the first deportation train to Auschwitz were under way in Mechelen, the patriotic underground newspaper *La Libre Belgique* urged its compatriots to demonstrate their sympathy to the Jews with the rallying cry: 'Greet them in passing! Offer them your seat on the tram! Protest against the barbaric measures that are being applied to them. That'll make the "Boches" furious!'

Although at the time hardly anyone could have been aware of the terrible fate awaiting the deportees in the East, many Belgians opened up their homes to the Jews, hiding them in back rooms and attics. Couriers of the Jewish Defence Committee kept the people in hiding supplied with money or food cards. The funds for this came indirectly from the Belgian government in exile in London and from Jewish aid organizations in America. Some Belgians even shared their pitiful rations with the hidden families.

In all the city halls and council offices there were officials who quietly issued additional food cards for people's relatives who had supposedly been bombed out, or whose nieces had suddenly turned up out of the blue. There were city officials who gave the Resistance blank forms to which only the false name had to be added and the right passport photograph glued. And then there were postmen who intercepted letters addressed to the Gestapo and the war commands if they suspected they might contain denunciations. They opened the envelopes, warned the people denounced in them and delivered the letters two days late, to give them time to go into hiding. 'Service D' – against defeatism and denunciation – was the name that the members of this group gave themselves. They probably saved 5,000 people from being handed over to the occupying police.

Everywhere posters put up by the military administration warned the populace against helping the Jews. Doing so would be a punishable offence. It was not an empty threat. Some of the helpful Belgians who hid Jews in their homes ended up in the St Gilles prison in Brussels, if they were lucky. Others paid for their generosity by being deported to a concentration camp.

After the war 200,000 Belgians were acknowledged as having been active members of the Resistance. It was thanks to many of these that the chances of survival of those hunted by the Nazis in that small country were relatively high. At any rate, over 50 per cent, about 30,000 of the 56,000 Jews registered in Belgium, escaped the Holocaust. In Holland only 12 per cent did so.

Unlike the Dutch Queen Wilhelmina, who fled into exile to London with the cabinet, Queen Elisabeth, who had stayed in Belgium, was not unmoved by the fate of her Jewish compatriots under the German occupation. The mother of Leopold III, who was under house arrest, and widow of the much-loved King Albert I, who had died in a climbing accident, Elisabeth was descended from the Bavarian Wittelsbacher dynasty. Deeply respected by her subjects, she was a great lover of art and music. She inaugurated the 'Concours Elisabeth', a prestigious music competition still in existence today.

As early as 1933 the German physicist Albert Einstein had reported on the anti-Semitic atrocities of the Nazis. The Nobel laureate, who, before his emigration to America, was spending six months with his family in the Belgian North Sea resort of De Haan, was a good friend of the Queen.

The Belgian Jews now placed all their hope in this woman. The chairman of the friends of the former First World War POWs, Lazare Liebman, had seized the initiative. He watched the merciless Nazi witch-hunt with horror. Only the Queen, he believed, had sufficient authority to moderate the Nazis. As a war hero who had won numerous military medals, the Jewish patriot made use of his contacts. He asked the head of the King's Cabinet, a fellow soldier, for an appointment to speak to the Queen Mother.

On the hot afternoon of 1 August 1942, three serious gentlemen, wearing yellow Stars of David on the lapels of their black suits, were welcomed by the chief court clerk in the entrance hall of the city castle in Brussels. Just around the corner lived General von Falkenhausen, who was only to learn of this extraordinary audience some time afterwards. The Jewish dignitaries climbed the wide stairs past the magnificently framed portraits along the walls, and were led into a sumptuously furnished drawing room. A meeting with Queen Elisabeth had been fixed for four o'clock that afternoon. To give greater weight to the discussion, Liebman had been recommended, by the highest authorities, to come in the company of official representatives of Jewry. So Salomon Vanden Berg and Eugène Hellendael, both on the committee of the Belgian Jewish Council, waited with him for the Queen, whom they planned to win over to the cause of the Jews.

Eugène Hellendael was an assimilated Jewish member of the haute-bourgeoisie, with close connections to the highest circles of Belgian society. But he was also among the sponsors of the Jewish Defence Committee founded by the Communist Hertz Jospa. When he had told Jospa of his intention to ask the Queen to intervene on behalf of the Belgian Jews, the Marxist had urgently warned him against taking such a course of action. Such a move, in Jospa's view, would be wrong from both a human and a political point of view, because it would discriminate against non-Belgian Jews, and in any case he considered it pointless. 'Anti-Semitism and the persecutions are the ideological foundation of the Nazi regime, and no one can touch it,' the Communist engineer had explained to the member of the upper middle-class. There was no point in 'asking Hitler's followers for mercy for a particular class of Jews'. Jospa's scepticism, it would later turn out, was not exaggerated. He was also to be proven right in his fear that Hellendael would only endanger himself by attempting to negotiate at the highest level.

'It was our last hope,' Vanden Berg noted in his diary the same evening. Unlike Liebman and Hellendael, he seemed to have enjoyed the meeting in the city palace. He proudly recorded the kind gesture that the Queen had made in leaving her Residence at Laeken to come to Brussels. With his apparently unmoved detachment, Vanden Berg was miscast as a petitioner. At least that was how things were seen by Lazare Liebman, who had initiated the conversation. Liebman would later tell his son how shocked he had been by Vanden Berg's cool and complacent behaviour. While Liebman and Hellendael put their heads together and, in a whisper, discussed their planned speech once again, Vanden Berg wandered casually through the room, without a sign of nerves, stopping every so often to admire a particularly lovely piece of furniture or an especially valuable painting. When the three men were received by the Queen, he left it to Liebman and Hellendael to describe the terrible suffering of their fellow Jews.

The Queen, Vanden Berg wrote in his diary, proved to be 'deeply impressed by the despair of the Jewish population in the face of mass deportation'. Shortly afterwards, in fact, she contacted her daughter, Princess Marie-José, the daughter-in-law of King Victor Emmanuel of Italy. She in turn contacted Hitler. And in the end the Führer assured

Elisabeth's daughter that humanitarian views would be taken into consideration in the deportation of the Jews. The happy news reached the Jewish notables a few days after their visit to the Queen:

This afternoon [the Red Cross representative wrote to Lazare Liebman on 4 August] I received a visit from Mr Streel, Secretary to the Queen, who brought the following facts to my attention in the name of Her Majesty. The object of your request to Her Majesty has been presented to the Führer in person, and he has passed on the following answer:

1. There is and will be no separation of families.
2. Someone will be sent from Berlin to ensure that those carrying out the orders will not exceed their instructions.
3. The deportees will be treated in a decent manner.
4. Small children may stay with their parents, which is to say that children and their parents will have the same fate.
5. No Belgians will be deported.
6. In Mechelen future deportees may have visits from their relations.

This answer was passed on to us by a third party. It is only a promise.

The Queen is aware of it, but she will also take a great interest, within the bounds of her possibilities, in the fate of the valued Jewish population.

This promise was to be unmasked in the course of the following months as an act of purest cynicism. Any supposed concession to humanitarianism later proved to be nothing but a ruse on the part of the Nazis. Permission to receive visits in the transit camp was a trap. It meant that the Nazis also learned of the addresses of the Jewish relations to put on their list. The promise not to separate families meant that large families were deported *en bloc* and sent to the gas chambers. The question of temporarily sparing Jews with Belgian citizenship from deportation – a particular consequence of the royal intervention with Hitler – had by this point already been decided by the RSHA. The head of the military administration, Eggert Reeder, had already won this special status for the Belgian Jews in Berlin, after a discussion with Himmler. The Belgian Jews were indispensable on the labour market; their loss, he argued, in conformity with the system, could create problems for the economy and thus damage the German cause. Above all, the important thing was not to unsettle the Belgian populace, not to attract attention.

There is also a secret telegram from this time, from Obersturmbannführer Adolf Eichmann to Ernst Ehlers, the head of the Security Police and the Security Service in Belgium: 'For the given reason I refer to the fact only stateless Jews can be removed on the Jewish transports to Auschwitz.' It was not Elisabeth's support, but the fear of uproar that led Eichmann and his henchmen to be so cautious.

At a meeting on 28 August in the RSHA, Eichmann then established how long the exemption of the Belgian Jews was to apply for. From the end of June 1943 they were to be 'evacuated' to Auschwitz. The timetable was to be adhered to with great precision. In a remark concerning a discussion with the military commander in June 1943, the secretary of the SS Security Service on Avenue Louise recorded General von Falkenhausen's gradual movement away from his original position, that the Belgian Jews were on no account to be deported. First of all, Falkenhausen tried to limit the transport to those 'Jews who were living illegally in Belgium'. Finally, the minutes captured the capitulation of the military commander to the policy of extermination: 'But in the end Falkenhausen had no compunction about taking immediate action against the Belgian Jews'.

By 1942 even Vanden Berg, who had been so proud to be received by Queen Elisabeth, no longer believed that the Belgian Jews would be spared from deportation. On 19 September he observed that: 'There has been no let-up in the arrests of foreign Jews. I am of the belief that in the end all foreign Jews will be deported. And I also believe that once they are gone, attention will turn to the question of the Belgian Jews.'

A few days later the Jewish businessman was summoned to see Kurt Asche on Avenue Louise. A total of twenty representatives of the Jewish Council crammed into the Obersturmführer's office on the morning of 24 September. The Nazi functionary was enthroned behind his desk, but looked, Samuel Vanden Berg noted in his diary, 'rather nervous'. In a raging voice the SS man bawled out the Jewish dignitaries lined up in front of him as though they were schoolboys. 'I know these people,' he railed. Some of them, he shouted, would deliberately carry out his orders badly, or even sabotage them. 'And some other gentlemen have had the impertinence to turn to the Queen in order to prevent the deportations.' But in the end, he observed, such appeals to the highest authorities had led nowhere, and the evacuation of the entire Jewish population would now commence.

'To avoid the familiar difficulties and attempts to interfere with that evacuation,' the Judenreferent concluded, 'Messrs Ullman, Benedictus, Hellendael, Blum, Vanden Berg and Rotkel are placed under immediate arrest. And will remain so until the other members of the association have proven willing to carry out our orders in an orderly fashion.'

The six members of the Jewish Council spent the rest of the day and the following night in one of the basement rooms on Avenue Louise. The next day they were brought as political prisoners to the concentration camp at Fort Breendonk. It took an intervention by the Secretary of State in the Ministry of Justice to free them from the imprisonment that Asche had ordered.

Eugène Hellendael, petitioner to the Queen, did not get off so lightly. As one of the senior figures on the Jewish Council, Hellendael had found himself in Asche's sights. He had used arguments from constitutional law to prevent the Israelite Community – the 'Communité Israélite de Bruxelles' – from being integrated with the Jewish Council, and thus placed under the control of Judenreferent Asche. The SS man could not bear to be contradicted, so the Nazi took his revenge upon the courageous Jew. Hellendael and his wife were observed leaving their house without wearing the Star of David as decreed by law. In punishment, not only the couple themselves, but also their two little sons and their grandparents were deported to Auschwitz.

In 1967 Kurt Asche was questioned about this particular event, under accusation of being an accomplice to murder. He stated that he had no memory of it. 'I can't remember any Jews who had infringed anti-Jewish regulations being put on the deportation trains to Auschwitz.'

The hunt for non-Belgian Jews became ever more ruthless in the late summer of 1942. The archbishop in Mechelen, beneath whose windows, so to speak, the trains to Auschwitz passed, received daily cries for help and petitions from Jews baptized as Catholics, but they were rounded up with the others. Cardinal Van Roey decided to take action. He sent his canon, Leclef, to the headquarters of the military administration on the Place Royale, to intervene on behalf of those Jews who had converted to Catholicism.

The Catholic dignitary returned to his bishop empty-handed. The official he spoke to informed him that the Gestapo alone was responsible for these measures. And in any case the German had told him that the authors of the anti-Semitic regulations in Berlin were not concerned with religion, but solely with race. Jews remained Jews, even if they had converted to Catholicism.

That afternoon was to give the canon another insight into the abysmal depths of the National Socialist contempt for humanity. In the archbishop's waiting room, Leclef found a woman in floods of tears. Through her sobs she told him of her efforts to free the two underage baptized children of a Jewish friend from the hands of the SS police. The friend's nineteen-year-old daughter and fifteen-year-old son were imprisoned in Mechelen transit camp and would, if nothing happened, be deported to the East. Initially the good Catholic woman had turned to the military administration, and had been sent from there to the Gestapo.

On Avenue Louise she was then received, according to Leclef's notes, 'with extreme rudeness by a certain Asche'. He strictly refused the request to free the two young people. There were no age limits, he explained, on forced labour. And apart from that he would tolerate no interference in his responsibilities. He would make all the decisions on his own. When the woman finally told the Judenreferent that the mother of the two young people was mad with worry, the little man in the blue suit merely declared scornfully that he might be interested in persecuting her as well.

'The current treatment of the Jews is truly inhuman and is arousing a general pity and rage,' Cardinal Van Roey wrote the next day to his colleague Magliome in the Vatican. There is no record of a reply from Rome.

Everywhere in the country, the Field Police and SS police were stepping up their checks. Anyone caught in the street without a Star of David was compulsorily dispatched to Mechelen transit camp. And anyone, like twenty-year-old Claire Prowizur, who was travelling on a tram at eleven o'clock one night, three hours after the curfew applied to the Jews, risked life and limb. As always, Claire and her husband Philippe sat far apart in the compartment, so as not to be identified as a couple if a check were carried out. They were both returning from a meeting of their Trotskyist group. Suddenly the tram stopped, and the doors were blocked so that no one could get away. Two Field Policemen boarded the vehicle and demanded to see the passengers' identification papers. Philippe was able to present a forged green passport identifying him as a Belgian. But at that point Claire had only the yellow identification card reserved for foreigners – although without the black stamp 'Juif – Jood'. Claire later recalled that dramatic moment:

> Philippe passes the check. His green card is perfect. I try to
> collect my thoughts as I wait. 'Calm down now, Claire, your
> card is yellow, but it doesn't have the Jewish stamp.' The field
> policeman stands stiffly in front of me. I show him the card.
> He checks it once, then again, looks at me, looks at the
> photograph and addresses me in his mother tongue. His
> voice is icy: 'Sprechen Sie Deutsch?' I look at him, pretend
> to be startled, frown, act as though I don't understand a word.
> 'Jew?' he asks pointedly. I look at him without batting an

eyelid: 'Pardon, que dîtes-vous?' He hesitates for a moment, hands me back my yellow card and walks to the next passenger. I've got away with it.

When the young couple fell into each other's arms in their flat shortly afterwards, they were both clear about one thing: it was time for black-haired Claire to transform herself into a blonde. And a friend, a practised forger, who had already promised a perfectly forged green identity card for Claire, had to be urged to make one for her as quickly as possible.

The SS, and also the representative of the Foreign Office in Brussels, Werner von Bargen, noted with concern that the Jews were escaping the clutches of their persecutors. On 24 September he wrote in a report to his superiors in Berlin:

> The deportation of 10,000 stateless Jews resident here, scheduled for 15 September, has been carried out. Although most of the Jews responded to the compulsory labour order at the beginning of the action, as matters developed we were obliged to resort to raids and arrests of individuals, since so many had failed to comply with muster orders. Many of the Jews in question are leaving their flats and seeking refuge with Aryan Belgians. These efforts are being supported by a considerable proportion of the Belgian population. Further difficulties arise out of the fact that very many Jews are in possession of fake Belgian identity cards. That also makes it easy for them to emigrate illegally to occupied and unoccupied France.

On 25 September 1942 the military commander prepared all the military commands for 'major actions', leading to the 'evacuation of the Jews'. The Field Police thus became embroiled in the witch-hunt of the Jews:

> After the labour deployment of 10,000 Jews in the East, the

complete evacuation of the Jews from the area of command has been got under way… Exempted from this are those Jews who are living in mixed marriages or who are exempted from wearing the Star of David. Otherwise, great care should be taken in the evacuation to ensure that families remain together, and this should be done in as inconspicuous a manner as possible…

Finally, in agreement with the Security Police, particular attention should be paid to the illegal emigration of the Jews, which has been on the increase of late. Steps must be taken to ensure that the Jews from the four major cities do not move illegally to the country or smaller towns while not wearing the Star of David.

From now on, leather merchant Léon Gronowski's days in his own house and shop were numbered. Since the Germans had transferred ownership of the shop on the Chaussée de Wavre to the Trusteeship Company, he was no longer his own master. Belgian friends had urgently advised him to seek another flat. The lives of the Jews were in too much danger to go on living at addresses known to the Nazis.

Gronowski's son Simon had spent four wonderful weeks in the summer of 1942 in the town of Diest, at scout camp. They were to be the ten-year-old's last carefree days of childhood. Tanned a deep brown, and with his knees grazed by wild adventures in the open air, he came home in August. This time his parents seemed less interested than usual in his holiday experiences. The alert little boy sensed the oppressive atmosphere in his parents' house in Brussels.

Ita Gronowski had – like some of her classmates in the Cymring school – already received the dreaded 'labour deployment order'. She had obediently turned up in Mechelen as she was required to do. But since she had taken Belgian citizenship at the age of sixteen, as the law required for those born in Belgium, she was sent home again. Jews of Belgian nationality were still exempted from the deportation. As far as Ita was concerned, this was merely a postponement – until September 1943.

In bourgeois Woluwe, a leafy district on the edge of Brussels, the Gronowskis found a small flat with the help of some friends. They had to leave their shop, house and garden, the pride of the hard-working immigrants. Léon Gronowski organized the move very carefully. He rented his own flat to the Rouffaerts, the parents of one of Simon's fellow scouts. Ita's piano ended up in the tenants' flat. Some furniture and, more importantly, all Gronowski's business supplies were put in storage; the family would live illegally, and without food cards, on the sale of those goods.

When they moved into their cramped new quarters at the beginning of September, the Gronowskis even took their little dog with them. In retrospect Simon Gronowski can clearly see that his parents were unaware, despite all the warnings, of the terrible danger they were in. Léon Gronowski was not particularly interested in politics. He was – as his son worked out later from his father's Hebrew diary – 'a dreamer with a poetic disposition'. He revered German culture, quoted Goethe, Schiller and Hölderlin, and nurtured illusions about the people 'of poets and thinkers', as the Germans liked to call themselves.

So the Gronowskis didn't exactly go into hiding, illegal though their lifestyle was. Simon and Ita's parents would often leave their safe flat to walk the dog or buy groceries. Enterprising Ita complained loud and long until she was allowed to go out with her friends every now and again. They had removed the Stars of David from their jackets and their coats. And Simon still ran charging about the Bois de la Cambre every weekend with his scout troop. Fifty years later Simon knows: 'To reduce the risks they would have had to hide my sister and myself away from them in the countryside.'

Meanwhile, unobserved by the occupying forces and above all by Himmler's SS thugs, a group of Jewish anti-fascists, Belgian Resistance fighters, social workers, Communists and Christians had set up a network to rescue Jewish children in Belgium. The Jewish Defence Committee, the underground organization for the defence of Jewish interests, was linked with all the other Belgian Resistance groups, armed and unarmed, left-wing and royalist, under the umbrella of the 'Front de l'Indépendance'. At the end of August 1942 they recognised the need to set up an 'Enfance' division, to look after orphaned and endangered Jewish children.

When the German police knocked on the door at night, and the trucks waited in the street with their engines running, the first thing that ran through the parents' heads was: How can I protect my children? Sometimes they managed to hide their little sons or daughters, who would then be discovered by neighbours the next morning, crying loudly. Mothers or fathers arrested by the Gestapo in the street remained silent, when interrogated at SS headquarters, about the fact that their children were waiting secretly at home for them. They relied on the idea that their children would be looked after by friends and neighbours. There were also parents who, fearing the worst, were willing to part voluntarily with their children and lodge them with a Belgian family. In all such cases the 'Enfance' division was called in.

Members of the Jewish Council helped to hide them. When concerned parents turned up at the office to inquire about the chance of lodging their children safely, they were sent home empty-handed after giving their addresses. Shortly afterwards a representative of the Jewish underground organization would turn up at their home. Within twenty-four hours the parents had to have a packed suitcase ready for their children, and the little ones, if they understood what was happening, prepared to part, with no idea of how that parting might end.

Finding lodgings for the children was the women's work. Yvonne Jospa, Hertz Jospa's wife, used her contacts with a large number of different social institutions. In the Borinage, a mining region of Wallonia, the qualified sociologist had worked on a programme to increase understanding between immigrant Italian miners and the local inhabitants. Now she travelled about the country to find families and institutions that were prepared to take in Jewish children. Yvonne, dazzlingly beautiful and with a soft Russian accent, received a warm welcome everywhere she went, from priests, farmers, the headmasters of boarding schools, abbesses and mother superiors, charity organizations, trade unions and philanthropic aristocrats. Even decades later she was amazed at their great willingness to help: 'No one ever turned me down.'

A young primary school teacher, Andrée Geulen, beyond suspicion as a Belgian woman from a bourgeois family, had taken on the difficult task of collecting the children from their parents. Heartbreaking scenes were played out before her eyes. Some mothers couldn't simply let their sons or daughters go away with this strange woman. The farewell was made even more difficult for them because for reasons of security they were not allowed to know their children's future addresses. Visits or letters would give away the children and their Belgian protectors.

On the way to their new lodgings, a farm, a children's home or a convent, Andrée – who, with her fair hair and cheerful nature seemed to some of her protégés like a fairy-tale princess – drummed into the children that from now on they would have new names. Little Sarah became a Susanna, Guscia became Gaby. From now on David was only to answer to the name Daniel, and Abraham to the name Albert. In this way 4,000 children in Belgium were saved from certain death. In no other country occupied by the Germans was the proportion of surviving children within the Jewish population as high as it was in Belgium.

The Goldsteinas family, from Lithuania, were also worried about their daughter. After studying in Belgium the couple had enjoyed a bourgeois life, and lived with six-year-old Abela in a well-to-do district of Brussels. But as stateless Jews, Henda and Mendelis Goldsteinas no longer felt safe when they heard of the first raid near the Southern Station. The witch-hunt, they thought, would also be continued in other parts of the city. Mendelis had nothing to fear from his colleagues at the sugar factory. In fact, his laboratory was the only safe place for him. The company even supported him financially when he and his wife decided to send their daughter into hiding. A friend who clearly had close connections with the Jewish Defence Committee, found a hiding place in the monastery of St Pietersleeuw for little Abela. Other Jewish children had already been placed there.

Abela had to get used to the fact that her name would henceforth be Janine Liégeois; she learned to pray like a Catholic, and attended the lowest class in the Catholic boarding school. She still can't forget being grabbed by a nun one afternoon and pulled away from her fellow pupils. The sister dashed off with her, helter-skelter, dragging her into the house by her hand and dashing up the stairs with her, up to the attic and finally on to the convent roof. The Security Service had been given a tip that the nuns were hiding Jewish children. And now the uniformed SS men were searching the convent for a dark-haired little girl like Abela.

That same evening some of her parents' neighbours came to collect her from the convent. Abela was no longer safe there. She found her next hiding place with two unmarried sisters who lived in a little village near Tournai; she was to be their niece, who had recently been bombed out of her home. Her parents had got hold of fake identity papers and now went by the names of Yvonne and Marcel Poncelet.

11 A General Under Pressure
Late January 1943

As usual, Hitler's governor in Belgium had spent the weekend in Seneffe. Alexander von Falkenhausen enjoyed the silence and seclusion. In his baroque castle he was entirely surrounded by people who – like his adjutants and his secretary, who had assumed the role of housekeeper – were well-disposed to him and ready to serve him. Elisabeth, the sixty-two-year-old's blonde ray of sunshine, was there as well.

The general withdrew to the warmth of his blazing hearth. Hitler's Russian campaign, which Falkenhausen called a 'crazy idea that flew in the face of any military understanding', had deeply affected his life. His favourite nephew and godson Alexander had been killed at the age of twenty-three in the Steppes near the Caspian Sea. A pointless sacrifice for a pointless campaign.

The general's relations with the ruling bodies in Berlin had deteriorated somewhat over the past few months. A special delegate sent by Heinrich Himmler, SS brigadier Richard Jungclaus, had recently arrived in Belgium. He had not so far deemed it necessary to pay the military commander a formal visit. The general had been told that he was sniffing around after him, supposedly collecting material against him.

Now Falkenhausen, with his extravagant way of life and his loose tongue, also supplied some material to the Berlin rumour-mill. Himmler was said to have asked Jungclaus to report on national issues so that the SS officer could, at the first possible opportunity, replace the independent-minded military governor who currently headed the administration.

The situation in Belgium was reaching crisis point so far as the occupying forces were concerned. The mood among the populace alternated between fury and euphoria. The collapse on the Eastern Front, according to the current reports of the Field Police, had 'raised hopes in Anglophile circles that Germany would soon be defeated'.

At the same time the country was seeing greater numbers of sabotage actions and attacks. The Resistance movement seemed to be growing stronger, since Fritz Sauckel, Hitler's authorized representative for the labour deployment, had ordered the forced dispatch of Belgian workforces to Germany. Hitherto, workers for the German factories had been recruited on a voluntary basis.

The general's objection that 'people forced to work do not achieve anything good, but only raise the risk of sabotage' had fallen on deaf ears. The military administration received an order from Sauckel to introduce compulsory labour service. And the high field commands, with their so-called 'Werbestellen', or recruitment posts, were instructed to come down hard on anyone who refused to cooperate. Anyone who failed to report to the recruitment post lost his right to food cards.

The Field Police working under the military governor had to deploy civilian man-hunters from the political far-right. Wallonian Rexists and Flemish nationalists now hunted down any of their young compatriots who tried to escape conscription. Falkenhausen was proved to be right in his guess that forced recruitment would cause all classes of society to rise up against the occupation. In his book *La Belgique Occupée*, the historian Etienne Verhoeyen writes that 'conscription for forced labour in Germany was a crucial contribution from Berlin to the development of resistance in all its different forms.'

Among the Nazi bosses in Berlin the ruling military commander was seen as a weakling because of his lenient response to the rebellious population. An article from the Swedish newspaper *Svenska Dagbladet* had been handed around the offices, describing Belgium as the stronghold of the Resistance. The diplomat Werner von Bargen, a friend of the general's, had leapt to the military governor's defence. In his function as head of the Brussels branch of the Foreign Office, he had attempted to ease the furious feelings in the capital with a telegram: '*Svenska Dagbladet* report on situation in Belgium greatly exaggerated. Incidences of sabotage do occur, but have so far only caused minor damage to transport and business. Military administration's reaction in all cases energetic and well-directed.'

The governor of Belgium's policy of moderation was met with incomprehension in government circles in Berlin, and in Belgium the security forces of the SS gave the lie to the general's good intentions. The general had no influence whatsoever on the SS police, the Security Service and the Gestapo, whose tentacles were spreading throughout the land. The SS police received their instructions directly from the Berlin RSHA. It had its own telegram connections and its own postal service, so that the military administration was entirely excluded. The Nazi Security Service was accumulating ever greater powers. The Field Police, which had at first been responsible for stamping out sabotage, espionage and subversion of the army, ended up having its authority restricted to purely military crimes.

Every evening, soldiers could tell how unpopular the Germans were by inspecting their uniforms. It had become a popular sport among young people to burn holes with their cigarettes in the grey cloth of the German military. The scene for this widespread act of resistance was the platform of a tram, where the passengers were crammed tightly together and smoking was permitted. The little acts of arson on the sleeves and backs of the German uniforms became such a nuisance that the military administration finally banned smoking on tram platforms.

The population was in ferment. The Belgians, subjected time and again to foreign rule, practised the strategy of permanent resistance. When it came to implementing the instructions of the military governing body, the Belgian administration went on what might be called a go-slow.

And the country's police force, the military administration had been forced to acknowledge, could not be deployed in the interests of the occupying forces. The Germans did not use Belgian gendarmes either for raids or to accompany deportation trains. There were fears that the guardians of order would evade the orders of the Germans to help their compatriots. The Nazis could only depend upon the fanatical Flemish and Wallonian far-right. The Flemish SS men had the reputation of being even more brutal in their treatment of political prisoners and Jews than their German superiors.

In Belgium – the home of petty-bourgeois anarchists – individualism was of the utmost importance, and all forms of submission to authority were condemned. Small wonder that the country remained utterly alien to the conservative Prussian Falkenhausen.

Time and again, the German police were forced to look on helplessly as saboteurs, attackers and snipers escaped their pursuers with the help of people who had nothing to do with the incident. The Gestapo hardly ever managed to catch a Resistance fighter redhanded. They escaped to the nearest café or shop, and were let out through the back door by owners or employees.

The perpetrators, according to a report from the diplomat Werner von Bargen to the Foreign Office, could effectively never have been caught. They had vanished 'within a few feet of the attacks'.

It was a difficult country for the Nazis, accustomed as they were to order and obedience. And without local informers and traitors to hand Resistance fighters and Jews over to them, the SS police would have had no success whatsoever. In the military administration's Activity Report Number 23, for the months of January to March 1943, if the National Socialist Security Police and the Field Police achieved 'outstanding success despite their numerical weakness' in the fight against terror and illegal organizations, it was chiefly because of the infiltration of the Resistance with spies and secret agents: 'As before, the most successful combat measure proved once again to be the activity of the Sipo [Security Police] and the GF [Field Police] based on intelligence from agents'.

In this respect the Gestapo clearly had high expectations of one of their prisoners, Pierre Romanovitch. The stylish and eloquent 'White

Russian', who was in St Gilles prison for fraud and impersonation of a police officer, had hinted under questioning that he might be a useful double agent in the fight against terrorism. He had, he said, excellent contacts within Resistance circles. On 26 January Romanovitch was freed. The court of the Brussels High Field Command 672 had unexpectedly overturned its judgement of September 1942 and abandoned proceedings against him.

12 Asche's Helpers: Traitors and Informers

Although masters of the same trade, the two men were very different in appearance. One of them, Icek Glogowski, was a beefy-looking man in his mid-forties, with quick, piercing eyes. The insignias of the bourgeois life, a light-coloured hat on his wide head in the summer and a brown one in winter, and a tight-fitting dark suit for all seasons, only intensified his proletarian appearance. The other, Pierre Romanovitch, was an extraordinarily elegant apparition. Tall and slim, his pomaded dark hair combed smoothly back, he wore a hand-made silk shirt and fashionable suit as though it were the most natural thing in the world. The Polish Jew Glogowski and the stylish 'White Russian' Romanovitch were forever going in and out of Gestapo headquarters. They earned their livelihoods as traitors.

Icek, or 'fat Jacques', as the hated and feared man was known to his co-religionists, was in the pay of the security service and thus a constant colleague of Judenreferent Kurt Asche. As a spy and unofficial cop, 'le gros Jacques' helped to fill the trains to Auschwitz. He wore the swastika on his lapel.

Romanovitch, who sometimes called himself a count, received freelance wages as an opportunistic informer. While Glogowski had sold himself lock, stock and barrel to the SS, Romanovitch preferred to work independently. The talented and conscience-free chancer was, in the words of a lawyer who investigated the Romanovitch case after the war, 'one of the most perfidious spies in the service of the Germans'. His tactic had always been the same. He had slithered his way into the trust of his victims by doing them favours, before handing them over to the SS thugs 'once he was sure of getting a good catch'.

When the Germans occupied Belgium, Romanovitch was one of the few who were able to derive positive benefit from the national humiliation. Since interrupting his studies at the 'Free University' years before, he lived primarily at other people's expense. He had never yet held an honest profession. His police files revealed the travelling salesman to be a professional swindler. Now he was living on the black market, currency smuggling and betrayal.

The preferred hunting ground of the 'White Russian', who was born in Kiev and had grown up in Brussels, was the café terrace of the Metropol Hotel in the centre of the Belgian capital. He would slowly drive down Boulevard Anspach at the wheel of his black Citroën, before parking his car as conspicuously as possible within the view of the café customers. Then he would casually peel himself out of his limousine. The very possession of such a car, an extraordinary privilege, raised eyebrows, because at this time almost all private cars had been confiscated by the Germans. Drifting like a dandy to one of the marble tables, he would swing his car-key around the index finger of his right hand. As the mood took him, a winning or a dismissive smile would play around his lips. He avoided hearty laughter, which would have revealed his poor teeth.

The comfortable wicker chairs gave a view of the lively boulevard, which at this time of day would be filling up with secretaries, businessmen, grey-uniformed soldiers and ladies. From here one could also view the coming and going of the hotel guests. The Hotel Metropol, built in an eclectic architectural style, was the place where international artists, actors and musicians like Django Reinhardt, Edith Piaf, Fernandel and Maurice Chevalier would always stay. Prominent Nazis met here as well. In one of the salons Adolf Eichmann, the architect of the Holocaust, had met the two most important representatives of the Brussels 'Central Committee for

Jewish Emigration', Obersturmführer Kurt Asche and Fritz Erdmann. Three weeks previously, the 'Final Solution of the Jewish question' had been launched on the authority of the RSHA.

Sometimes Pierre Romanovitch had Malka Cymring at his side. She was the younger sister of Charles Cymring, the headmaster of the Jewish school of the same name. Malka was spectacularly beautiful, thin as a rake, with a narrow face and an incredibly cool gaze. She was married to a Belgian and thus – at first, at least – protected against deportation. She made no secret of her relationship with Romanovitch. The elegant couple enjoyed appearing together in public.

'Comte' Romanovitch was able to assume all kinds of different roles. Sometimes he played the mysterious Russian aristocrat, sometimes the wily businessman. His Brussels police files reveal that he even presented himself as a German policeman. Thus, for example, on one occasion he attempted to intimidate a householder in order to expropriate his garage for his own Citroën. On another occasion he cheated a business partner by pretending to be a plainclothes German policeman. At the beginning of 1941, when the Jews still had their rights, Romanovitch was convicted of swindling a Jewish money changer. He had offered the agent Max Cohen a hundred British pounds in exchange for Belgian francs. When Cohen opened the envelope, after Romanovitch had made off with the British currency, he found it contained nothing but worthless paper coupons.

Romanovitch's criminal record was a long one. In August 1941 he was condemned to eight months in prison by the German military court for swindling and impersonation of a police officer. After this, under the German occupation, Romanovitch would see the inside of the St Gilles prison another eight times for deception, currency smuggling and unauthorized border-crossing. But Romanovitch's periods of imprisonment became shorter and shorter; sometimes he was released after only three days. For the Gestapo, the crook was something of a wild card in their fight against the Belgian Resistance. The Brussels Gestapo clearly saw the wily 'White Russian' as a potentially lethal informer.

Everyone with eyes to see knew that Icek Glogowski was a traitor. In the company of the Gestapo, he hunted out Jews who had gone into hiding. From the safety of a German police car he would peer out at passers-by on the pavement, searching for suspects. Sometimes 'fat Jacques' would make a sudden appearance in cafés or restaurants, or turn up unexpectedly outside a flat where Jews were in hiding. The stockily built man seemed to be everywhere in Brussels.

Why was Glogowski so willing to hand his co-religionists over to the SS thugs? On 3 September 1942 his family had been deported to the East with the twelfth transport. In one of the carriages Glogowski's wife Eva and his three children – nine-year-old Elka, seven-year-old Simon and five-year-old Léon – had travelled towards certain death in Auschwitz. Had their father bought his way out of the deportation as a spy? Or did he practise the terrible trade because he couldn't bear to see others living safely when his own family had disappeared?

He was registered as a local employee on the wages list at Gestapo headquarters, and lived with a German SS man within walking distance of his workplace. His days passed in orderly fashion. In the morning at about nine he walked into the Gestapo office on the Avenue Louise. Shortly afterwards a limousine swept out of the portal of the building, Glogowski sitting in the depths of the marked police car. His ability to scent out his own kind was infallible. Among the passers-by he could practically smell those who were not wearing their Stars of David, and who had assumed another identity. On those trips, the car would regularly stop. Glogowski, very agile despite his bulky physique, and his German companion from the SS, would leap out, hurl themselves on a passer-by and menacingly demand to see their ID. Onlookers would look on helpfully as the victim was dragged into the car after a violent exchange of words.

Sometimes the spy would be given a tip-off, and appear unexpectedly at the flat of someone who had gone into hiding. This happened to Rudolf Schmitz, who had moved from Cologne to Brussels with his family in 1939. The judicial files of the Nazi trial against Kurt Asche contain a report by this Holocaust survivor. Under the heading

'Written in a pub in Brussels in September 1945', Schmitz reconstructs his unforgettable encounter with 'fat Jacques'. He had hidden his three children in a convent and lived with his wife, withdrawn from the world, in a little flat in the centre of Brussels:

> It's a rainy day. I come back from shopping for food. Because I've got wet I change my clothes and hang my things up to dry. I make myself comfortable and am completely engrossed in the newspaper for about half an hour. The door opens slowly, and there in front of me stands a tall man in a green loden coat, pointing a gun at me. 'Where are the others?' he asks, and points to a postcard that he takes out of his pocket. 'Six to seven people are supposed to meet here in the evening. Talk!' I don't reply, and he hits me on the right hand with the gun. 'Maybe you'll talk now.' The door opens again, my wife comes in, followed by Jacques. Jacques, the Jew, who has devoted himself to leading his fellow Jews into disaster. He tries to hit my wife for attempting to hide, but then he gives up and reaches for the key-hanger, puts house-keys and a torch in his pocket, rummages through the drawers, pockets my leather gloves, and rifles through everything to see if there's anything worth stealing.

Many of the Jews fingered by Glogowski had unimpeachable identity cards proving that they were Belgians. But denial was in vain. In the cellar of SS headquarters, male Jews had to drop their trousers before the scornful eyes of 'fat Jacques'. If they were circumcised, the thugs laid into them.

Sometimes Kurt Asche would stand in the doorway, watching what was going on. He was even known to encourage his brutal henchmen. The pleasure the Judenreferent took in the bloody scenes was plain. Even in SS headquarters the Asche–Glogowski duo had a bad reputation. They were famous for frisking and robbing their victims even before their personal details had been taken.

After the war a Flemish SS man from Ghent, who had worked at the police station on Avenue Louise in 1942 and 1943, described Obersturmführer Kurt Asche as an unpleasant colleague:

> His subordinates were SS Sturmscharführer Rodenbusch, SS Sturmscharführer Frank, the German interpreter Müller and the Polish national Glogowski, a spy for the office of the persecution of the Jews... Asche tolerated the mistreatment and excesses of his subordinates towards Jews in the custody of the Gestapo. I myself often saw him beating people who were brought into the building. It happened in the hallway and the cellar, before the prisoners were locked in the cell. His chief accomplice in this kind of behaviour was Glogowski, who distinguished himself by a particularly
> high level of violence. Using this blunt approach, Asche forced the Jews to confess their true identity... Many of the Jews were bleeding because they had been injured during their maltreatment by Asche and particularly by Glogowski. Within a few months, I heard, four or five Jews were supposed to have taken their own lives after being mishandled by Glogowski under Asche's instructions.

A description of Glogowski circulated among the Jewish resisters. This most dangerous of cops was described: 'Medium height, black hair, dark complexion, Jewish appearance, long nose, longish face.' He was dressed in a brown coat and wore a dark hat. His habit of rounding off lunch in the Gestapo canteen on the Square du Val de la Cambre with a quick stroll, between quarter to two and five to two, along the Rue du Monastère, would give two partisans on bicycles a good opportunity to attack and kill him on the side-street that led off the Avenue Louise. Having accomplished their mission, the attackers then planned to escape uphill via the Rue du Bourgmestre.

It was one of many plans to liquidate the police spy 'Jacques le mouchard' – 'Jacques the grass'. Youra Livchitz was also said to have been involved in the hunt for Glogowski. But 'fat Jacques' was a cunning adversary. As a night-porter in the dodgy district around the station, he had probably developed a keen nose for dangerous situations, and learned to be just ahead of potential attackers.

Jacob Gutfrajnd, in his book *Les Partisans Armés*, describes the vain attempts of his Resistance group to eliminate Glogowski: 'The story of our courageous and selfless struggle, which demanded so many victims, was darkened by one accursed shadow, the notorious Jacques.' In the battle against Jewish informers Glogowski had absolute priority:

> According to our information, he went to the races every Sunday. That was when we planned to attack. When the spectators surged out of the hippodrome, three of our men posted ourselves at the exit. They spotted Jacques and approached him. Standing right behind him, covered by his two companions, was the man who planned to shoot him. He already had his finger on the trigger, when someone pushed in front of him. The spy broke away from the crowd and ran to the tram, which was just arriving at its stop.

On another occasion the disappointed potential attackers tried to catch him as he left his flat on the Rue Vander Kinderen. But this time the gun cartridge jammed. Jacques fired back and fled. After that the Gestapo always collected him in the car in the morning and brought him home again.

Finally the young underground fighters hoped to be able to catch the clever informer in a trap. Several of them arranged to meet in a café near the Josaphat Park in Schaerbeek, an area very popular with Jews. The ones who looked particularly Jewish sat there as decoys, while a number of others took up position in a nearby café and the rest spread out around the area. One of them rang the Gestapo and reported that Jews were sitting in a café in Schaerbeek. And the woman spying for the Resistance group from her observation post on Avenue Louise reported that a car, with the traitor Jacques in the back seat, had set off. But the partisans waited in vain for their victim.

On the way to the café Glogowski had spotted a Jew on the street and taken him back to police headquarters.

Icek Glogowski ruthlessly dispatched hundreds of fellow Jews to their deaths. He would not even spare children. 'Fat Jacques' must have struck the pious sisters in the convent on Rue Clemenceau as the devil incarnate when he turned up with two German SS officers, demanding to search the building for hidden children. Among the children playing in the playground, he actually did spot several little Jewish girls. The following morning, he announced, they would come back and collect the children. The nuns were to ensure that they were dressed for a journey and supplied with a packed lunch.

Mother Superior Marie-Angèle, who was sheltering twenty-eight little Jewish girls in the boarding school, was beside herself with fear for her charges. She alerted people in the Jewish Council and the bishop's office in Mechelen. But by now they knew that interventions had no effect on the racial fanatics in Avenue Louise.

It was about nine o'clock in the evening when a young man and a young girl accompanied by a priest demanded to be let in. The young people explained that they were from the Resistance and wanted to save the children from deportation. The cleric tried to prepare the Mother Superior for what was about to happen in the next few minutes: 'We're in a state of desperation. Only force can help us now.'

Paul Halter, the twenty-three-year-old commander of the armed partisans, had learned of the forthcoming cleansing action on Rue Clemenceau. An acquaintance who ate regularly in the soup kitchen of the Catholic community of Anderlecht had been told the terrible news by the priest. Along with four friends, Paul hatched the plan to attack the convent and free the children. The priest assumed the role of mediator between the pious sisters and the young Resistance fighters.

After giving a brief warning the young people stormed the convent. Guns at the ready, they kicked the door in. First of all they locked the Mother Superior in her room. Then they tore out the telephone cables and ordered the nuns to assemble in the office. There they tied the nuns to chairs, drummed into them not to call for help for an hour, and locked the office. Two young nuns were entrusted with the task of helping the smaller girls to get dressed. 'Quickly, quickly,' the nuns encouraged their little pupils, 'the white knights want to save you.'

When the group left the convent, ten parents who had been informed about what was happening were waiting by the door. As disciplined as a school class, the other children marched in crocodile formation behind their young liberators. They had prepared a bivouac for the little girls in an illegal workshop. New hiding places were found for all the liberated children, and they all survived the Holocaust.

Their saviour, Paul Halter, was later arrested and deported to Auschwitz. Only there did the true dimension of this courageous kidnapping dawn on him. 'I realized what would have happened to the girls.' All children under the age of sixteen were sent straight to the gas chambers upon their arrival in the extermination camp. Halter, dubbed a baron by the Belgian king, took part in the first international meeting of children hidden during the Nazi era, in May 1991 in New York. There he was able to hug five of the girls who had been saved by him and his co-fighters. Forty-eight years after their risky escape, these women still had vivid memories of their 'white knight'.

13 The Waiting Room for the Holocaust

By day, light fell into the cellar through the upper part of the barred windows, just above street level. All they could see of the passers-by who walked heedlessly past the windows was their legs and footwear. Sitting on a wooden bench and wearing her nurse's uniform, the young woman was filled with yearning as she stared after the footsteps beyond the iron grille over the window. She envied the pedestrians their liberty. Régine had already spent several days and nights in the cellar of 453 Avenue Louise. Since being arrested at a friend's flat she had been here, in the basement of Gestapo headquarters, waiting with other prisoners to be transported to Mechelen transit camp.

Twice a day an emissary came from the Jewish Council, bringing food for the prisoners. If Régine wanted to go to the lavatory, she had to knock loudly and was then accompanied to the toilet door by a Flemish SS man, rifle at the ready. Now and again, the door to the dark room would open, and a desperate new arrival would be shoved in.

The air-raid on Gestapo headquarters on 20 January had profoundly shaken the SS police. Four workers, including the head of the Security Service, had been killed by fire from the English plane, and five had been seriously injured. The Nazi functionaries were still puzzled about who the pilot of the RAF plane could have been. He must have had excellent local knowledge. He had steered straight towards the building and sprayed it with shells. It was a bitter defeat for the 'master race'. Their stupid feeling of superiority had been severely shaken. The highly disciplined SS police headquarters had temporarily been thrown into complete chaos. Nonetheless, the witch-hunt of Jews and opponents of the Nazis continued unabated.

And Kurt Asche was merciless in his rejection of any attempts by advocates to intervene on behalf of any of the prisoners. At his trial, the Judenreferent of Avenue Louise was quoted as saying that the 'purpose of the measures' was a general evacuation and 'the complete separation of the Jews from the Aryans'.

Even the military administration was often powerless to deal with him. On 18 January, a young girl, accompanied by a representative of the Jewish Council, called upon Kurt Asche. Unlike her parents, who had been taken to the cellar of Avenue Louise a day before, she had Belgian nationality. The daughter was convinced that the arrest of Esther and Majer Mileband must be a mistake. After all, she was able to show the Nazi functionary a confirmation certificate from the military administration, according to which the couple had been 'exempted from the labour deployment'. Asche rapidly picked up the telephone to bark at the military commander, to tell him of his displeasure that he had interfered in the matters of the Judenreferat.

Then the Obersturmführer turned back towards the girl, and his eyes behind his thick glasses narrowed to slits. There was nothing he could do for her parents. This was no longer a labour deployment, but an evacuation of the Jewish population. And as a Belgian Jew, her turn would come. Or if she preferred, she could go straight down to the cellar without further ado. On 22 January the girl's parents were registered in Mechelen transit camp, numbers 202 and 203, for the twentieth convoy to Auschwitz.

The National Socialist man-hunter drew the net tighter and tighter. Even the phlegmatic furniture manufacturer Samuel Vanden Berg no longer felt himself to be safe despite owning a special identification card from the privileged Jewish Council. In January 1943 he recorded in his diary:

The war in Russia is not progressing quickly enough for
us. Despite all promises that we are protected by our ID cards,
we are in great danger. The important thing is
always to wear the Star of David in full view, otherwise
one provides a pretext for arrest… Although everything
seems outwardly so quiet, one never knows if one will be
sleeping in one's own bed again that evening. Our nerves
are in shreds.

Vanden Berg was clearly deeply affected by the arrest of an old
acquaintance. He himself had found a hiding place for seventy-eight-
year-old Augusta Rose in Woluwe. And now the owner of the house
told him that 'a terrible misfortune' had occurred. Germans had come
to get the Polish woman, pushed her violently around and given her
only an hour to pack all her belongings together. When the landlady
asked them why they were treating the poor woman so badly, the men
replied, 'our job is to free the world of this plague.' On 26 January,
upon her arrival in the Mechelen transit camp, Augusta Rose was registered as number 242 for the twentieth transport.

A day later Régine Krochmal was brought with several others in a
truck to the Mechelen barracks. Among the fifty people who were
taken at dawn from the basement cells and led to a truck parked in
the courtyard were Claire Prowizur and her husband Philippe. The
young Trotskyist couple had been betrayed, by a Communist whom
some friends had asked them to take in for a night. They had gone on
talking with the convinced Stalinist until late in the night, before
their guest, for want of a bed, lay down to sleep on a cutting-table
covered with fabrics. The following day, as agreed, the man had
vanished.

In her memoirs Claire describes the hours leading up to her arrest.
Like so many of those arrested by the Nazis, she reproaches herself for
not having trusted her instincts at the crucial moment. That was on
26 January at 9 o'clock in the morning, when she left the house with
her husband and suddenly saw their guest from the previous night in
the street:

He was walking along the pavement towards us, that stranger of the night, in the company of a woman. We met and passed with a barely noticeable nod. And then there was a shock. Why did Philippe and I feel that shock at the same second? No, it was impossible. And yet the doubts remained!

What reason could there be for those doubts? Why that fear? We must have been mistaken. Were we both being oversensitive? No, we had nothing to fear. We had merely met an acquaintance in the company of a blonde woman. After all, I was blonde too, and not all blondes were dangerous…

That same afternoon Claire met the daughter of the friends who had passed their guest on to them. Since her parents and little brother had been taken from their hiding place by the Gestapo a few days before, twenty-year-old Ety Ajzenberg had been wandering around Brussels without anywhere to stay. Someone must have denounced her family. Ety herself had only managed to escape being hunted down because she had been in transit when the Gestapo had appeared at her parents' house. Now Claire and Philippe wanted to help her. For the time being she was to stay with them.

A loud knock on the door of the flat startled the young people awake in the middle of the night. A glance at the time – three o'clock in the morning – made them rigid with fear. At that time of night it could only be the Gestapo. Escape was impossible. Philippe opened the door and three men in black, revolvers levelled, pushed their way in. As they tore open the drawers and cupboard doors and rummaged through all their belongings, Ety and Claire quickly got dressed. A leather briefcase standing on a chair attracted the attention of the SS policemen. When the man in black opened it, anti-Nazi pamphlets fell out. Philippe stammered that he had bought the briefcase the previous day in the flea market. This remark was met with a punch to the face, so hard that it made his nose bleed. When Claire went to help her husband, she too was beaten. Still, Claire was able to gather together a change of underwear. Escorted by the violent policemen, the three of them left their little flat. The door was sealed with a sticker: 'Confiscated'.

They passed through the dark streets in a black police limousine. After a short journey the car stopped in the courtyard of Gestapo headquarters on Avenue Louise. The young people were dragged from the car and taken to be questioned. Philippe was the first to enter the interrogation room. As he had an impeccable Belgian ID card, he refused to reveal his true identity no matter how much they beat him. Finally he had to drop his trousers. 'Now we've got the filthy Jew', his tormentors crowed when they saw that he was circumcised, and beat him all the harder. He returned from his interrogation ashen pale, his face swollen. Then it was the turn of the two young women. 'There was no point,' Claire later remarked, talking about her more lenient questioning, 'in getting us girls to drop our trousers.'

A few hours later Claire and Philippe climbed into the truck that was to take them and the other unfortunates to Mechelen. One of the others in the dense crowd in the back of the vehicle was the little nurse, Régine. Normally radiant, her light brown eyes looked as though their light had been extinguished. She no longer paid any attention to her surroundings. 'I was incredibly shattered after all those nights on the wooden bench. Even today I can't remember how I got to the barracks, or with whom.'

The heavy oak swing doors were quickly closed again when the truck drove through the blue basalt portal bearing the inscription 'The Habsburg Court' and into the rectangular courtyard. The Nazis were not keen on having eyewitnesses see what was happening inside the Dossin barracks in Mechelen. People climbed down from the truck, exhausted and downhearted, each clutching a bag or suitcase containing their most basic belongings. Two uniformed SS officers were waiting for them. All of them, adults, children and fragile old people, were sent to stand in rows of three at a door bearing the sign 'Reception'.

Chaskel Prowizur, Claire's father, stood at the first-floor window of the building opposite. As always when a new cargo of human beings appeared in the barracks yard, his eyes scoured the new arrivals, fearful that he would discover his wife or one of his children among them. He had already observed this wretched scene several times before, trembling with fear. And on every previous occasion he had been relieved not to find his family members among the prisoners.

At the beginning of January, Chaskel Prowizur had been arrested by Jacques, the Gestapo cop, while walking along the Chaussée de Vleurgat. He had certainly been careless. Against the advice of his daughter and his son-in-law, he had refused to abandon his daily strolls. He needed the fresh air, he had argued, because of his asthma. And also he felt sufficiently well disguised under a chauffeur's cap that he wore when he went out. But Glogowski, who was driving through the streets of Brussels in the back of the black police limousine on that cold January morning, was not taken in. Chaskel was arrested, and ended up shortly afterwards in Mechelen transit camp.

His daughter Claire had tried to buy his freedom, just as she had, a short time before, on behalf of her Trotskyist organization, freed her comrade Ernest Mandel from St Gilles prison. The deal had been struck through an intermediary, an attractive Jewish woman of about forty, who used her connections with the Gestapo for that kind of business. Claire had handed over 100,000 Belgian francs for the freedom of comrade Mandel. The young Trotskyist also hoped to use the help of this go-between and the financial support of her party to free her father from the barracks. But this time her intermediary had to disappoint her. No Jew had ever succeeded in getting himself released from the barracks. Nonetheless she managed to get Chaskel Prowizur crossed off the list for the nineteenth transport, which had left Mechelen for Auschwitz on 15 January. But now, on that grey morning of 27 January, he had to watch his brave daughter and her husband Philippe jump out of the truck and join the queue of new arrivals in front of the reception office.

Three long tables stood side by side in the office. Behind them sat SS men, and young women at typewriters. At the first table Claire was curtly asked for her personal details. When she explained that she didn't know where her other family members were, the German said scornfully: 'We'll get you all.' The secretaries typed her name, her address, her place and date of birth and her profession into their typewriters. The brief details fitted exactly into a single line: Klara Prowisor, 30.5.22 Altona, stl., tailor. On each fresh sheet of paper that was clamped into the typewriter – with two blueprints for carbon copies – there were about fifteen such brief biographies, each with the abbreviation 'stl.', meaning '*staatenlos*' or 'stateless'. To avoid quarrels with foreign embassies, who might be interested in the location of an arrested citizen of their country, all foreign Jews were simply described as stateless by the occupying Germans. Thus no one was responsible for them. Since Ety Ajzenberg, the girl who had spent the night with the Prowizurs, was born in Belgium, and had taken Belgian nationality at the age of sixteen, she was on a different list.

At the next table the internees had to hand over all their papers, their jewellery and all valuable objects. They were handed a cardboard sign bearing the number under which they were registered on the reception list. From now on, at all times they were to wear this rectangular piece of grey card, with their names written on the back, on a piece of string around their necks. Claire was given the number 255, and her husband Philippe was registered as Frain Szyper, number 254. Régine Krochmal, who stayed very close to the young couple during the reception process, was now number 263: 'a piece of string, a file number, our personalities were to be destroyed, our personal characteristics erased.'

Apart from their consecutive registration numbers, all the cardboard signs bore the same Roman numeral: XX. That was the number of the transport with which the prisoners would leave the camp at some point over the next few weeks or months.

Jewellery, money and watches were sealed up in a paper bag, along with keys to flats or houses. Only wedding rings were not confiscated. The individual objects of value were noted down on the paper bags, as well as the name of their former owner and that person's transport number.

At the third table, the expropriated people had to confirm the contents of the envelopes. When Claire thought it was all over, she was sent into an adjoining room. Two men, one man sitting behind a desk in plain clothes, the other in SS uniform, were waiting for her.

'Take your clothes off,' she was ordered. She hesitantly removed her clothes. Naked, covering her private parts with her hands, she watched the SS man painstakingly going through her underwear. Then he picked through her thick curly hair, stuck his index fingers into her ears, her nose, her mouth, in search of a secret hiding place, and even forced her teeth apart. Never in her life had Claire been exposed to such appall-ing treatment. At last she was allowed to put her clothes back on.

Then Claire had to go through what they called the luggage check with her bag, which she had left in the courtyard. The man in charge of this procedure was an old drinking companion of Kurt Asche's, SS Untersturmführer Karl Mainzhausen. He was usually drunk by mid-morning. He lashed out blindly if he caught someone trying to hide something from him. Often he struck the prisoners only because they were too slow in opening their suitcases.

The reception process in Mechelen camp lasted three hours. Finally all the prisoners received a blanket, a plate, a beaker and a spoon. Then they were shown to the dormitories, which occupied the upper storeys of the rectangular building. Ety had to separate from them, and go to the dormitory with the Belgian Jews.

Suddenly Claire found herself in her father's arms again. 'It wasn't a happy reunion,' she noted decades later. 'It was a mixture of tragedy and joy.' Ety met up again with her family that day, too. Her parents and her nine-year-old brother Peretz had already been delivered to Mechelen on 21 January, and registered under the numbers 88, 89 and 90.

The feeling of happiness at having found her father again only lasted for a short moment for Claire. The terrible reality of this inhos-pitable waiting room for the Holocaust quickly sobered her up again. Roughly cobbled together, dual-level wooden frames served as bed-steads. The straw mattresses were drenched in the sweat and dirt of the previous tenants. No cupboards, no chair. Belongings had to be stowed under the wooden frames.

A good-looking young man delivered a brief introductory lecture to the new arrivals. Later they learned that the Jew Dagobert Meier had previously been an opera singer in Antwerp, and was now in charge of the 108 Jewish manual workers. Meier explained the course of their days and the rules of conduct. Wake up at six, breakfast at seven, then the work would be assigned. Lunch was at twelve, dinner at six in the evening. When the light was put out at nine o'clock, there had to be complete silence. The beds had to be impeccable, the blankets folded perfectly. No one was permitted to miss the roll-calls, which could take place during the day or even at night.

In the middle of the dormitory, about sixty feet long and twenty feet across, there were two tables. Here, at seven o'clock in the morning, the senior inmates of the dormitory put down the pots containing a black brew: coffee substitute. It was rumoured that bromide was added to this infusion so that the internees didn't develop excessive sexual desires. Men and women, children and old people, were all lodged together. All class differences were abolished. The prostitute slept next to the devout orthodox Jewish woman, the little receiver of stolen goods next to the bank director.

On the half-landing between two equal-sized dormitories, each sleeping one hundred people, stood two iron canisters, which served as chamber pots. There was no running water either on the landing or in the dormitory, so vermin were rife. The inmates were plagued by lice, worms and fleas. On the ground floor there were the washrooms, with primitive washbasins, and next to them the toilets, about ten stinking latrines. Each morning people stood in line outside this 'latrine for Jews only'.

Their bellies were constantly rumbling, all their thoughts revolved around food. They were allotted 250 grams of bread each day, along with one teaspoon of jam and another of sugar, and at lunchtime the prisoners were served a tin bowl full of thin cabbage soup. And in the evening, once again, some bread and two spoons of cabbage soup. Bread was the currency: it was for bread that people cheated, betrayed and stole. Possession of bread or other food meant power, respect and influence. After a few weeks, all the inmates who had to make do with the rations authorized by the directors of the camp were recognizable by their emaciated faces and their dragging gait.

Better fed were those who received the occasional parcel from friends and relations. Letters and parcels were distributed once a week. All consignments were opened by Jewish staff. Next to them stood two SS men, who immediately grabbed the most valuable pieces. Often all the recipients were left with was a pitiful remnant of the parcel, which had been dispatched with such love and amidst such great privations.

The camp was governed by the principle of what Régine Krochmal calls 'dehumanization'. 'Impossible for us to believe that outside the walls there were laughing people, friendship, food, flowers, music, books ...' Let alone solidarity. A perfidious system of small favours for a very few caused resentment and discord in this very mixed and haphazard society.

In his memoirs, *A Holocaust Memoir: Doctor 117641*, the American professor of psychiatry Louis J. Micheels describes the mechanisms of intimidation and oppression in the Dossin barracks. The Dutch doctor, born, like Youra Livchitz, in 1917, was one of the 1,631 inmates of the twentieth transport to Auschwitz. He is one of the few survivors of the death camp. Micheels quickly understood the situation in Mechelen: 'I realized that in this sort of camp our customary system of values had almost ceased to exist, and with it the possibility of uniting the prison population against the oppressor.'

Like most of those stranded in Mechelen, the young Dutch doctor had been betrayed. He and his fiancée Nora had entrusted themselves to a group of people-smugglers, who were to take them out of Holland, through Belgium and France and into Switzerland in return for a large sum of money. Instead of bringing them over the border to France, the Flemish-speaking driver who had taken them on in Belgium took them straight to Avenue Louise. Louis and Nora spent a month in St Gilles prison, before being transferred to Mechelen. There, in order to remain together, they presented themselves as a married couple.

Life in the camp, Micheels observed, brought out people's worst qualities. Louis and Nora were constantly hungry. With no contact with the outside world, and no chance of ever receiving a parcel, the couple were at the bottom of the camp hierarchy. They learned the techniques of survival in a wolf-pack and behaved like beggars, constantly in search of food. They quickly discovered that if possible they should be last in the queue for the soup pot, because the deeper the ladle went, the more nutrition there was in their portions.

One day Louis made friends with a Belgian, the only non-Jew among the prisoners. He was a homosexual who liked dressing in women's clothing. In the eyes of the Nazis that meant that he had given up his right to a humane existence. As the transvestite received large food parcels, he offered to give the starving young doctor his own soup ration. Once the food had been distributed, Micheels was to go to his dormitory. But when Micheels asked his roommates where the Belgian was, they started shouting at him and punching him. Finally they pushed him down the stairs. 'I felt humiliated, helpless and enraged. I could not believe that one Jew could treat another so cruelly, especially when he did not have the physical strength to defend himself.'

Anyone who, like the young doctor, fell under the category of 'prisoner', was on the lowest rung of the camp hierarchy. Jews with Belgian citizenship had a higher status because – temporarily – they were under the personal protection of Queen Elisabeth. None of the prisoners had any idea at this point that the Nazis would later break their promises not to deport the Queen's Jewish compatriots. The Belgian Jews felt comparatively safe. Many of them had made their wooden bunks in the dormitory as comfortable as they could, with proper bedclothes, pans and pots. They had preserves, cigarettes and soap, because they had non-Jewish friends and neighbours who could go to the Post Office without putting their lives at risk, and who were thus able to send them parcels.

Above the Belgian Jews in the hierarchy were those Jews who were able to show that they had one Aryan parent, the 'Mischlinge' (halfbreeds). Equal to them were those who were married to an Aryan, so-called 'Mischehen', or mixed marriages. According to the Nazi racial laws, members of these two categories were exempted from extermination. They worked in the camp as deliverers of parcels or bathroom attendants, in the kitchen, or ran one of the workshops.

Then there were the Jewish office workers and secretaries, most of them pretty young women, who had been employed because of their knowledge of languages and their typing and shorthand skills, and had made themselves indispensable in the course of the months. Certainly, they were dependent upon the favour of their German superiors, so as not to find their own names on the next transport list.

For everyone else, the barracks in the medieval Episcopal city was merely a huge waiting room. The prisoners who set off from here on their last, terrible journey were only temporarily tolerated within those walls. 'In the camp, people were useless,' writes Louis Micheels. 'The only purpose of their existence was to serve the oppressor's sadistic needs. The SS was fascinated by and even encouraged internal conflict or self-destructive, competitive behaviour.'

But there were also prisoners who saw through the system, who stuck together and helped one another. They formed a little elite in this classless society, one distinguished by humanity and courage. Many of them belonged to the Resistance and had heard about the mass-shootings and organized atrocities of the Nazis in Poland. All of their thoughts were directed at ways of escaping the Nazi killing-machine. Among them were Claire and Philippe Szyper, the young Trotskyist couple. And Szymon Baruch Birnberg – number 245 on the deportation list – who, with his friend David Gorski, number 230, had arrived a day before them in Mechelen. Philippe knew David, who was seven years older, from his time in a left-wing Zionist youth organization. But once Philippe had joined the Trotskyists, they had severed all contact. In Mechelen, where they faced the same fate, the convinced Stalinist Birnberg and the equally hardline Trotskyist Philippe Szyper started talking to one another again. And they discovered that they had been betrayed to the Nazis by the very same Communist, that man in the pay of the SS, to whom Claire and Philippe had given shelter for the night in their little flat.

14 The Bourgeois Terrorist
Late January 1943

What German policeman could possibly have suspected the elegant woman going about her daily business in high-heeled shoes, in a made-to-measure suit and with a fashionable hat on her well-tended perm? And if the German police had indeed been suspicious, they would have found nothing of note in the well-dressed lady's handbag. An examination of her papers would have shown that she was a Belgian woman who had moved to Brussels from the provinces, and who lived on the Place Brugmann. A respectable bourgeois address, as befitted such a lady. On the square in the district of Uccle, spacious mansion blocks had been built for people in the upper income bracket in the early 1930s.

What Madame de Castro actually did have to hide she kept well hidden in the false bottom of her fashionable hat. They were forged IDs, which she was to deliver at a particular time to a particular address on behalf of the businessman Maurits Bolle.

This lady, apparently above all suspicion, was a Jew. Like Maurits Bolle, she and her late husband came from the Netherlands, and had moved to Brussels in the early 1930s. Her daughter Inès was a friend of Bolle's daughter Hélène. She, in turn, was a colleague of Youra Livchitz. The girls had been inseparable since their schooldays in the lycée in St Gilles. They were both members of the Belgian guide movement, and often spent their weekends together at guide camp.

By now Hélène was in the final year of her medical studies at Liège University, and Inès was working as a physiotherapist at the St Pierre hospital. Through Hélène, she had met the whole of Youra's clique. Even today she talks in the slang of those times, of the '*bande des amis*', the gang of friends. Inès recalls celebrating New Year's Eve with Hélène during the first year of the war, with Youra and his friends at the Theosophist Society. It was a relaxed party.

Youra was a good mate of her friend Hélène 'and nothing more'. It was indirectly thanks to the young physician that Inès de Castro had taken papers in psychology and philosophy when sitting her finals as a physiotherapist, because Hélène had arranged for her fellow student to assist her. 'Youra was very knowledgeable about it all,' Madame de Castro says in retrospect, 'and above all he was very good at explaining things.'

Inès worked for the Resistance as well. She answered to 'Papa' Bolle, Hélène's father and a friend of her parents. Even before the occupation, the Dutch businessman had helped refugees from Nazi Germany across the border to France on his own initiative, until he was recruited by Hertz Jospa for the Jewish Defence Committee.

Inès did not transport the documents entrusted to her in a hat, like her mother, but in a pastry box bearing the inscription of a well-known patisserie. Sometimes, when a German policeman boarded the tram she was sitting in, she would pick up the little white Spitz terrier that went everywhere with her and put it on her lap to hide the box. A clever distraction, she still thinks today: 'People were only interested in the sweet little dog. And I felt safe.' Only in retrospect did she realize the danger she had placed herself in. 'Somehow this courier service was the most natural thing in the world for me. We were young, and quite dashing about it.'

Inès's father died in 1940. The flat on the first floor of the modern mansion block on the Place Brugmann was actually too big for mother and daughter on their own, but 'Papa' Bolle, who had supplied them both with impeccable Belgian IDs, had a use for the extra room. It became a nocturnal staging post for refugees who were to be smuggled out of the country.

The two women always learned beforehand on what day and at what time their guests would arrive. A go-between brought them to the front door and told them to take the lift to the first floor. In the flat a hot meal – ingredients supplied by Maurits Bolle – and a freshly made bed awaited them. For many it was an unfamiliar blessing after days or weeks of flight.

Early in the morning, the refugees followed Inès to the tram, got out with her at the Place des Héros, and walked along behind the young woman until she greeted a man. That was the agreed sign that her nocturnal visitors were to follow this pedestrian on the next stage of their escape route. Then Inès's mission was accomplished.

Robert Maistriau, who had attended the lycée in Uccle with Youra Livchitz, says half a century later, 'Basically, everyone who was politically aware wanted to do something. But in the end only a few risked the step towards the underground, with all its consequences.'

Most of Youra's friends from school and university tried to combine the two disparate elements: their bourgeois lives and their activities for the Resistance in 'Groupe G'. That possibility was closed to the Jew Youra Livchitz. Since summer 1942, when the raids had begun, he was, as a Jew, in constant danger and a threat to his non-Jewish friends.

Robert Maistriau had been following the emergence of 'Groupe G' from its very inception. He had met the heads of this underground organization through Youra and his friend Robert Leclercq. Leclercq was the group's head of information. Richard Altenhoff, who was responsible for the acquisition of arms and explosives, had met Maistriau now and again at games of croquet. The English game had lost none of its attractions during the first few years of the war.

It must have been in late January 1943 when Robert Maistriau was invited by an older friend to take part in a meeting in the Bois de Soignes. He cycled to the agreed spot, where Henri Neuman, Walter de Sélys Longchamp, Richard Altenhoff, Robert Leclercq and Jean Burgers planned to train in self-defence that Saturday afternoon. In a clearing, they imitated the fast and complicated grips that the lawyer Neuman displayed for them. The Asian close-combat method was called Judo. 'We had a lot of fun,' Maistriau recalls, 'but I can hardly believe that any of us would have thought of the right Judo grip if it had come to the crunch.'

Another episode from the first few months of 1943 has stayed with Robert Maistriau. Richard Altenhoff had asked the younger boy to go with him to a canal lock near Charleroi. As an engineer with a public building company, Altenhoff was very well informed about the transport infrastructure. Another advantage of his profession was that he could move around the sites of subsequent acts of sabotage without arousing suspicion.

On this outing Altenhoff wanted to sound out the possibilities of destroying the lock mechanism and making the canal unnavigable at least for a few days. Maistriau had been chosen to select the act of sabotage at a later date. But the task turned out to be one that Maistriau was incapable of performing. To put the mechanism out of action, he would have had to climb into the cold and cloudy water. And that was something that the keen and otherwise vigorous young man was unable to do, since he had a phobia about leeches. Even in old age, Maistriau, who later carried out very different acts of bravado as a member of 'Groupe G', is amused by Richard Altenhoff's exclamation at the time: 'Just what I need! You're not afraid of armed Germans, but you're terrified of leeches!'

In his book *Avant Qu'il Soit Trop Tard*, Henri Neuman describes the almost imperceptible transition by these bourgeois boys to ever riskier actions. The engineer Richard Altenhoff, who travelled around the country to carry out inspections for the state building company SOCOL, had discovered an army depot of straw and cattle-feed in Vilvoorde. It could be reached by bicycle from their homes. After an initial inquiry, Altenhoff and Neuman decided to set fire to the depot. Neuman remembers this particular attack because it was the first time that the two young saboteurs set off with loaded revolvers. They had strapped their Colts to their calves. Fuses and explosives were hidden in the cast-iron frames of their bicycles.

At the scene of the action itself they waited until the patrols had disappeared, climbed the fence and laid their fuses. By the time they got back to their bicycles the fire was already spreading. Shortly afterwards the night was lit up as bright as day. The fire became so powerful that even the adjacent army wood depot went up in flames.

The act of sabotage receives a brief mention in the military administration's list of attacks for the month of February: '14.2.43. Fire in the barn at a farmhouse, 75,000 kg of pressed straw burned.'

On the way back to Brussels the two saboteurs encountered fire engines, their sirens howling. Henri and Richard cycled side by side, having firmly decided to shoot the first person who stopped them to check their papers. Possession of weapons was punishable by death. But they met only two Belgian policemen, who politely advised them to avoid certain crossroads, because they were guarded particularly heavily by the German Field Police. When they reached Henri Neuman's apartment, safe and sound, even Richard Altenhoff, who usually abstained completely from alcohol, downed a large glass of brandy to relax. 'So this thoughtful and peaceable young engineer had turned himself into a daring man of action,' Neuman writes, concluding this episode in his memoirs.

15 The Fight Gets Tougher
February 1943

At the end of a day at Pharmacobel, Youra had got used to dropping in on Marcel Hastir on the Rue du Commerce at least once a week. Although the thirty or so students at the painting school would usually have finished their classes, the building was never silent. Friends or friends of friends would always be found squatting in Hastir's warm studio – thanks to Marcel's gift for organization, he was never short of fuel, even in a harsh winter like this one.

A few weeks previously Youra and his friends had been jubilant. They were filled with hope that the war and the occupation were finally coming to an end. The bombardment of Gestapo headquarters by the Royal Air Force fighter plane had given them all a tremendous boost. On the other side of the Channel they were able to rely on friends, on the Allies, who were prepared to help the oppressed little country.

But the German occupying forces soon recovered from that defeat. The cure for their injury was an even stronger dose of repression. That in turn stirred up a popular fury against the authoritarian invaders.

Times had grown harder for the young people. It had become risky to meet up in cafés or stand around in groups. The German Field Police could suddenly turn up at any time, check IDs and recruit young Belgians for labour deployment in Germany. Those young people would replace German industrial and agricultural workers who had been called up and were now bleeding to death on the

Eastern Front. The Field Police were even searching cinema audiences, looking for people who were fit to work, and who were trying to get out of being sent to German factories. According to a measure that had recently been passed, all men between the ages of eighteen and fifty, and all unmarried women between the ages of twenty-one and thirty-five had been compulsorily conscripted for the labour deployment in Germany.

Unlike the deportation of the Jews, organized by the SS police, which occurred in great secrecy and provoked no public outcry, the compulsory recruitment of the Belgian workforce was the dominant subject of conversation during those cold winter months in Belgium. Every family had at least one member who was affected by the new measure, and who tried to escape it. In his first quarterly report of 1943 the military commander with responsibility for the places in question described the explosive mood in the country:

> As regards internal politics, the worsening attitude and the growing mood of hatred were fired by the implementation of compulsory service. In the wake of the planned increase in workforce numbers and the inclusion of all classes of the population, groups of all political colours had increasingly closed ranks.

That evening Youra discovered his old classmate Jean Franklemon in the group that gathered around Marcel Hastir. 'Pamplemousse' and his street-players had been using the second floor of the building for rehearsals of Jean Cocteau's *Les Parents Terribles*, and he was now listening to their host, whose stories from the reality of the German occupation were far more exciting than any play. Jean had abandoned his unloved maths studies at ULB, and was now studying at La Cambre Art School. His switch to art was clearly visible in his appearance. The tall, slim young man now wore his dark hair longer than most of his contemporaries.

A short time ago, the house on the Rue du Commerce had been searched. Once again it proved advantageous that Marcel, with his mischievous brown eyes, had good contacts with a few cultural devotees in the German propaganda department. These workers in the Brussels branch of Goebbels's Ministry of Propaganda, whose headquarters was in the same street, were francophone and enjoyed chatting with the educated Belgian artist. As a result he had been warned, by a press officer who was well disposed towards him, that the German police planned to search the building the following day. It was believed that young people wishing to escape the labour deployment to Germany were hiding in the school.

The same night Hastir and his friends removed all suspicious material. Most of it was temporarily stored on the roof of the house next door. But what were they to do with the duplicating machine on which Hastir's 'students' regularly ran off their anti-German flyers and the underground paper *Radio Moscou*? If the police found it in the painting school, they would all be arrested as terrorists and end up in Breendonk camp. Hastir, who had previously always managed to winkle himself out of the most desperate situations, had a bright idea on this occasion, too. A few houses along lived an old man, a pathological collector, who took all the things he picked up on his travels and stored them in his backyard. So the valuable machine temporarily disappeared under the mountain of trash and rubble.

Another lucky escape. But which of them would be caught next time? Marcel Hastir remembers: 'It was a life of high excitement, a constant conspiracy.' Everyone who went in and out was constantly infringing the rules of the occupying forces and had an involvement with the Resistance movement. People like Jean Robert Leclercq, and Jean Franklemon, a member of the Communist Party. Franklemon's parents were also putting themselves at risk by taking in endangered Resistance fighters, and a Jewish child lived in their house under a false identity. Another friend of Youra's who often popped into the studio was Szmul Rzepkowicz. He was just as passionate a card-player as Franklemon. He was known as the 'King of the Matrix' because of his skill at forging papers. But he and Youra were guilty in the eyes of the Nazis above all because they infringed the National Socialist racial law.

Some of them had believed until recently that resistance was something like a game of cops and robbers, in which the clever robbers led the stupid cops a merry dance. By now experience had taught them otherwise. Recently the military administration had started fighting back with renewed intransigence. The violence on both sides escalated.

The spiral of terror had begun in November, when three pro-Nazi community heads, including the mayor of Charleroi, were liquidated by partisans. At first the Resistance fighters' strategy of obstructing collaborations between the occupying forces and right-wing Belgian activists actually seemed to be successful. In several towns council members stepped down for fear of such attacks.

But this placed the Governor General under pressure. Falkenhausen had so far adhered to the military rule of only executing hostages if German Wehrmacht soldiers were murdered. And the Communist attackers had so far avoided giving the general a pretext for such retaliatory actions by attacking German soldiers.

But now Wallonian Rexists and Flemish nationalists were urging him to punish attacks on their people by shooting hostages. Only in that way could law and order in the state be upheld. And the general gave in. In the Military Commander's twenty-third Activity Report he announced the enforcement of this new regulation:

> Since the Flemings and Walloons who are working with us
> (Waffen-SS, Flemish and Wallonian Legion, NSKK, the
> Auxiliary Police and railway guards) are basically able to
> demand these measures because they are often hit in attacks
> on German Wehrmacht members, the Military Commander
> has ordered the shooting of a large number of terrorists.

Falkenhausen first had eight political prisoners from Breendonk concentration camp executed in retaliation for the assassination of the mayor of Charleroi.

After this bloody demonstration of power, the armed Resistance swore revenge. They felt strengthened by a decree issued by the Belgian government in exile. Anyone who collaborated with the enemy or denounced his compatriots, the Belgian cabinet in London had declared, could expect the death penalty once the war was over. 'The traitors will fall in greater numbers than ever before, and the revenge of the partisans will come down on the heads of the Germans themselves,' the Communist guerrillas announced in their underground newspaper *Le Partisan*. And they kept their word. Between Christmas 1942 and 12 January 1943, six uniformed Germans, including two council members of the military administration, were ambushed and shot.

This time the general did not hesitate. He ordered the execution of more Communists and terrorists. They died without even being questioned. The military administration was to persist with these reprisals until the end of the occupation. In just two years, Falkenhausen had 240 hostages executed. In the far larger territory of France, where General von Stülpnagel had put the police force under the charge of an SS police chief, the number of executed hostages rose only very slightly in over two years and 254 hostages were executed.

Nonetheless, the guerrilla fighters refused to be intimidated. 'Despite draconian counter-measures by the military administration, particularly the shooting of many hostages,' the Brussels representative of the German Foreign Office reported to Berlin in mid-January, 'the terrorist circles do not appear to be impressed.'

None of the young people sitting together on that late afternoon in the Rue du Commerce had ever taken an interest in a pastoral letter from the bishop of Mechelen. But this time it was different. The most recent public appeal from the head of the Catholic Church, which the priests read out on Sundays from their pulpits, was the subject of intense discussions. Bishop van Roey had condemned the bloody attacks of the Resistance. For some it was a long-overdue appeal to reason, for others a cowardly act of submission. 'Where is this bloodshed leading?' read his letter. 'The consequences are clear: insecurity and general turmoil, discord and deadly hatred. The safety of the people must be the supreme principle. In the name of this principle we ask that these bloody actions stop, so that calm and patience may return in the hope of a just peace.'

In Hastir's circles it was agreed that the pastoral letter was not directed solely at the Communist Resistance, but defamed the Resistance as a whole. By condemning the attacks of the partisans, but not devoting a word to the crimes of the occupying forces, the cardinal placed himself on the side of the German occupiers. The situation for the Resistance was already difficult enough. Now the Catholic leader was also trying to drive a wedge between his sheep and the rebels. And that was exactly how things were seen by the representative of the German Foreign Office in Brussels, who confirmed approvingly in a telegram to his superiors in Berlin: 'Open conflict with Catholic clergy so far avoided. Cardinal Archbishop of Mechelen has on the contrary most severely condemned assassinations in a pastoral message.'

That afternoon Youra had noticed that Jean Franklemon was following the conversation with an unusually serious expression on his face. This time 'Pamplemousse' wasn't telling jokes or doing imitations, he wasn't saying a word. And finally Jean came out with what it was that was bothering him. He had learned from a friend in the Party that the Gestapo had arrested dozens of Communists over the past few weeks. In Charleroi the organization was more or less crushed. And there had been a number of arrests in Brussels.

Youra immediately thought of his brother Alexandre. The elder Livchitz had gone underground as a member of the armed partisans. For several days not a word had been heard from him. There was actually nothing strange about the fact that he only dropped in at irregular intervals, since it helped to protect his relations.

Eight o'clock in the evening meant curfew for the Jews. Anyone who was caught on the street after that time risked being arrested. Youra didn't want to worry his mother, who was sure to be waiting for him already. So he left his friends behind in the studio. In the street he was enveloped by darkness and cold. It had started to rain. According to weather reports, the downpour was expected to turn to snow over the course of the night. With his collar turned up, hands deep in his pockets, he set off homewards on foot.

Behind him Youra heard a car approaching. When the car had caught up with him, he quickened his pace. This didn't bode well. Without moving his head, Youra's eyes scoured the house-fronts for the chance of escape, an open door or a brightly lit pub. Then he heard a bright woman's voice calling his name. Malka Cymring had lowered the window of the black Citroën, and was delighted that she and her companion Pierre Romanovitch had surprised the young doctor. She had recognized Youra by the spring in his step, a distinctive feature of that tall athletic figure. Malka had an eye for such things.

The couple invited him to get in. They would drop him off on Avenue Brugmann. Malka, with her narrow, lively face, had known Youra for a long time. She was the younger sister of Charles or Chaim, the former head of the Jewish students' organization at the 'Free University'. Now the Jewish Council had appointed Charles Cymring headmaster of a Jewish secondary school, although its pupils were gradually disappearing behind the barrack walls of Mechelen. Malka had introduced Youra to the elegant 'White Russian' Romanovitch only a few days before, at Bistro Vitefili by the Porte de Namur. The students' and artists' pub was considered 'kosher'. The landlord and landlady were, like their guests, opposed to the Germans. And the noise and smoke deterred strangers from coming in.

In the pub, Romanovitch had talked urgently to Youra Livchitz. It was quite clear he was trying to impress the young medic. The shady 'White Russian', who had offered his services as a spy in Gestapo headquarters, presented himself as a Resistance fighter. He was a businessman, he said. And all the information that he received from his German partners he passed on to the 'White Army'. It was all extremely risky, and would be punished severely by the occupying forces. When he mentioned as though in passing that he had just spent a few months in the St Gilles prison, Youra actually seemed impressed. He started to trust the sly crook.

Now Youra was sitting dry and cosy and relaxed in the back of the black limousine, listening to Romanovitch. To the pearly laughter of his lovely companion, he was telling the latest anti-German jokes. Only when they said goodbye at Avenue Brugmann did the 'White Russian' turn serious. Youra could always depend on him. And perhaps they would soon have the chance to do something together. They would see one another again before long.

16 A Bright Idea
End of February

Hertz Jospa paced nervously back and forth in the little room. It was early morning, and still dark in the street outside. The lights were not yet lit even in the red-brick building opposite, the hospital of Ixelles, which he could see from his room. Jospa was too worried even to read. Although he usually spent hours poring over his books, he could find no peace today. The bulb of the dim lamp on his desk fell upon an open book, and other volumes and papers for which there was no room on the table were piled up on the floor. Since he and his wife Yvonne had been forced to leave the flat they shared, and had gone into hiding, they lived in this temporary chaos. It was a makeshift bedroom at the home of some friends, and for safety reasons they could only go there at night.

Jospa was worried. His journey to Charleroi the previous day, full of interruptions in the over-filled train, had been a gruelling one, and the situation of the comrades in the industrial town had left him deeply depressed. They had already been impatiently waiting for him. The Yiddish announcement 'Joschpa kimt' – 'Jospa's coming' – had been enough to mobilize the Jewish members of the Communist Party. They hoped the thoughtful young man from Brussels might be able to give them encouragement and hope after the disastrous events of the past few weeks. But this time it had been difficult for Jospa even to boost their confidence by a small degree. Thirty-four Communist partisans had been arrested in the region of Charleroi after a Party member had fallen into the clutches of the German Security Police. The man had given in to questioning and handed over names and addresses. Now the organization was robbed of its toughest fighters in the Charleroi region. But in Brussels, too, the ranks of the Resistance were thinning out. The partisan army had lost several members of its mobile task force. Jewish fighters had been particularly badly affected. The ones who had been discovered without weapons were waiting in Mechelen for the next transport to the East. The others, whom the Gestapo had found with pistols were, *Le Soir* reported, to be executed as terrorists.

The hated German Security Police probably had information from within the ranks of the Resistance. That was the only way Jospa could explain their success. The commanders of two Mobile Task Forces had been arrested. One of them was responsible for the incendiary attack on the Jewish files, the other, a Spanish veteran, the Hungarian Sandor Weisz, had ordered a bomb attack on the Marivaux cinema, when the Flemish nationalists issued invitations to a screening there. This defeat of the underground movement put a spring in the step of the German occupiers. The military administration was proudly able to report to the RSHA in Berlin that the Belgian underground movement had suffered severe setbacks. It was true that 'terrorist attacks on members of the army and members of the "renewal movement", had risen until mid-January.' But then,

> the excellent and well-planned work of the Security Police
> and the Security Service had quickly succeeded in unmasking
> the Communist organization responsible for the attacks and
> acts of sabotage, and arresting several leaders as well as a large
> number of Communist partisans… As ever, the most
> successful combat measures proved to be those that were
> built on the basis of the information service.

This referred to the work of spies and informers.

What Jospa feared the most was the infiltration of Gestapo spies into the closed ranks of the Resistance. He had been living under-ground for months. He and his wife possessed excellently forged IDs that would stand up to any checks. Helpers in the town councils did not only supply the Resistance with original IDs, but also ensured that through faked change of address reports the identity of the owner could be checked seamlessly against several different addresses. Jospa insisted that his friends only call him by his code-name, Joseph. His wife Hava was now called Yvonne, an impeccably French name. Her black hair, which she had formerly worn tied smoothly back with a centre parting, now fell in blonde curls around her shoulders.

Hertz and Yvonne had had to part from their little son Paul, who was staying with non-Jewish friends. Every now and again his hosts told them when they were taking him for a walk. Then, without being seen, Yvonne was able to convince herself that the little boy was clearly doing well in his new home.

Yvonne hadn't come home that night. Jospa's wife had travelled across the country, as an organizer of the 'Enfance' department of the Jewish Defence Committee, to seek lodgings for Jewish children. This time her task was to persuade the headmaster of a Catholic boys' boarding school to take in a few boys whose parents had been arrested. Hertz Jospa was sure that the lovely and eloquent Yvonne would be able to find a place for the boys. She had never returned from such a trip unsuccessful. The members of the CDJ had so far been able to place about a thousand children in new homes.

Since their marriage in the Register Office of the Brussels district of Ixelles, Yvonne and Hertz Jospa had lived under the sign of their shared political commitment for the neglected and the oppressed. The young sociologist who worked as a social worker in the Borinage, the poorest region of Wallonia, and the scientific laboratory director of a Brussels pharmaceuticals company were convinced Marxists and Communist Party members. At the time of the Spanish Civil War they had helped volunteers against the Franco regime from Central and Eastern Europe to pass through Belgium. Since 1936 they had been active in the League Against Racism and Anti-Semitism, in which, as a fighter for human rights, Yvonne worked with tireless commitment in the battle against xenophobia and discrimination until her death in January 2000. In the 1990s it was undesirable aliens and asylum-seekers for whom the campaigner fought.

At the time of the German occupation her husband Hertz Jospa was one of the leading figures in the Belgian Communist Party. But even among the bourgeoisie the good listener with the kindly dark eyes enjoyed great respect. The businessman Benjamin Nijkerk, an independent Zionist, and the Dutch businessman Maurits Bolle held the intelligent Communist and his organizational abilities in high esteem. They became friends in the fight against Hitler's fascism. In those days capitalists and Marxists were united by their will to help their persecuted fellow Jews. The Jewish Defence Committee, which looked after the interests of the Jews within the Belgian Independent Front, the Front de l'Indépendance, was financed with 750,000 Belgian francs a month by the 'American Jewish Joint Distribution Committee'. Benjamin Nijkerk, who risked his life with each journey that he took, collected the money in Switzerland. From this kitty he provided the sparse wages of the Jewish partisans and fed children and adults in hiding.

The office of the Jewish Defence Committee was only ten minutes on foot from the place where the Jospas slept on the Rue Léon Cuissez, in the home of a Belgian businessman. The house was entered through a shop, so that the coming and going of the members of the CDJ was not particularly conspicuous. The second-floor office, which only looked like a work-room by day, was reached by a flight of stairs at the back. At night it was turned into a normal bedroom again. After working hours, all documents and papers were hidden elsewhere, lest they fall into the wrong hands during a house-search. Only those who announced their presence at the arranged time and with the agreed knock were allowed in.

That morning Youra Livchitz was to be one of the few allowed into the office of the Jewish Defence Committee. For days the young doctor had planned to visit Hertz Jospa. He was worried. Lately, the bad news seemed to be coming in thick and fast. In the office of the Communist and co-publisher of the Yiddish underground journal

Onzer Wort, many different strands of information came together. It was there that he would hear more about the political state of things. And Youra also learned over time that a conversation with the thoughtful and incorruptible Bessarabian compatriot helped to put his own jumbled thoughts in order.

When Youra had come home the previous evening, he had found Alexandre, his beloved 'Choura', waiting for him. There had been no word of his elder brother for two weeks. And now he sat like an exhausted warrior in his favourite chair by the fire, and was terribly hungry. Rachel Livchitz was in the kitchen making macaroni and tomato sauce, a favourite dish of both her sons.

At such a time, when no one could tell if they would ever see each other again, Saps, as everyone called her, had been grateful for every hour that she was able to spend with Youra and Choura. As a social assistant with the Israeli community, she heard about the most awful tragedies every day.

Couples were torn apart, parents spent months waiting in vain for a sign of life of their sons and daughters who had been sent to the work deployment; children whose mothers and fathers had disappeared on one of the trains to the East, stayed behind as orphans. Each day could be the last that a Jew spent in freedom, so long as the Nazis were in power in Belgium. Sometimes the fifty-four-year-old asked herself whether, as a young woman in Munich, she had really lived in that country from which all the evil in the world now seemed to flow.

The four years that she had spent in the Bavarian capital with her husband had given her the impression of a very different Germany. She remembered the abundance of culture on offer, the exhibitions, plays and concerts, the openness to all new intellectual trends. Now Theosophy, and Rudolf Steiner's Anthroposophy, doctrines that had attracted many people in Germany in those days, were on the Nazi index. The 'land of thinkers and poets' was now ruled by the resentful and the narrow-minded – and the Jew-haters.

This appalling hatred also affected her and her sons. Rachel Livchitz had deliberately not brought her children up in the Jewish tradition. That would have contradicted her liberal attitudes and her Theosophical conviction of the equal value of all religions. Her life in Brussels was anchored far more in the Theosophical than in the Jewish community. She had found her friends among its members. They were academics, artists and intellectuals who were open to everything new, who loved music and literature as she did.

The idea that her son Alexandre, now thirty-two, played an important part in the partisan army as 'Commandant Jean' filled Saps with pride, but also with fear. She knew that he had recently been involved in an attack on a police station in Molenbeek. They had got away with 62,000 food cards and twenty-four revolvers. Choura did not brag about his heroic actions against the occupying Germans. But she sensed that her eldest son was taking part in much more dangerous missions, and that his life often hung in the balance.

She grew even more worried when Choura told her that evening that several of his comrades in Brussels had been arrested. The Gestapo clearly had access to Resistance information or else it would not have been capable of such a coup. Two of Choura's comrades had been interned as 'Communist terrorists' in Breendonk concentration camp, because weapons had been found in their possession. By now three Brussels partisans were in Mechelen transit camp, fearing deportation. The Gestapo had been able to prove only that they were Jews.

While the fortress of Breendonk was hermetically sealed, information was constantly leaking out of Dossin barracks. Some of the privileged Jews who lived in a so-called 'mixed marriage' with an Aryan, or who were descended from one Aryan parent, performed functions in the transit camp that brought them in contact with the outside world. It was through those channels that information flowed.

But that evening Choura also had some good news to report. Two Jewish partisans had recently reappeared among their units. It had long been assumed that they had ended up in a German concentration camp. On 15 January, they had jumped from the nineteenth deportation train that had set off from Mechelen while it was still on Belgian soil. One of the escapees wanted to make his experiences public in an underground newspaper. Maybe then other Jews could be encouraged to take every available chance to escape.

Youra, the brothers had agreed between themselves, would inform Hertz Jospa about it. The Jewish Defence Committee was certainly interested in further details of this possibility of escape.

The elder Livchitz had not left until shortly before midnight. Because it was too late and too risky to return to the district in which he was currently hidden, he planned to stay with their mutual friend Minnie Minet. The spirited pianist was always prepared to have surprise guests calling in. Her bohemian Saturday soirées no longer took place, and the social lives of Youra and his friends were much the poorer without those colourful events. At the last party a German military truck had driven up in the Rue Van Goidtsoven, loaded all the guests on board and had their personal details examined in High Field Command. They had clearly had some kind of tip-off that the musical offerings on those evenings were only a disguise. Fortunately, on that occasion, the Field Police were obliged to set Minnie and her invited and uninvited guests free again. But it had been a serious shock.

At eight o'clock in the morning Youra phoned his laboratory at Pharmacobel to tell them that he would be late for work. Then he tried to contact Maurits Bolle. The Dutchman, the father of his fellow student Hélène and a close comrade of Jospa's in the Jewish Defence Committee had, unusually, spent the night at home. Since Bolle had become committed to the Resistance, he only lived sporadically in his haute-bourgeois house on the Avenue Lepoutre. He generally slept over at friends' houses so as not to put his family in danger. Hélène was just completing her final year of medical studies at Liège University.

Bolle offered to inform Jospa that Youra would visit him in his office at eleven o'clock. He himself had arranged to meet him at ten-thirty. It was this rigid time-keeping that helped people survive in the underground.

Hardly had Youra put the phone down than he dialled again. This time he phoned Jacqueline Mondo. He had begun an intense flirtation with the pretty medical student as tutor on a freshers'-week course; and she was still in love with him. He wondered if she fancied a little morning stroll, because it was still much too early for his meeting with Jospa. Unusually, this February morning seemed to be turning out brighter and milder than the bitter, grey winter days just past. Fresh air and a chat with his girlfriend would do him good.

Jacqueline was enthusiastic about the idea. They would meet near her parents' house by the Etangs d'Ixelles. The CDJ office was not far away. After a quick breakfast Youra took the tram, which stopped right outside his front door. In huge letters on the outside of the tram Belgians were exhorted, in French and Flemish, to go and work in Germany. They would get good money there, and good health care. Someone had added a death's-head, the sign that SS men wore on their caps and belt-buckles.

Shortly afterwards, Youra was walking hand in hand with Jacqueline around Ixelles pond, listening to her vivacious chatter. The young girl was from a bourgeois Belgian family, her father was a city auditor, and her mother ran a fashion boutique. They too were in the Resistance. The Mondos hid English pilots who had been shot down over Belgium and parachuted to safety, and helped to smuggle them back to Britain.

It was precisely half past ten when Youra walked into the stationery shop. Youra Livchitz was one of the few who knew the way through the shop to the office on the first floor. When he had given the agreed knock and the door had been opened, the delicious aroma of real coffee-beans swept over him. A rare luxury in these hard days of war. But the businessman Bolle, whose liking for the good life had left its mark in a slight paunch, clearly had an inexhaustible supply of this elixir.

With Youra, three generations were now gathered in the little temporary office. Livchitz was twenty-five, Hertz Jospa thirty-eight and 'Papa Bolle', as he was known to the friends of his daughter Hélène, was fifty-five. The two older men liked the young, idealistic physician. They were both convinced that Youra Livchitz, with his intellect and winning manner, would have a great future as a doctor. If the times ever changed.

Hertz Jospa, the convinced Marxist, had the gift of filtering the essential elements out of a large quantity of diverse information and drawing non-ideological, unprejudiced conclusions. This time, too, he impressed his two listeners with his clear analysis. Things weren't looking too bad on the Eastern Front. The Red Army was on the march in Leningrad and the Caucasus. A hundred Wehrmacht divisions had been routed, and 300,000 German soldiers were Soviet prisoners of war.

But on the home front, in Belgium, the armed Resistance to the German occupying forces had endured severe losses. In an almost toneless voice Jospa recapitulated the shattering reports from his comrades in Charleroi. In Brussels, too, the situation was rather depressing. Jospa's information accorded entirely with what Youra had heard from his brother the previous evening.

Jospa had heard rumours of a successful escape by Resistance fighters from a deportation train. He was glad to have these confirmed by Youra. If these men had risked jumping from the train, it showed that there was an awakening spirit of resistance among the deportees. Over the past few months Jospa had constantly had the same image going through his head: the picture of a flock of sheep willingly following the slaughterman to the butcher's block.

He was often in despair about the fact that attempts by the Resistance to keep the population informed through newspaper articles and flysheets had so little effect on the upright Israelites. Most Jews actually believed that the trains to the East were bringing them to work camps, where they could wait for the end of the war in harsh conditions with their families. Everything else they took to be Soviet black propaganda.

But now individual sheep had removed themselves from the flock, and actually escaped their butchers. Perhaps that was the beginning of a silent rebellion that had to be kept alert and reinforced. Perhaps there were still ways and means of sabotaging the Nazis' smooth-running deportation machine. Jospa's eye fell on the front page of the central organ of the Communist Party, which lay on the table. 'YES! THERE IS A CHANCE OF MAKING THE DEPORTATIONS COLLAPSE!, was the headline of an article on the first page of *Le Drapeau Rouge*. His two companions also stared spellbound at the bold headline.

But they quickly had to acknowledge that the article didn't refer to the Jews. It was a call from the Communist Party to the working class to stop the forced deportation of Belgian workforces to Germany through strikes and boycotts, and thus to damage the enemy munitions industry:

> Hitler is firmly resolved to show no scruples in siphoning off all workforces from the occupied areas to compensate for the huge losses he has suffered at the hands of the Red Army. It would be incorrect to claim that the occupying forces cannot be kept in check. The workers have always managed to do that in the past when they have worked together and with solidarity.

In various enterprises in Wallonia, the article reported, there had been strikes against forced labour in German factories.

How much more hopeless, in comparison, was the situation of the Jews. No one would strike for them, no one would call a boycott on their behalf. Nonetheless, from now on, Jospa could not shake off the thought that there might be a chance of saving some of the internees waiting in Mechelen for the next convoy to Auschwitz.

17 Profiteers of the Deportation
Late February 1943

That clear winter night in late February 1943 had etched itself deeply into Claire's memory. By now the young Trotskyist had spent four weeks in Mechelen transit camp. Over the past few days the news had been whispered among the internees: Stalingrad was continuing to hold off the German army, which had endured massive losses. Hitler's army was sinking into snow and mud. The German soldiers, inadequately equipped for the Russian winter, were suffering from hunger and cold.

The atmosphere in the Dossin barracks was thick with rumours. The mood of excitement among the prisoners had even communicated itself to their SS guards. The men in uniform were furious because of the reason for the quiet euphoria among the prisoners: the increasingly likely defeat of Hitler's army and the hope that the German occupation of Belgium might be about to come to an end.

Confident that the fortunes of the war were about to turn, and that their imprisonment in the camp would not last much longer, Claire had gone to sleep beside her husband Philippe on the roughly assembled plank bed in the dormitory. Suddenly sirens roused them both from their deep sleep. It was midnight. Floodlights flared in the barracks courtyard, and a voice barked from the loudspeakers: 'All prisoners come forward for inspection.'

They all rushed to get dressed, because it would be bitterly cold outside. Mothers helped their drowsy children into their jackets, and old people buttoned up their coats with trembling hands. Then they pushed their way down the stairs from the dormitory and into the barracks yard.

The tall figure of Obersturmführer Schmitt was silhouetted at an illuminated window on the first floor, to the right of the front gates. The forty-one-year-old Senior Lieutenant was in charge of both the transit camp and of Breendonk concentration camp. Standing beside him was a beautiful, young, red-haired Jewish woman, whom Claire had never seen before. Behind the couple jostled bawling SS men. They were enjoying the spectacle in the football-pitch-sized barracks yard, where the people, freshly roused from sleep, were running about in confusion. And they were yelling at their colleagues in the throng below to impose order with their dogs and guns.

Over the loudspeaker the prisoners were ordered to stand in neat rows and be quiet. But the sobbing of the frightened women and the crying of the children would not let up. Claire Prowizur, who had stayed rooted to the spot, stared up at the camp commandant. She watched him drawing his revolver and aiming into the crowd. In that moment Claire believed she could read the thoughts of the SS officer up there at the window: 'That night we were more than merely his enemies, we already embodied the beginning of the end for the Nazis.'

The camp commandant fired. But at that very moment his Jewish lover put her hand on his gun and averted the barrel. The bullets flew into the clear February sky. No one was hit.

By about two o'clock in the morning the horrific episode was over. Claire and Philippe were allowed to go back to the dormitory with all the other prisoners. This time the plank bed with the straw mattress seemed like a safe stronghold.

The camp commandant's excesses didn't always end so harmlessly. Philipp Schmitt was a tall, good-looking man, whose bright, ice-cold eyes seemed never to miss a thing. Every little error, every act of carelessness was punished with whiplashes or arrest. His most serious weapon was his Alsatian, 'Lump', who went everywhere with him.

When Schmitt appeared in his SS uniform and high-sided boots, with the dog at his side, in the barracks yard at Mechelen or Breendonk concentration camp, the prisoners tried to make themselves scarce. On several occasions he had set his dog on men who had not been sufficiently servile in their greeting. The prisoner Hermann Hirsch, from Frankfurt, had to have a leg amputated after one such attack. When he arrived in Auschwitz with the twentieth convoy, number 800 on the transport list, as an invalid he had no chance of escaping selection for the gas chambers.

Even today, journalist Ernst Landau can point to the scar on his thigh where the Obersturmführer's dog tore into him whilst at Fort Breendonk. The young Viennese had been arrested while working on a Belgian underground newspaper, and imprisoned in the concentration camp for twenty-eight months. He has terrible memories of the SS thug Schmitt: 'He was a cruel sadist.'

And it was well-known that the Obersturmführer was growing rich on the back of his prisoners. In Mechelen transit camp Schmitt had access to two store-rooms to which he alone had the key.

In the years after the war, former Jewish workers from the transit camp described the underhand dealings of the SS chief in Mechelen. In their eyewitness accounts before the Belgian military court, the same names of particularly malevolent or grasping Nazi functionaries came up time and again: Schmitt, his deputy Max Boden, Karl Mainzhausen, responsible for the baggage checks, and Erich Krull of the Brussels Trusteeship Company. Also repeatedly mentioned is a short man with thick glasses, who appeared at regular intervals in the Dossin barracks and in Breendonk: Judenreferent Kurt Asche.

Economics graduate Erich Krull had his office next to 'reception'. He was the representative of the Trusteeship Company in Mechelen, the organization that was confiscating the entire possessions of the Jews in the name of the Reich. The same authority had already expropriated Léon Gronowski's leather goods shop and placed the furniture factory of the dignitary Salomon Vanden Berg of the Jewish Council under compulsory administration.

In Mechelen transit camp it was Krull's task to strip the internees of their last possessions: jewellery, money, watches, razors, fur coats and fountain pens. Under his auspices these valuable objects switched to the possession of the Brussels Trusteeship Company. This in turn was a branch of the Berlin Eastern Ministry for the occupied zones, Western section, which had the final say about the possessions of the 'evacuees'.

Of the cash that the Trusteeship took from the prisoners at reception, the camp administration was allowed to take 30 francs as an administration charge for each internee, and to keep 1,500 francs for expenses and lodging.

An ingenious bureaucratic procedure was supposed to give new arrivals the impression that they would at some point get their possessions back. What other reason could there be for the prisoners' jewellery, cash, diamonds and house-keys being put in bags in the 'reception' office, and the bag then being inscribed with the name, address and transport number as well as a list of the contents? Bag in hand, the prisoner then entered the office of the Trusteeship Company, where accountant Erich Krull waited for fresh booty.

Krull was the same man in civvies who had looked on with a smirk as Claire Prowizur had stripped naked on the day of her arrival in Mechelen. The humiliating procedure was supposedly necessary so that two SS men could search her clothes and her body for hidden precious objects. The economist was not only 'well known for his brutality and his thefts', as Eva Fastag, a Jewish woman who had worked as a secretary in the reception office, would later remember. Krull was also distinguished by his 'scandalous treatment' of women and girls. 'He took great pleasure,' said Fastag, 'in being present when women were examined.'

At his desk Krull took possession of the bag of confiscated valuables. He made the owner give a signature as confirmation of the contents of the bag. Then a so-called 'property list' was drawn up, recording all the details of the internee's assets. Krull, who came on very attentively, knew how to entice details of files, properties or business involvements out of some of the new arrivals. When he did so, they were robbed of their goods. Their fortunes swiftly entered the possession of the Brussels Trusteeship Company.

Krull did not record all the data in the official property list. The book-keeper of Nazi booty also kept a private file of his own. If an internee gullibly told him that he had left valuable paintings or precious silver behind in his flat, the Trusteeship employee initially kept the information to himself. After all, he had the owner's address and house-keys. And along with his other accomplices at the transit camp it was easy for him to strip the flats of valuables before they were cleared by the Antwerp-based branch of the Eastern Ministry.

The next phase of expropriation in the transit camp was overseen by Karl Mainzhausen, a mate of Kurt Asche's from the Security Service in Brussels. The big, coarse-looking SS man was responsible for checking the luggage of the new arrivals. Criminal Assistant-in-Chief Mainzhausen didn't even bother trying to cover up his thefts. He helped himself quite openly when something he considered valuable fell into his hands as he went through the bags and cases.

That February of 1943, when the deceptive hope arose among the prisoners in Mechelen that the days of the German enforced rule were numbered, SS Untersturmführer Mainzhausen was clearly also convinced that the war was coming to an end. As a precaution, on the occasion of his two-week leave, he brought his stolen goods to safety. Mainzhausen, as Eva Fastag observed at the time, had organized a truck in which he took the food, clothes and valuables that he had stolen from the Jews to Germany.

The fourth member of the band of corrupt Nazis in Mechelen was Max Boden, the head of personnel and administration in the camp. For Claire Prowizur, this short-legged man in his mid-fifties would have come closer than most of the Jewish prisoners to the Nazi caricature of a Semite, if he had only been stripped of his uniform and his whip and pistol, the insignia of his power.

On the very first day of their arrival, some prisoners became acquainted with the malicious brutality of the deputy camp director. When all the new arrivals had passed through 'reception' and had their luggage checked, and been assigned their places in the dormitory, they had to present themselves in the courtyard for inspection. Boden walked up and down the ranks and selected the more elegant, well-dressed newcomers. They were assigned to latrine service. With bare hands and kitchen sieves they were to fish the toilets for banknotes and jewellery, because some prisoners preferred to throw their valuables into the latrine rather than hand them over to the Nazis.

After this terrible work in the latrines, the SS guard forbade the men to wash themselves and their clothes. They were not allowed to go to the wash-room until the following day. Any banknotes, precious stones and jewellery found in the toilets were carefully cleaned and brought by Boden to the office of Trusteeship representative Krull. Camp commandant Schmitt and luggage-checker Mainzhausen would be there as well. 'They shared out their day's booty between themselves,' the Jewish secretary Benita Hirschfeld later told the Belgian court martial.

About once a month the Brussels Judenreferent Kurt Asche would turn up in Mechelen with his colleague Fritz Erdmann. The two SS men inspected the offices and workshops and observed the work of the secretaries. Their arrival always terrified the Jewish staff. Time and again the little Obersturmführer would pick out one or two of the privileged Jewish workers and persuade the head of administration, Boden, to put them on the list for the next transport. Asche did not believe that Jewish staff should be given special treatment. No one was to be exempt from the deportation.

Stocky Asche and coarse Mainzhausen often put their heads together. The two former colleagues from the Jewish Department on Avenue Lousie still saw each other frequently on their nocturnal expeditions through Brussels. Their common interest was alcohol, prostitutes and the acquisition of 'Pinke-Pinke', Asche's term for money.

Under Commandant Schmitt a black economy had developed in the transit camp. The tailors and furriers among the prisoners worked thirteen hours a day, seven days a week, in the two tailors' workshops and one leather workshop. They made clothes, underwear, belts and bags. There was also a paper workshop, where the bags for the objects retained by the Trusteeship Company were made.

As deputy head of the camp, Hauptscharführer Boden had a

strange quirk. The long-nosed man, who walked with his back bent, was led about by a boy of about five, an orphaned Jewish boy whose parents had been deported. 'Bubi', as Boden called him, was a miniature version of the Nazi thug. Like Boden, the child wore a uniform made specially for him, with gleaming boots and, in his belt, just as in the full-sized original, a whip.

Bubi was Boden's constant echo. On a Friday or Saturday evening, when prisoners spoke to the deputy commandant about a problem, he turned with apparent horror to his little companion, raised his arms into the air and said: 'But it's Shabbat. Isn't it, Bubi? It's Shabbat.' And the child in the SS uniform echoed, like a good boy: 'Yes, it's Shabbat.'

On cold winter days the Hauptscharführer liked to stage a scene in the barracks yard that always delighted him and his little mascot. Boden appeared, with Bubi at his side, in an apparently generous mood at the open window of the first floor of the part of the building reserved for officers. He jovially waved the people standing around in the courtyard close to him and asked in his bad Yiddish, 'Do you want cigarettes? I'll throw you some down from the window.' People came running from all corners to pick up one of the cigarettes that Boden was throwing into the crowd. Too late the men and women noticed that the squat SS functionary up at the window was pouring buckets of water over them. Then, as they fled the icy water, drenched to the skin, the malicious whinnying of the Hauptscharführer and the bright, cheerful laughter of the child rang out over the courtyard.

There was a steady supply of new prisoners to fall for the deputy commandant's malevolent game. Mendelis Goldsteinas wasn't one of them. The chemical engineer had quickly seen through the humiliating prank. He kept well back.

Like so many of those who ended up in Mechelen, he and his wife had also been victims of Jacques Glogowski. The Jewish cop in the service of the Gestapo had spotted an acquaintance of theirs in the street and gone after him: a Jew from Lithuania, like themselves. Desperate to escape, this man had fled to the nearby Goldsteinas apartment and thus given away their hiding place.

It was the end of their identity as Belgian couple Yvonne and Marcel Poncelet. They had just enough time to tear up their forged IDs, which were no use to them now, and flush them down the toilet. Under the watchful eyes of 'fat Jacques' and his companion, they packed their bags with their most necessary belongings. Henda Goldsteinas put on her white, wonderfully warm woollen scarf, a birthday present from her husband. She would need it in the cold East where the Nazis sent people like them. The Goldsteinas had only one source of consolation as they drove to Avenue Louise in the black police car: they knew their daughter was safe. Abela was living as Janine Liégeois with a Belgian family in the countryside.

On 19 February the Goldsteinas were registered in the Dossin barracks as new arrivals numbers 779 and 780. The previous day, Hena Zwerm, née Wasyng, had completed the reception procedure in the transit camp. Her cardboard sign bore the number 736. The thirty-year-old woman had been widowed shortly before. Her husband had been shot and badly injured in a Brussels street as he attempted to escape arrest at the hands of 'fat Jacques' and his Gestapo henchmen. He died of his injuries in the St Pierre hospital. She herself was betrayed by the owner of a shop in Ghent, a client of her late husband's who had offered her help. The Zwerms had hidden their two children with a Belgian family before they themselves went into hiding.

The dormitories of the Mechelen barracks slowly filled up. For nurse Régine Krochmal, condemned to inactivity, the weeks since her arrival passed by 'like a bad dream'. She worked out that it would not be long before the next transport started. The quota required for a convoy was said to be 1,000 prisoners. With every lorry that unloaded its human cargo in the barracks yard in the early hours of the morning, another fragment of hope vanished that the date for the next departure for the East would be delayed.

18 The Nazis Have Problems
Early March 1943

Everyday life had resumed at number 453 Avenue Louise, after the pilot's attack on Nazi headquarters. The clear-up work was over, the damage was largely repaired and the dead had been buried.

To accommodate the SS, another building had been confiscated in the chestnut-tree-lined avenue. The inhabitants of the elegant mansion block had to find themselves new lodgings, because the office space in the chancellery and the subsidiary offices had become too small for the three hundred workers of the National Socialist police organizations.

The new building had one important feature: a closed-off courtyard that suited it for the deportation of the Jews. Here the black Gestapo limousine could drive up and let the victims of the witch-hunt climb out unobserved. And in the early morning the arrested Jews, protected from the eyes of the curious, could be driven from the cellars to the trucks that would bring them to Mechelen.

As part of the move to number 374, Kurt Asche had been given a new office on the third floor. It was more spacious than his old one. But his chances of promotion had started vanishing by now. Six weeks after the bombardment, the job of his superior Thomas, who had been killed during the pilot's attack on the Gestapo headquarters, was still vacant, but the head of the department was showing no sign of filling the post. SS Sturmbannführer Ernst Ehlers seemed to want to wait for a while. The lawyer had heard rumours about corrupt colleagues.

Kurt Asche had to be careful. So far, rumours of fraud and profiteering referred particularly to Mechelen transit camp, and Commandant Philipp Schmitt. It was not outside the realms of possibility that Asche, too, could soon find himself in the sights of Ehlers, who had announced that he was going to 'clear the Augean stables'.

The important thing for the Judenreferent was not to draw attention to himself. He showed a certain skill in this. With the basic principle of always being inconspicuous and keeping himself in the background he had managed quite well so far, so long as alcohol didn't get in the way. Then the otherwise bland SS Obersturmführer was impossible to ignore, with his bright red face and his shrill voice.

In plain clothes on his nocturnal expeditions through the bars of Brussels, Asche attracted no attention or curiosity in the twilight milieu in which he felt particularly at his ease. A man in early middle age, with the appearance of a bad-tempered accountant, he got what he wanted even when he wasn't inspiring fear and respect with his uniform.

He avoided his old local in the Rue du Berger, since it had been mentioned in police headquarters that a Jewish waitress had been boasting about her friendship with a certain Kurt Asche. The Nazis called such relationships 'Rassenschande', or 'racial disgrace'. And that was a punishable offence. Ellen, the young woman who had first given him such hours of pleasure, and then caused him so much vexation, no longer worked in the brothel. She had been sent on a transport to Auschwitz six months before.

With Karl Mainzhausen he now preferred to frequent a pub in the city centre, very close to his apartment on the Rue du Pont Neuf. The landlord, a Jew from Germany, didn't just have alcohol on offer for Asche, Mainzhausen and their friends. In the back room of his bar young girls waited for custom.

To Asche's annoyance, one of his subordinates in Mechelen was to take over Commandant Philipp Schmitt's post. The corrupt network of SS accomplices was in danger, because the man selected by the head of the Brussels police headquarters was considered to be extremely correct. Officially, the young Sturmscharführer was only supposed to stand in for the camp commandant during his home leave. In fact, however, it was plain that Hans Frank was being sent to Mechelen to check that everything was in order. Police chief Ernst Ehlers had heard 'unpleasant rumours', that the work of the prisoners in the workshops was being exploited, and the profits falling into 'unknown hands'.

The Brussels branch of the RSHA did not enjoy a good reputation in Berlin. The Belgian SS chancellery was not considered particularly efficient. To the annoyance of Asche's superior, Adolf Eichmann, there had been delays in the implementation of National Socialist racial policy. And in no other occupied country had the deportation of the Jews been put into effect so slowly and with such hesitation. When it became known that SS officers tolerated cases of corruption within their own ranks, it was to be feared that heads would soon roll at the top of the Brussels Security Service. SS Sturmbannführer Ehlers wanted to avoid that by taking measures of his own.

In the upper storeys of Avenue Louise, there had been another serious problem after 15 January. Sixty-four inmates had escaped the nineteenth deportation train before it reached the German border. That was an embarrassing matter for those organizing the implementation of Nazi extermination policy in Belgium. Their colleagues in Auschwitz were able to use the transport list, which was brought along on the train, to operate precise checks on the number of arrivals.

The Cologne Jew Rudolf Schmitz was one of those who were able to get away from the nineteenth transport to Auschwitz while it was still on Belgian soil. In the account of his experiences which Schmitz wrote after the liberation of Belgium, he gives a detailed description of his escape from the train:

> On the evening of 14 January, the Schutzpolizei
> [constabulary] who are to take over the transport arrive
> from Cologne. On 15 January, some SS men, whom we don't
> know, turn up to regulate the loading. After gulping down
> our soup, we are beaten out of our dormitory. And then we

board the train according to the numbers that we are wearing around our necks. They shout: 'Windows shut! We've got live ammunition!' The doors are bolted. The journey begins. Behind our compartment is the carriage with the police. We – that is to say, a few prisoners – have agreed in advance to jump off the train during the journey, at a slope near Louvain. Because we are already aware that what lies ahead cannot be good. I am the first to open a window in our compartment and look outside. The policemen, about seventeen of them, seem to be asleep. I try to persuade my wife to climb out of the window and jump down. But she won't, she's frightened. Meanwhile eleven people leave our carriage, including a man with a child in his arms. I fetch my wife and show her how easy it is. Because the train is moving slowly and stopping from time to time. The Belgian engine driver is probably pretending it's defective. I don't want to jump down before my wife has done. So the night moves on slowly. I reflect, think about our eight years of marriage, about the idea that the SS, possessed by the devil, will separate me from my wife, and about my three children, whom I have hidden in a convent in Belgium. I want to see them again. That makes me decide to jump out on my own. I take the food out of the luggage left behind by the people who have jumped out, and put it in my wife's rucksack so that she will have something to eat until her arrival. Then I throw my rucksack out of the window and kneel to jump out of the window. When my wife realizes that I'm serious, she grabs me by the leg and pleads, 'Don't leave me on my own.' In reply I tell her to follow me. But she won't come. I jump out.

Up until this point, escape from the train was a comparatively easy matter, because third-class passenger trains were used for the transport of the Jews from Mechelen. The doors were locked, but the windows were left open.

Escapee Rudolf Schmitz had unfortunately jumped out on a guarded bridge, the Pont de Vise, near Liège. He was arrested only minutes later by two German military sentries. He stayed in the military prison in Liège until 9 February, before being transferred back to Mechelen. At 'reception', Schmitz encountered an unpleasant old acquaintance, the strictest of the luggage-checkers, Karl Mainzhausen. The SS Untersturmführer beat the runaway so severely that his right eardrum burst.

The Antwerp diamond-grinder Samuel Perl had 'hopped off' the nineteenth transport, as he put it, and been caught again. The young man, whose entire family had been deported during the great raid of 15 August in Antwerp, had at first settled in the part of southern France that was not yet occupied by the Germans, but had then, when the French police began to persecute the Jews, returned to his Flemish home town and gone into hiding there. Denounced by a Belgian diamond-trader, he was first interned in Mechelen in December 1942. Eight days after leaping from the nineteenth transport, the twenty-two-year-old Perl then fell into the net of the Gestapo once again, in January 1943. In Mechelen, the Trusteeship official Erich Krull put him on special treatment because he had been found with a fake ID and diamonds. Perl had to pull down his trousers in the accountant's office, and bend over the desk. Dr Krull struck him with his whip until the blood flowed. Then the bureaucrat pressed his burning cigar on to the naked man's bare flesh. He bit his lips to suppress his cries of pain. 'That was when I learned the real difference between cigars and cigarettes', the diamond trader said many years later, summarising his experiences with the sadistic Trusteeship administrator. 'The burning cigar wasn't nearly as painful as the cigarette that Krull stubbed out on me afterwards.'

The two escapees of the nineteenth convoy, Perl and Schmitz, were made to wear numbers crossed through with a red line. Samuel Perl was number three, Rudolf Schmitz number four on the special list. And in order to mark them both out visibly as particularly dangerous subjects, they had their hair shorn off by the camp barber, a custom that the new head of the camp, Hans Frank, was to maintain. Perl can still remember him issuing the threat: 'I'll see to it that you all get to Auschwitz next time.'

Rudolf Schmitz and Samuel Perl, who were by now among the longest-term inmates of the barracks, clearly noticed the difference between the recently fired commander and the new one. Under Frank things were 'better and more orderly', treatment was 'more decent', according to Schmitz's report in September 1945. For Perl, the greatest difference between the two SS functionaries lay in the fact that 'Frank didn't do any of the beating himself, he tried to be correct'.

Daily hours in the workshops were reduced from thirteen hours to eight. Production was now restricted to SS uniforms and gun-holsters. Otherwise the workers were allowed to carry out repairs for the prisoners. This preferential treatment was later to enable some of them to escape the transport to Auschwitz. Also abandoned were the bothersome 'movement games' that took place in the barracks yard under Mainzhausen's strict supervision, backed up by former Austrian army officer Ernst Meier: women and children had to go to the right side of the courtyard, men to the left, as directed by the blasts of Meier's whistle, and perform gymnastic exercises such as knee-bends and sit-ups until they were exhausted.

The new regime under Hans Frank meant that, at eight o'clock each morning, there were twenty minutes of freestyle exercises led by a Jewish gymnastics teacher. Sick people, children and the mothers of younger children were excused. The most momentous change for the prisoners was that they were now allowed to receive three parcels a week. The dispatches were delivered to Mechelen via the Jewish Council. This new regulation meant that there was less of a risk that the senders of the packages would be identified and perse-cuted as Jewish relatives or 'Jew-lovers'. Under Schmitt the practice had been for the guards in Mechelen to receive packages on a partic-ular day of the week, and to take the names and addresses of the senders.

Louis Micheels, the young Dutch doctor, and his fiancée Nora, had finally started receiving food parcels. Somehow his parents had learned that their escape route to Switzerland had been betrayed while they were still in Belgium. With a full stomach, the young couple found life in Mechelen much easier to bear.

The nineteenth convoy had set off in mid-January without Louis and Nora. Micheels was able to work temporarily as an assistant physician in the sick-bay. He had repeatedly visited the Jewish Dr Bach, to offer his services as an assistant orderly. He knew that his chances of survival were greater in that position. Jewish staff and their families received extra portions at mealtimes. And they were immune from deportation. However, the Dutch doctor recognized that Dr Bach and his orderly, a medical amateur, 'did not tolerate any intrusion into their zealously guarded domain'. They gave him the cold shoulder. But in January, unexpectedly, Micheels was ordered to deputize for three weeks. 'I thought that even if we were scheduled for the next transport,' the young doctor worked out, 'we would then be warmer and our chances better.' Louis Micheels had dropped back down to the status of a simple prisoner, number 33 on the list. But thanks to the parcels that were being sent to the barracks, at least he was no longer suffering from that gnawing hunger.

Régine had also visited Dr Bach to offer her services. He was very sorry, the German doctor informed her, but he had no use for her. Nonetheless, she dropped in on the friendly doctor every now and again, wearing her nurse's uniform with its blue cap. She didn't want to give up hope entirely of being employed as a Jewish assistant.

Régine had been in the camp for more than a month when one day she received an undamaged parcel. Thanks to the new regulation, the SS luggage checkers were no longer able simply to loot the dispatches. She found a message hidden in a tube of toothpaste. Her friends in the 'Austrian Liberation Front' told her that an important member of the Resistance would soon be arriving in the transit camp. The young woman eagerly saved soap and bread, valuable means of survival in the camp, to give them to the prominent Resistance fighter.

The climate in the camp had noticeably improved since the sudden disappearance of Commandant Schmitt. Meanwhile Hans Frank tried to untangle his predecessor's machinations. He sealed both of the rooms in which Schmitt had hoarded his booty. In the course of his inquiries Frank came across a Jewish businessman who was constantly going in and out of the transit camp. Léon Krynek, who was fifty-four, appeared to be very affluent, having made a Ford V8 available for Commandant Schmitt's private use. Krynek, Frank established, was 'the middle man between Schmitt and certain Belgian companies'. The goods manufactured in the camp workshops were disposed of through him.

Krynek led an extravagant life in his house in Rue du Luxembourg in Brussels. There the businessman received and entertained SS officers from Avenue Louise. He generously gave the Nazis boxes of expensive cigars and French cognac to get on their right side. And they were only too happy to be spoilt by the generous Jew. Krynek had 'incredible contacts in Belgian business circles', Frank explained at his trial after the war. On one occasion the Jewish businessman passed on to Schmitt a whole truckload of spirits that had been confiscated by the Belgian price control office. Schmitt then kept it in his storeroom in Mechelen.

But Léon Krynek's survival strategy of getting on the right side of the enemy was not an effective one. In Schmitt he had chosen the wrong man. When the camp commandant was convicted as a conman by his younger fellow Nazi, Frank, Krynek's fate was also sealed. He ended up as number 1526 on the list of the twentieth transport to Auschwitz.

After Schmitt, who would be next to have his frauds exposed? Kurt Asche felt keenly that he was under observation. Fear of discovery made him cautious. He was now no longer amenable to attempts at corruption. One day in February the president of the Brussels attorney's office appeared in his office. A Jewish colleague, Joseph Silber, had been arrested and brought to Mechelen. The senior attorney wanted to buy back his freedom for 200,000 Belgian francs. The SS Obersturmführer, who was in charge of the deportation list, would not budge. So Joseph Silber, who had no idea at the time of this intervention on his behalf, ended up as number 848 on the list for the next train to Auschwitz.

Only if he could be completely sure that his fraud-ring was not busted, Asche would take the money and simply owe the service he had promised in return. An arrested Jew would not complain about him, so long as he had even a remote prospect of being freed. That was exactly how Asche had dealt with one affluent prisoner, the owner of a private bank in Berlin. He had accepted the bribe money, promising him that he would ensure that he was struck off the deportation list, and since then not a word had been heard from him. Nonetheless, the banker Fritz Wallach (number 522) had still hoped until the last minute that he would be summoned to Asche's office and freed from the camp. Wallach had paid the Judenreferent 25,000 marks for his freedom.

The departure date for the next train to Auschwitz was postponed. They lacked the means of transport. The war required its tribute. 'The removal of the Jews has had to be temporarily postponed for want of railway carriages. It will be resumed once this shortfall has been made up, which in the opinion of the military administration will not be before the autumn,' the diplomat Werner von Bargen informed the Foreign Office in Berlin, in an envelope sealed with the word 'Secret!'

At the same time the Berlin RSHA saw itself obliged to strengthen its security measures after the experiences of the nineteenth convoy. All loopholes were to be closed. According to a new law, from now on, Jews were to be transported only on cattle-trucks. Kurt Asche would later deny that the switch from passenger trains to animal carriers occurred in order to prevent attempted escapes by the deportees. At his trial in 1967, the SS man claimed that the measure had been introduced because 'the German population had protested about the transport of Jews in passenger trains'.

19 The Plan Takes Shape

'Time passes so quickly that I can't believe that another fifteen days have gone by,' Samuel Vanden Berg noted in his diary at the beginning of March 1943. According to his diary entries, the chairman of the Jewish Council enjoyed an almost tranquil life within his family circle, largely untouched by all the wretchedness around him. The furniture manufacturer continued to manage his company under the supervision of the German Trusteeship Company, participated in meetings of the Jewish Council and the synagogue administrative council, and played cards with friends and relations.

> Actually, nothing of any great importance has happened
> over the past two weeks. We played bridge on Saturday
> and Sunday as usual, and spent several evenings at home
> throughout the week, so that the week had barely begun
> before it was over again. We are still eating well, our health
> is holding up, but my eyesight seems to be deteriorating
> somewhat. Nicole is taking drawing classes, I think she has
> a certain talent. André still plays the piano. That isn't
> particularly interesting so far as his future is concerned, but
> it is a very good distraction for him given all the evenings
> he has to spend at home. Business is still going quite well,
> but we are worried about the compulsory closure of many

trading-houses, which has already happened in Germany.
So far as we know, the war is not progressing quickly enough.
The Russian offensives seem to have slowed down, the
bombing of France and Germany, on the other hand, seem
to be becoming more frequent, and I wouldn't be surprised
if that were the English offensive on the continent, if there
were such an offensive, but one begins to lose courage. A
letter came from Hellendael, who is working in a coal-mine
in Silesia, poor fellow…

This sign of life from his former colleague on the Jewish Council, who
had fallen into disfavour with Asche and been deported, reinforced
the furniture manufacturer in his assumption that the Nazis were
actually bringing the Jews to work camps. For Vanden Berg, who still
thought that the SS police in Avenue Louise could be kept happy with
submissiveness, Resistance fighters like Jospa were a thorn in his side.
They caused unnecessary trouble, and possibly even encouraged disobedience. Vanden Berg, the Jewish notable with Belgian citizenship,
and the stateless Communist engineer, Hertz Jospa, couldn't have
been further apart. Jospa's sole purpose in life lay in saving as many
Jews as possible from their terrible fate.

A small new issue of *Le Flambeau* had been published at the beginning of March. The duplicated pages of the underground newspaper
of the Jewish Defence Committee were passed around from hand to
hand. These news items and commentaries conveyed a quite different
picture of the situation in the country and at the Front from that
communicated by the official press, which toed the Nazi line.

People were still unwilling to believe that the Germans in Poland
had moved on to the genocide of the Jews. Reports to that effect were
dismissed as Communist scare stories. 'A cultured people like the
Germans wouldn't do anything like that,' was the constant cry, and it
may have inspired the editors of *Le Flambeau* to have put the daily
persecutions of the Jews by the German Nazis under the heading
'Culture'.

Little Rue de Vleurgat, which ends up in the quaint and traditional area of the Old Market, has been sealed off by police cars. The Gestapo are hunting the Jews. A small Citroën marked 'Pol' waits for the victims. A member of the Gestapo hauls the ostracized people out of the house at the back of a dilapidated building: a weeping little boy of six and his two-year-old brother. The little boy in the agent's arms smiles innocently into his uncle's eyes. The Nazi is embarrassed, shamed by the child's guileless expression. He walks towards the car, hesitates for a moment. Is he really supposed to put the child in the Pol 'hearse'? His heart starts thumping under his grey uniform. But Hitler's poison is stronger. The child is handed over to his executioner…

This touching episode is followed by an account by Meyer Tabakman, a Resistance member, under the heading 'I Got Away':

'I Got Away' isn't the title of a thriller. No, this really happened. The nineteenth transport train that's supposed to take me to Poland is travelling at 60 kilometres an hour. The doors are closed, and every five minutes the track and the train are lit up by floodlights. The Nazi deportation has become a reality, its meaning is the same as death. I decide to escape. There is the lowered window of the lower door of the carriage. And with one jump I land on the cold ground. I lie there, stretched out on the ground, until dawn. I feel a terrible pain in my left arm. After my escape I go home with a broken arm. An individual case? No, every time a train sets off, dozens of deportees resist death.

Before his arrest, the partisan had been a member of Alexandre Livchitz's company. The publishers of the newspaper hoped that his escape would prompt imitations. For how long, Hertz Jospa wondered, would his fellow Jews go quietly like lambs to the slaughter?

Not dozens escaping from the deportation train with their own hands – no, hundreds should have been escaping the clutches of the Nazi thugs. Hertz Jospa could not shake off the idea of stopping the train to Auschwitz and rescuing those who were being dispatched to their deaths. The idea seemed so obvious to him, the plan so logical, that when he was interviewed for the Wiener Library after the war, he rattled off the individual steps of this 'large-scale operation' as though it were a simple series of instructions: 'Ambush and attack the train, fight the German guards, exploit the general confusion to open the doors of the carriage, order the prisoners to escape and give each of them a 50-franc note so that they can continue on their way on their own...'

On some days in March 1943 it was so warm and spring-like that Jospa was able to meet his fellow fighters Benjamin Nijkerk and Maurits Bolle in the Bois de la Cambre. Sitting on a park bench by an enchanted-looking forest path, they felt safe from 'fat Jacques'. Their conversations revolved around their plan to rescue the deportees. The conditions for such an action seemed favourable.

First of all, a fairly large group of partisans was being held in Mechelen: men who would not wait fatalistically for their deportation like the majority of internees, but who wanted to resist their fate; prisoners who were resolved to do anything and would find ways and means of contacting the outside world. The Communists Szymon Baruch Birnberg, number 245 on the list, and David Gorski, number 230, had been imprisoned in the transit camp since the end of January. Shortly after that, Sandor Weisz – a Hungarian veteran of the Spanish Civil War with a legendary reputation among the armed Resistance fighters – had been arrested and registered under the number 362. The attack on the Marivaux cinema, when the Belgian SS sympathizers of the German–Flemish Labour Association 'Devlag' were assembling for a screening, had been carried out under his command.

The Jewish partisans Léon Kutnowski – number 383 – and Henri Silbersztejn – number 338 – had been arrested in the centre of Brussels by two long-coated Gestapo agents. In all likelihood these young men were in much the same state of mind as Kutnowski, as he was to describe it several weeks later in the underground paper *Notre*

Voix: 'Keeping outwardly silent, enduring everything and waiting for the chance to act, to free ourselves and take revenge.'

Jospa and his friends were able to assume that the railwaymen would not retaliate in the event of an attack on the train. Resistance against the occupying German forces had intensified among train-drivers, engineers and track workers. The majority of the personnel of the state railway organization SNCB sympathized with the Communist Party. For the most part, the railway staff stoutly refused to be drafted into labour service in Germany. The journal of the Belgian Communist Party, *Le Drapeau Rouge*, had reported in its February issue that only one in forty-five railwaymen had agreed to be conscripted, none at all in Ghent, and that in Essen the railway workers had gone so far as to demolish the recruitment post.

The driver of the deportation train would not be a willing helper of the occupying forces. But who was to carry out the ambush? The committee itself had neither the men nor the opportunities for such an attack. 'The important thing now,' Hertz Jospa wrote years later, describing the difficult search for volunteers, 'was for a group of people to decide on this plan and carry it out.'

At first the Belgian partisan army members were the only ones who came to mind. They were equipped for armed struggle, had military training and access to a countrywide network of dedicated comrades. The ranks of this underground movement also included many Jewish fighters, who must have had a personal interest in protecting their fellows from certain death.

Jean Terfve, a Communist from the leading squad of the partisans, listened carefully to Jospa's words. But the longer and more glowing Jospa's defence of the plan, the more impossible did the obstacles appear to be. To ambush the train, Terfve warned him, they would need at least twenty partisans armed with rifles and grenades. They would have to attack the German guards at either end of the long convoy. And furthermore, they could expect a bloodbath if the German guard unit immediately started firing. An incalculable risk for the underground army, which had already been severely decimated over the previous few weeks. And how would the escapees make their way home? There were no vehicles on hand to ferry them away from the scene. The minute they sought refuge among the locals, they would endanger the many Belgians who were refusing labour service, the *'refractaires'*, who were hidden around the province. The SS and the German Field Police would be sure to search every house in the vicinity after the attack.

And in any case, the action as a whole was not in line with the partisans' usual *modus operandi*. They struck, and they vanished. But this time large numbers of people would have to be evacuated from the scene of combat. There was not enough time for precise planning, since the departure times for the deportation trains were only ever revealed a few days in advance. Jean Terfve shook his head. 'Too daring and too dangerous,' was the assessment of the partisans' representative, Jospa recalled.

Disappointed, Jospa told his friends in the Jewish Defence Committee of his conversation with Terfve. They took his refusal badly, but would not give up. They still believed in their plan, which was filled with the spirit of rebellion. The attack on a deportation train would, they hoped, finally startle people out of their dull resignation. Furthermore, Terfve had not fundamentally advised them against their action, and had encouraged Jospa to make contact with other resistance groups.

Above all 'Papa' Bolle, who had helped many of those who were being persecuted by the Nazis to escape, did not accept the objections of the partisans. Certainly the risks involved in such an attack were very great. But was any resistance activity free of risks? After all, the deportation trains travelled at night, so that the attacks would take place under cover of darkness. Then there was the element of surprise, because the Germans would probably assume that no one would be capable of such an attack. 'He who saves a human life, saves an entire people,' says the Talmud, a motto that both the bourgeois businessman Bolle and the Communist Jospa had adopted as their own.

Wasn't Youra Livchitz in close contact with a group of Resistance fighters who all knew each other from the 'Free University'? This group of young intellectuals, who had specialized in sabotage attacks against the enemy's transport system, was possibly more flexible than the rigidly hierarchical partisan army. If Bolle knew this former student friend of his daughter Hélène, Youra would do anything within reason to carry out this rescue action for the deportees. That was Jospa's view of the young medic as well.

And wasn't Youra's brother Alexandre an experienced fighter? The two of them could form the core of a troop that would carry out this unusual mission. Every now and again Jospa had witnessed the silent complicity that prevailed between the two brothers. Sometimes it only took a glance from Alexandre to bring Youra back down to earth. Youra, in turn, ensured that his older brother was not left out; with a little gesture he would draw the reticent Alexandre back into the conversation. They were very fond of each other, and were always of one mind on important matters.

The meeting place was the chemist's shop of a friend of Maurits Bolle on the Place Brugmann. Shortly before close of business, the stout Dutchman Bolle, the engineer Jospa and Youra Livchitz would disappear one by one behind the lime-green, floral-decorated door of the 'Pharmacie'. The three men would wait in silence in the dark back room until the last customer had left and the shop door had been bolted. When the chemist had withdrawn into the flat above, Jospa started talking about the plan. This time he didn't have to try and find arguments to convince his partner. Youra Livchitz was electrified. It was an action entirely in line with his convictions, strongly influenced by the Indian philosopher Krishnamurti, who had enthralled Youra and his friends from the Theosophical Society at their camp in Ommen. Such a deed would be a declaration of war on egoism, apathy and violence, and it would restore a little humanity to this shattered world.

Youra was sure that his friends in 'Groupe G' would see the plan much as he did. It was a shame that he couldn't speak to Robert Leclercq immediately. By Saturday afternoon at the earliest his friend from the Hennegau would be coming to Brussels. But as the philologist had by now been promoted to the Resistance organization's head of information, it was uncertain whether he would find time to drop in on him and Saps on the Avenue Brugmann.

And he had to speak to Alexandre. His elder brother was an experienced fighter in the partisan army, he would be able to assess the risks of such an undertaking. He would certainly be keen on the idea of freeing these poor people from the claws of the Germans. But 'Commandant Jean' had gone into hiding. Youra would have to wait for his brother to contact him.

Time was marching on. In Mechelen transit camp, it was said in the Jewish Council, there were already supposed to be more than eight hundred prisoners. The rescue mission would have to be prepared as quickly as possible.

The easiest member of 'Groupe G' to contact was Richard Altenhoff. As an engineer with the building company SOCOL he had the privilege of his own office and telephone. So Youra had only to phone his former fellow student to arrange a meeting on the Rue de Louvain, company headquarters. Youra had met ginger-haired Richard in the debating circle 'Libre Examen'; he was reticent about making contributions, but always had something weighty to say when he finally spoke. Altenhoff already enjoyed a position of trust in his company. As far as his colleagues were concerned, Altenhoff, who still lived as a bachelor with his younger brothers and sisters in the home of his widowed mother, devoted his life entirely to his job. But his true commitment was to 'Groupe G'. Almost automatically, his technological know-how and his many contacts with state and council bodies meant that he was responsible for logistics and the acquisition of the materials required for the sabotage.

Richard Altenhoff listened attentively as Youra told him, his eyes gleaming, about the planned liberation mission. Stopping the train seemed to be the least of their problems. 'Groupe G' was in the process of forging contacts with the railwaymen to paralyse rail transport with explosives. But what would happen next? There would be a shooting match between the liberators and the guards. The members of his organization were saboteurs, not underground fighters. They had no knowledge of arms. But Altenhoff was fascinated by the plan. He wanted to pass it on to his friends.

'Despite the great humanitarian interest of such an operation, we decided, after a straw poll and taking thorough advice, not to take part in it,' says Henri Neuman, summing up the discussion in 'Groupe G': 'Given the very limited funds at our disposal for our own actions, and for want of men with experience in handling weapons, we thought it was too difficult, in fact practically impossible, to carry out this action.'

Richard Altenhoff shared his friends' scepticism. But he didn't want to abandon the plan entirely. He would stay in touch with Youra. That was much the opinion of Robert Leclercq, who now began racking his brains for someone to support Youra in the attack on the deportees' train.

On 12 March a call was put through to Youra at Pharmacobel. The voice of the caller, who didn't give a name, was familiar. It was flirtatious Wilhelmine, the close friend of Minnie Minet, who had been listening in on the regulars at their relaxed Saturday evenings on Rue Van Goidtsnoven. Her voice trembling with excitement, she asked Youra to call in on her as soon as possible. It was a matter of urgency.

Youra knew straight away: something had happened to Alexandre. Pretty Willy Baudoux had been very much in love with Youra's brother. Wilhelmine had been divorced for two years. But her husband's name still protected Willy – née Cohen – against deportation. In Judenreferent Asche's file, their union was registered as a 'mixed marriage'.

When Youra rang the doorbell at the Baudoux household, 386 Chaussée d'Alsemberg, Willy tore the door open as though she had been sitting waiting for him. On the sofa in the living-room lay Choura – a pitiful sight. He tried to force a smile from his ashen face when he saw his brother. He had two bullets in his leg. The bleeding wounds had been given rudimentary treatment.

Alexandre Livchitz had been injured in an assassination attempt on a high-ranking collaborator. With his comrade Raymond Baudoux, his beloved Willy's ex-husband, he had planned to eliminate the head of Belgian Central Police. They waited for the senior police officer near the Ministry of the Interior. But on that particular day Detective

Superintendent Cortin was accompanied by two plainclothes armed guards. 'Commandant Jean' would not let himself be put off by that. A mistake, as it turned out. Because his bullets missed their target, and Cortin's companions fired back. Choura was hit twice, in his left calf and his right foot. Despite his injury, Choura managed to escape his pursuers. With Raymond's help he reached Willy's flat. Here he would be safe, at least for the time being.

When Youra examined the painful entry-wounds, he realized his brother was going to need an operation. Who would take such a risk? All doctors were forbidden to treat bullet wounds. If a hospital doctor was prepared for such an undertaking, there was always the risk that the injured man would be given away to the Gestapo by an informer. Youra had to satisfy himself with cleaning the wounds, thus ensuring that they did not become inflamed.

20 Kurt Asche Gets Organized

On sunny days Kurt Asche liked to cut short his lunches in the officers' canteen on Avenue Louise to 'get a breath of fresh air', as he put it. His walk took him to the nearby Bois de la Cambre, where the roller-skating rink was very busy when the weather was fine. The inconspicuous little man with the thick glasses stood there watching the young women and girls in their short skirts circling to the music from the loudspeakers. He usually wore a blue suit. He wouldn't have risked appearing in this crowd of cheerful people in his SS uniform. And he was careful not to open his mouth, because often when he tried to make himself understood in his native language people reacted in an unfriendly and inhospitable manner.

In March 1943 the response of the German occupiers had become even more severe. The military administration had had one of the most popular men in the country shot. Department-store owner Martial van Schelle was a prominent athlete and sponsor, who had provided the Belgian capital with a swimming-pool and an ice rink. He organized spectacular sporting competitions and climbing and skiing tours. It was bad enough for such a busy man to have been imprisoned for months in Breendonk fort, supposedly because he belonged to a terrorist organization with nine of his compatriots. Now the German military commander had had the national hero executed without trial, as a hostage.

There was also bad blood because of a new law introduced by the occupying forces: the military government had forbidden the 30,000 Belgian scouts to wear their uniforms. On weekends, therefore, scouts and members of the Belgian Hitler Youth fought furious battles in the Bois de la Cambre and the Forêt de Soignes; for the scouts refused to give up wearing their belts in their Sunday meetings in the countryside. This in turn caused the children of the Nazi collaborators to set themselves up as junior policemen and take the scouts' beloved belts off them.

Even Cardinal van Roey, who had distanced himself from the Resistance a few weeks previously, now called for disobedience to the occupying forces. The Germans had started requisitioning the church bells from the parishes. The religious instruments were to be melted down in the war factories into guns and ammunition for the Front. In the Catholic province of Flanders, priests and parish members fetched down the bells from the steeples to hide them in the ground so that the Germans wouldn't find them.

Those Jews still living in Belgium had quite different concerns. The net was drawing more and more tightly around them. The ones who were hidden were living in cellars, attics and uninhabitable roofspaces, and no longer dared to go into the street or to see the doctor. They were entirely dependent on the goodwill, the patience and the generosity of their Belgian acquaintances or neighbours who granted them refuge and kept them supplied with food in their hiding places. They were all liable for punishment according to the legal system of the occupiers, which was becoming ever more ruthless. Anyone helping the despised Jews was punished by being sent to a German concentration camp.

Only those privileged Israelites who had 'carte blanche' from the Jewish Council were, like the representatives of the Council set up by the Nazis, exempt from deportation. Each month a committee member of the Jewish Council presented the military administration with a list of particularly meritorious citizens, noted scientists and artists, who might be eligible for this special status. The official responsible for exemptions, Wilhelm von Hahn in the High Field

Command, would have liked to be generous with his approval, but every time he voted in favour of an exemption, his positive vote was defeated by the fanatical little anti-Semite in SS headquarters. Asche mercilessly crossed out his list.

The German lawyer Emil Kochmann from Gelsenkirchen Buer was one of those who fulfilled all the requirements for special exemption. Kochmann, who had escaped to Brussels to get away from the Nazi thugs, had been awarded the Iron Cross First Class and the Cross of Honour for Front soldiers in the First World War; he was married to an Aryan woman, and his son Wolfgang fought as a corporal in Hitler's army. With other Jews who had found refuge in a castle in Wallonia, he was brought to Mechelen. In vain, son and daughter applied to the High Field Command for their father's release from the transit camp. They were referred on to Obersturmführer Asche at the Brussels Security Service, who did not deign to reply to their request. The family received 'a printed card' from Birkenau concentration camp, 'and then nothing more'. Kochmann's daughter wrote to the state attorney's office in Kiel on the occasion of the trial against the tireless persecutor of the Jews, Kurt Asche. 'I hope with all my heart that these people will not go unpunished.'

With their practically Prussian sense of legality, the representatives of the Jewish Council had still not understood that racial hatred and the arbitrary use of power were the only reliable constants in the 'final solution of the Jewish question'. On 11 March the Jewish Council attempted another intervention on behalf of the internees with Kurt Asche in Avenue Louise: 'An intervention on behalf of the Hilsberg family is being examined. If the information that we have been given should prove to be correct, release might be considered.' But the couple from Warsaw were not permitted to leave Mechelen transit camp. The tie-maker and his wife became numbers 1131 and 1132 on the list of deportees.

The Obersturmführer's fanatical anti-Semitism and brutality were notorious. Even among Party members he was noted for his uncontrolled aggression. After the war, the German Criminal Secretary Alfred Kirsch went on record as saying that he had been standing with

Asche outside the office when a truckload of arrested Jews entered the barracks yard. The men, women and children were to be lodged in the cramped cells in the cellar. Among those who got out of the truck was a woman with a severe limp. Asche yelled at her to walk faster. When the apathetic-looking woman didn't react, he dashed up to her and struck her in the face. Criminal Secretary Kirsch claims to have told his colleague to moderate himself: 'Comrade Kurt, you shouldn't do such things in public.' But Asche had turned on his heel and left him standing there.

Meanwhile Salomon Vanden Berg was extremely alarmed when Asche's colleague Fritz Erdmann had left in the middle of March for a lengthy home leave. For health reasons the SS man was allowed to take a break of several weeks.

> That would be extremely unpleasant [Vanden Berg confided
> in his diary] as he appears to place a particular value on
> the white IDs that he allows people to show. You wouldn't
> know whether someone else will take the same attitude.
> This Erdmann is more polite than the others and seems to
> be rather more human. So far he has more or less protected
> the directors and employees of the Jewish Council...

This meant that Kurt Asche would have sole responsibility for the organization of the next convoy. It was time for him to be put to the test. Now the Obersturmführer could finally prove himself. And talk about his extravagant night-life and his corruptibility would finally fall silent. Adolf Eichmann, his superior in Berlin, would discover that Asche was his best man in Brussels. For it was in Berlin rather than in the Avenue Louise that decisions about his promotion through the SS hierarchy would be made.

At his trial in Kiel the Judenreferent would later declare that he had been 'effectively removed as the head of the Referat' from autumn 1942 because he had had disagreements with his office director, Ehlers. He had had 'practically nothing to do with Jewish matters, and merely worked with forgotten files'. Asche would even deny ever having had 'direct contact with Jews'. 'All important matters were dealt with personally by Thomas' – the same Alfred Thomas who was killed in the air-raid by the Belgian pilot on 20 January 1943.

In March, Asche's police units were at work night and day. It was becoming increasingly difficult to track down the people in hiding. But 'fat Jacques', Asche's secret weapon in his ruthless hunt of the hated Semites, remained entirely dependable. So far his hunting-ground had been restricted to the centre of Brussels and the traditional emigrant quarters of Anderlecht, Schaerbeek and St Gilles. Now he was increasingly extending his spying activity into the bourgeois residential areas. It was here in the tree-lined villa districts that the more cunning and cautious Jews had gone into hiding.

Among them was the furrier Samuel Heuberg. He had left his flat in Anderlecht along with his wife and daughter, and now lived under a false name in the peaceful and idyllic Avenue Jacques Pastur in Uccle. With his Belgian ID, registered under the name of Simon Huberty, he felt fairly safe from the Nazis. One March afternoon he suddenly found himself facing three Gestapo agents in the street near his flat. He attempted to flee, but they caught him and dragged him, struggling violently, back to their police car. There they set upon him.

Addressing the court martial in Brussels in 1948, the furrier remembered his tormentors very clearly. First, the notorious Jewish spy Jacques Glogowski had stopped him and struck him in the face with the handle of his revolver; the second to have done so was a twenty-eight-year-old butcher's son from Düsseldorf; the third had been the chauffeur. In the cellar of 347 Avenue Louise the beating continued under the instructions of a man whose unpleasant voice had etched its way particularly deeply into Heuberg's memory. He seemed to be the head of the brutal trio. Heuberg describes him in the court records as 'short, about 5ft 6in tall, rather stout, rimless glasses, brown hair and his nose tilted slightly upwards, aged about thirty-five.' From a photograph he identifies him as Kurt Asche.

Furious about Heuberg's evasive answers, the men struck his head against a fuse box and pistol-whipped him. On Asche's instructions they took the bleeding man's ring, his watch, his cigarette-case and his wallet, and shoved him into a cell. Samuel Heuberg realized that the police had immediately set off towards his flat on the Rue Jacques Pastur to fetch his wife and daughter, who arrived shortly afterwards. The following morning Samuel, his wife Laura and eleven-year-old Sylvia were brought to Mechelen transit camp. They were given the consecutive transport numbers 1194, 1195 and 1196.

Greed and envy remained the SS police's most generous sources of help. Either out of resentment or because they were expecting a bounty, neighbours and people who happened to know handed over the hidden Jews. Thus a woman betrayed the address of a Jewish trader to the Gestapo because she thought he had paid her too little for three rings and a platinum chain. Simon Visschraper, aged seventy-two, was immediately arrested. For the Belgian informer the betrayal hadn't been worth it. She didn't get a single piece of her jewellery back from the Judenreferat. But old Visschraper – transport number 1463 – could expect certain death in the gas chambers.

The family of the leather goods dealer Léon Gronowski was also betrayed. 'I never found out by whom,' Simon Gronowski says bitterly. Perhaps they had been spotted taking their little dog Bobby for regular walks.

It was Wednesday morning. Simon was sitting with his mother and his sister Ita at breakfast. His father was in hospital with an acute infection. He was due to be released in a few days. Suddenly there was a long, insistent ring at the door. 'We were worried and practically paralysed. And all our plans to flee through the gardens proved to be hopeless. I don't know who opened the door to them, but there were already two Germans in plain clothes standing in the room,' Simon Gronowski remembers fifty years later, as though it were yesterday.

One of the invaders shouted: 'Gestapo! IDs!' Simon's mother sat as though petrified at the breakfast table. Finally she handed him her ID. The SS man compared the details with his information and seemed content. This really was the Gronowski family. Then he hesitated. 'Where is Herr Gronowski?' he asked. 'My husband has died,' Simon's mother replied with great presence of mind.

They were told to pack their bags very quickly, because they were being taken to Mechelen transit camp, a name that chilled them to the bone; they had heard so much about that ominous place. 'Take your fine clothes with you,' recommended one of the two cops when he saw Ita standing hesitantly by her open wardrobe. Simon packed his precious, fringed scout's socks, knitted by his mother. The men tied the dog to the banisters. Outside the front door they climbed into a little grey car that would take them past the massive-looking barracks of Etterbeek to Avenue Louise.

Later that afternoon they were loaded, along with other internees, on to a tarpaulin-covered truck. Through an opening in the tarpaulin Simon was able to catch glimpses of passers-by, cyclists and squares full of people. Even today, at the age of sixty-seven, he can remember what went through his head at that time. 'Outside everything is going on quite normally, as though nothing had happened. None of them knows that we are sitting in this truck.'

At 'reception', Simon and his mother were given numbers 1233 and 1234. Their sleeping-places were in dormitory 18 on the second floor. It was here that they would spend most of their time over the coming weeks. Simon's sister, as a Belgian citizen, was given the identification B274 and was sent to the dormitory for Belgian Jews, who still thought they were under the special protection of Queen Elisabeth.

Every day Asche was told of the new arrivals in the transit camp. And once a week he sent a report on the number of internees to the RSHA in Berlin. On 20 March he was able to report a population of almost 1,300 camp inmates to his superior, Eichmann. At Brussels Security Service they were hoping that that departure would be soon, because the hygienic conditions in the barracks were becoming increasingly intolerable, a breeding ground for potentially terrible epidemics. There were already headlice. And the guards were more afraid of infectious diseases than anything else.

21 The Silent Rebels of Mechelen

At about six o'clock in the morning the call 'Get up, Jews!' rang out around the dormitories of the old Habsburg barracks. Simon and his mother hurried to the wash-room, so that they wouldn't have to queue for too long at the primitive basins and latrines. From seven o'clock the eldest members of the room distributed the hot ersatz coffee and the bread rations to the hundred inmates in the dormitory. At eight o'clock it was time for sport in the barracks yard. Only after the thin soup at lunchtime was 'Simkele' – little Simon – able to go and play in the yard. There the children would chase each other around among the feet of the adults, for whom this daily walk in the yard was also the only variation in the grey monotony of the transit camp.

On these 'walks' there were moving scenes of greeting almost every day. The prisoners would meet neighbours, friends and acquaintances who had, like themselves, fallen into the hands of the Gestapo. One afternoon Ita, Simon's sister, met her former classmate Jacques Angielzyk among the men who were doing their round in the yard. They fell into each other's arms. They had attended the Ecole Cymring together, after being excluded, as Jews, from the state grammar schools. Was it really only a year since they had gone hiking through the Ardennes on a class outing in the lovely month of May? Jacques remembers more than fifty years later that 'those were the last weeks when we were still able to smile'. Jacques' parents had had their only son adopted by a Belgian couple to protect him from anti-Semitic persecution. For that reason he had returned to his old class in the Athénée de Bruxelles after a brief interlude at the Jewish school. Nonetheless, because he had been denounced as a Jew, he entered Mechelen transit camp as number 1314 under the name of Jakob Grauwels.

The daily walk in the courtyard was a great source of news and contacts. Here information about the latest situation on the Eastern Front was passed on by the new arrivals, hopes were awakened and fears aroused, old hostilities were kept up and new friendships forged.

One day a newly arrived prisoner addressed the young nurse Régine Krochmal. The older man, even smaller than dainty Régine, wore the traces of torture on his face. A broken nose, a black eye, two missing teeth, a bloodstain on his cheek: it all suggested a Gestapo interrogation. She knew straight away that this man was the Resistance fighter who had been mentioned in a secret message as being particularly influential. Simon Brauner, fifty-six years old and number 1004 on the list, was from Poland, where he had held a senior position in the Communist Party until his flight to Belgium. When Régine asked him about his job in the Belgian Resistance, the modest man had replied, 'Régine, the job, membership of a group, religion or nationality doesn't mean much, the important thing comes from the heart.' Brauner's answer became a motto for Régine Krochmal, and one that she followed into her old age.

She gave the important Resistance fighter everything she had saved for him – soap, bread and a few valuable foodstuffs. But the crusted traces of blood did not vanish from Brauner's face. Clearly he wasn't using Régine's soap. The young nurse discovered that he had passed on all her gifts to the children in the camp.

Unlike Régine, who was suffering from the 'climate of dehumanization and lack of solidarity' in the camp, young Simon Gronowski perceived little of this oppressive atmosphere. He had not been particularly unhappy in Mechelen, he remembers fifty-five years later. 'After all, I was with my mother and my sister, and I felt protected by them.' The Rouffaerts, the parents of his scout friend, to whom Simon's father had transferred his house, sent them food, so that they didn't have to rely on the starvation rations in the transit camp, where the degree of brutality to which the prisoners were exposed was determined by the amount of alcohol consumed by their jailers. This was true even under the command of Frank, who, was considered relatively 'correct' in comparison with his predecessor Schmitt.

One favourite game of the inebriated Nazis was called 'foot-checking'. At some point in the night the light would burst on in the dormitory, and someone shouted 'Foot check!' Uniformed SS men went from bed to bed and shone their torches on the feet of the internees. The fear of the prisoners startled from sleep seemed to bring them particular pleasure. They used their whips to lift the women's blankets. If they found that a prisoner had not washed his feet sufficiently, the 'filthy Jewish pig' was sent to the barracks yard. There the prisoners had to wait in their pyjamas or their underwear until all feet had been checked. On particularly icy nights, the deputy camp head Max Boden poured water over the 'dirty Jews' and made the drenched prisoners stand in the courtyard until dawn. After one such cold March night, the prisoner Bernard van Ham was delivered to the hospital with pneumonia, and died shortly afterwards. 'Heart failure' was the cause of death recorded in his papers.

One episode from this period made a profound impression on all survivors: the night of Jonas Polak's punishment. The young man from Amsterdam had managed to flee the transit camp, but had fallen back into the hands of the SS shortly afterwards. In the middle of the night all prisoners were ordered into the central barracks yard to watch the punishment of the runaway. Simon Gronowski was a witness to the terrible drama. Once and for all the Jews were to understand that any attempted escape was condemned to failure.

Polak was led into the middle of the yard in handcuffs, tottering on his feet, his face swollen, his eyes bloodshot. Hauptscharführer Boden turned towards the prisoners, who were trembling with cold and horror: they should be pleased, he said, that the runaway had been caught. If he had succeeded in his escape, they would all have had to bear the consequences. 'Spit on the mangy dog, show the traitor your contempt,' Boden ordered his audience. 'But we swallowed back our saliva,' writes Claire Prowizur in her memoirs, 'and waited in silence.'

Boden called for volunteers to step forward and whip Polak. No one moved. When no one responded to the second order either, the SS officer himself started thrashing Polak. The rod came hissing down ten times on his naked torso, and each blow left a bloody gash. Then a prisoner was chosen to carry on the torture. The man hesitantly took the whip. Only three blows, and far too gentle, the Nazi thought. Boden took the whip and thrashed away until his victim collapsed on the ground. Then prisoner number 1235 was taken into the dark, damp dungeon cell of the barracks, and would not leave it again until the departure of the twentieth transport.

Many years later the lawyer Simon Gronowski would scour the attic of the Brussels Ministry of Justice for the files of the trial of the Nazi whose punishment he had witnessed as a little boy. In the statements of Boden, who had to account for himself before the war court in Brussels, Gronowski recognized the savage and ruthless SS officer who still saw himself as a guardian of justice and order: 'Yes, I struck people, yes, I whipped people, but only to maintain order in the camp.'

Bloody demonstrations such as this had very different effects on the prisoners. For most of them, dull and resigned in the vast waiting room as the departure date approached, it was confirmation that all resistance, any attempts at escape, were pointless. They complied, particularly since they didn't know that the gas chambers awaited them in Auschwitz. 'We were ignorant and innocent,' says Simon Gronowski, 'we didn't know that we had been condemned to death long before.' Somehow the large number of internees also gave them a feeling of certainty: 'Mass extermination like that perpetrated by the Nazis was simply unthinkable.'

Even the Jewish nurse Gerti Scharf, who had worked throughout the whole time in Mechelen transit camp, only learned of the gas ovens in Auschwitz after everything was over. They had imagined that very bad things awaited the deportees, she said later in a television interview. They had heard of hunger and plagues, and were grateful to be able to stay in Mechelen. The optimists among the internees had even believed they would find a great green ghetto in Auschwitz, where they would live and work with their families. SS Commandant Frank was forever embellishing this version with new additions: an idyllic place awaited the prisoners, surrounded by forest, somewhere remote and in the middle of the countryside. The food was ample and delicious. And in the evening, once the work was done, there was even entertainment. Gerti Scharf and her colleagues would further disseminate the fairy-tale of the lovely concentration camp to make the prisoners less afraid of the journey.

The members of the Resistance knew more, even if they were unaware of the extent of the organized genocide. The Germans, they believed, would exploit their labour under inhuman conditions. Extermination through labour, that was imaginable, and they wanted to escape that fate. A spirit of silent revolt spread particularly among the young people. These secret rebels, members of the armed and unarmed Resistance, left-wing, apolitical and bourgeois, would not be deterred from their purpose. In fact they were even more resolute in their decision to do anything they could to escape the Nazi thugs. The diamond-grinder Samuel Perl from Antwerp, who had already 'hopped off' one deportation train, says: 'I simply had to do it again.'

In the dormitory, little Simon practised jumping down from the top wooden bunk with the other children. Somehow the eleven-year-old had conceived of the idea of fleeing the train. He'd be able to do it, because he had already mastered the art of jumping off the tram in Brussels while it was still moving.

Meanwhile it had also trickled through to the camp: the Germans would be using goods trucks for the next transports. None of the Jews were to escape their fate, the Final Solution. Throughout Europe the SS had learned that the number of escapes in the use of windowless railway trucks tended towards zero. And how could the weakened prisoners escape this prison cell on wheels?

From now on this question vexed those prisoners who had sworn to escape the deportation train before the border. Because only in

Belgium, where the German occupiers were so hated throughout all sectors of the population, would the Jews would have a chance of survival. These prisoners were, like the businessman Joseph Silber, convinced of this: 'Nowhere else would we be able to count on such solid support as we could from the Belgian population.'

For a long time Silber thought he was alone with his thoughts of escape, until he met up with an old acquaintance from Antwerp at the beginning of April. This Nathan Mitelsbach was also a businessman, and belonged to a patriotic resistance organization. In the camp he looked for similarly minded people, who were to work together for the break-out from the deportation train. Silber was all for it. 'I enthusiastically accepted the offer,' he went on record as saying in March 1981 on the occasion of Asche's trial. 'It came as a great relief for me no longer to be alone with the idea of resisting deportation.'

'Little conspiratorial groups were forming everywhere, a network of conspiracy came into being,' Claire Prowizur writes in her book. The silent rebels had quickly discovered which of the Jewish staff would support them in their plans. Their helpers had to have chutzpah, they had to be shrewd and they couldn't be fearful. And they were to help them get hold of the tools with which the rebels would free themselves from the closed carriage.

All of these conditions were embodied in the figure of Albert Clément. Fair-haired, athletic and blue-eyed, Antwerp-born Clément had been a privileged prisoner in Mechelen since October. As he was married to a non-Jewish Belgian he came under the heading of 'mixed marriage', and had been assigned to the Jewish staff in the transit camp. Clément belonged to the 'Service Entretien', or building maintenance. And whenever there was a shortage of nails, screws, plugs and tools, the thirty-year-old, who had previously earned his livelihood as a travelling salesman in household goods, was able to go off in the company of a guard to do some shopping outside of the barracks. In an iron goods shop in nearby Borgerhout, the customer from Dossin barracks, with his grim-looking guard, was a regular feature. When the shop-owner was tying up the parcel with the goods he needed, he often added the occasional tool that wasn't on the bill.

Like so many decent Belgians, he had pity on the Jews who had been persecuted and carted away by the Germans.

The Jewish cobbler in Dossin barracks, Rubin Liberman, also hoarded sharp blades, pliers and saws for the would-be escapees. All those who, like Joseph Rafalowicz – number 517 – or Frain Szyper – number 254 –worked their eight-hour day in one of the workshops, also tried to set aside tools and iron bars. There was another lucky circumstance. The new camp commandant Frank had allowed the prisoners to receive cutlery – including knives – in their parcels. So some of the inmates came into the possession of blades in this way.

'We knew more or less which prisoners would jump out of the train and risk their lives,' Claire Prowizur writes in her memoirs. Her father, her husband Philippe, her friend Szymon Birnberg and his mates would all risk escape: 'The hope of freedom drove us all.' The two Dutchmen from their dormitory also wanted to make the jump, father and son, forty-five and twenty years old, both tall, fair and with a reddish complexion and a loud voice. They even planned to jump first to give the others courage.

In the group of those who had already fled, who had been put on a special list and were under particularly intense observation, the prisoners placed their hopes on one Viennese Jew. He had a reputation as a champion escapologist. Samuel Perl can no longer remember his name, but he still recalls what was respectfully said about the Austrian: 'If anyone can break us out, he can. He could get through any fortification.'

22 Brave Men Wanted

Everyone in the flat was ready for the operation. Youra had got hold of alcohol, bandages and plaster. Now he and his brother were waiting for the surgeon. Dr René Dumont planned to come to 386 Chaussée d'Alssemberg at six o'clock in the evening. The two bullet-wounds that Alexandre had suffered during the attack on Belgian police superintendent Cortin were threatening to become inflamed. Action had to be taken.

At that time, if an injured Resistance fighter required medical help, Dumont's name was the first that always sprang to mind. The surgeon from the university hospital of St Pierre had already had to carry out many emergency operations of this kind in the Spanish Civil War. Youra still knew his slightly older colleague from his time as an assistant doctor in the University Hospital. But unlike his student friend Hélène Bolle, Youra was not part of the circle of young intellectuals who had regular discussion evenings about Marxism–Leninism with the Communist Dumont.

In her memoirs, Claire Prowizur describes the doctor as 'tall and thin, marked by his years in Spain'. Now a grandmother living in Tel Aviv, she gratefully remembers that the helpful surgeon extracted her from an apparently impossible situation. Dumont had undertaken a termination of a pregnancy for her, in her little attic room, assisted by her husband Philippe. For the young couple in hiding from the Nazis it was an act of mercy. The birth of a child would have made them easy prey for the Jew-persecutors.

That evening the surgeon was to operate on Alexandre Livchitz. At precisely six o'clock there was a ring at the door. People turned up on time for conspiratorial meetings. When Dr Dumont had removed the bandage, he knew straight away that both bullets would have to be operated-out as quickly as possible, or else the patient would die of blood poisoning.

In Alexandre Livchitz's file in the archive of the Brussels Social Ministry there is a report from 1950, in which René Dumont recalls his visit in the following terms:

> Early in 1943 I was called to Mr Alexandre Livchitz on the Chaussée d'Alsemberg, I can no longer remember the house number. There I found Mr Alexandre Livchitz, suffering from two injuries from a firearm. One bullet had penetrated his left thigh, where it firmly remained. I was able to remove the bullet in his right foot, and as the skin was broken I applied a plaster bandage with the help of Mr Youra Livchitz, the injured man's brother. The patient was then tended by his brother, and a short time later the second bullet was removed by an operation in Edith Cavell Hospital.

Alexandre was almost more downcast than his younger brother. He, the battle-tested partisan chief, would not be able to give the orders in the ambush on the deportation train. He was out of action. The refusal of the organized Resistance to take part in this rescue mission had left them very disappointed. But their refusal also gave them a sense of how dangerous the undertaking was. If the partisan army and 'Groupe G' balked at the mission, how could Youra and Choura find people brave enough to take the risk?

Together the two brothers recalled former school-friends and fellow students, and discussed the dependability and courage of friends and acquaintances. Alexandre, the older and more cautious brother, thought that many of those whose names were mentioned during these discussions were not up to the task: they were too fearful, too talkative, too unfit, not trustworthy. Malka Cymring's boyfriend, the 'White Russian' Pierre Romanovitch, whom Youra had described to his brother as a blank page, was too much of a risk for such a delicate mission. For a coup such as this they needed absolutely reliable comrades like Robert Maistriau. The twenty-two-year-old was certainly inexperienced, but Youra knew him to be a stable and reliable fellow, clever and prudent. Youra still remembered how Robert had talked about going into the Resistance 'to do something against the occupying Germans'.

Maistriau had also been recommended to him by Robert Leclercq. Their former fellow pupil from the Athénée d'Uccle had already made contact with 'Groupe G'. Youra hadn't entirely given up hope that Richard Altenhoff might join in. The engineer shared the concerns of his friends in 'Groupe G' about the dangerous mission. But Altenhoff was attracted by the fact that this mission was not about sabotage, not about destruction, but about the saving of human lives.

Youra and Alexandre only ever talked about the plan when Willy was out of the house. They didn't want her to know what was going on, and thus put her in even greater danger. She was already putting her life at risk by taking in partisans who were being sought by the Gestapo. Willy organized food supplies for the convalescent, and spent time almost every day with her closest friend Minnie Minet. Her contact with Rachel Livchitz was less cordial. Saps was not happy about the fact that her son had gone into hiding with Willy, of all people. After all, Alexandre was as good as engaged to the lovely Irène Gromberg. And Irène, a social worker with the Jewish Council, was now going through the most hellish torments, knowing that her beloved Choura was lying on the sofa of her rival, Willy.

Behind the regular, feminine features of Wilhelmine Baudoux was a person who paid little attention to the feelings of others. In retrospect she spoke of her 'selfishness in love'. She told her son much later, that 'war makes love even more intense. You can't imagine the emotions it unleashes in you to smuggle news or even weapons for your lover.' Alexandre had the good fortune to have her affection. He was the recipient of all of her care. 'Typical Willy,' the female guests at Minnie Minet's Saturday artistic soirées would say when the tall, full-bosomed beauty flirted with all the men she happened to fancy, whether they were married or not. Only the generous and vivacious Minnie didn't find her best friend's behaviour repulsive.

At the same time, in the Jewish Defence Committee, Jospa, Bolle and Nijkerk were planning their rescue mission. The most difficult part seemed to be the evacuation of the people they might free from the deportation train. What ways and means were there to get the escapees away from the scene of the attack? They could see only one solution: the people would have to fend for themselves. And for that they needed money. The thing to do, then, was to distribute money to the inmates. A 50-franc note would be enough to buy them a ticket. Treasurer Benjamin Nijkerk had set aside 20,000 francs for the operation. The Dutchman had twice taken the long journey to Switzerland to collect money that had been transferred by the 'American Jewish Joint Distribution Committee'. Part of this donation was to be spent on the rescue mission of the deportees.

The news that reached Jospa from Mechelen transit camp made him cautious. Cryptic messages were reaching the outside world from the barracks, and not only in letters and cards. Some prisoners used the opportunity of their occasional meetings with visitors to exchange information with their comrades on the outside. These conversations, restricted to a quarter of an hour, took place in a strictly guarded room, and the visitor was obliged to apply for them in writing, days in advance. His personal details were closely examined, and the reason given for the meeting was weighed up. If everything was acceptable, the meeting could go ahead in the presence of two SS guards. The Resistance fighters inside the camp, for whom conspiratorial behaviour had become second nature, and their no less crafty visitors, were frequently able to trick their guards, particularly since they often spoke only their mother tongue, German or Flemish.

In this way the Jewish Defence Committee learned that there were trustworthy people on the Jewish staff who were able to leave the camp every now and again to accomplish certain tasks. The name of Albert Clément, for instance, came up.

No one could believe it was a coincidence when, one morning in the camp – the usual queues were forming outside the washrooms – two taps above the basins were suddenly unable to take the pressure, and fell off simultaneously. Cold water thundered out of the wall in a wide arc. Sabotage, the SS officers privately assumed and yelled, 'You just don't want to wash yourselves, you filthy Jewish pigs.' The men from the maintenance service were called. To repair the damage they would need new taps and new pipes. There were no replacements in the workshop. So Albert Clément was sent off with a uniformed guard in a car to buy the necessary material in Borgerhout.

When he returned to the barracks, he didn't have the things he needed for the repair with him. He was also in possession of a bundle of 50-franc notes, which the owner of the hardware shop had hidden in one of the boxes. Clément was to pass on the money to the silent rebels in the camp, on behalf of the Jewish Defence Committee.

Youra was also to receive money from the Jewish Defence Committee so that he and his colleagues could distribute the notes to those who would be freed from the deportation train. The young doctor still didn't know how many friends he would be able to mobilize for the ambush. One desirable candidate with the right mixture of adventurousness and reliability for this daring undertaking was no longer available. Szmul Rzepkowicz, the brilliant forger of documents and passionate card-player – and one of Youra's closest friends – was now himself a prisoner in Mechelen. His number on the transport list to Auschwitz: 1405.

Perhaps Jean Franklemon would join in. Youra's old schoolmate, who shared his passion for theatre and music, was not only artistically and musically talented, he also had a great gift for organization, from which the troupe of the 'Comédiens Routiers' benefited. Street theatre had long had its place in the Brussels art scene. At the same time 'Pamplemousse' was someone who liked to turn his ideals into action. He had joined the Communist Party, because according to his conviction, it was the only one on the side of the weak and the oppressed.

Having had enough of the theoretical anti-fascism debates at university, he had joined the Spanish Civil War.

Youra knew that he would meet Jean late in the afternoon, once his courses at Cambre Art College were over, in the corner café on the Place Flagey. It was the art students' local. 'Pamplemousse' was particularly drawn to it because it had an old piano. Late in the evening he would sit down at the instrument, and a little while later all the guests would join in with the chansons he played. He had brought back one song from the Spanish Civil War, which he liked to sing with particular intensity: '*Venceremos*' – 'We Will Win.'

When Youra walked into the café he saw Jean in his usual double role – as participant and observer – sitting in the circle of the youthful bohemians. 'Pamplemousse' was able to do two things at once: talk and draw portraits of the other people at his table. Today he clearly didn't have his drawing-pad with him, because he was drawing a portrait of one of his friends on a serviette.

Youra gave him a sign that he wanted to talk to him on his own. And before he rose to his feet, Jean passed the serviette, complete with pencil drawing, to the sitter. The two friends went outside to avoid being disturbed. They set off on the wooded path towards the Etangs d'Ixelles, but had no eyes for the green buds and yellow blossoms of the hazel bushes heralding the spring. Youra described his plan and told Jean of the refusal of the armed Resistance fighters to carry out the ambush. The young medic didn't need to paint the picture of the wretchedness of the Jews. Jean's parents had taken in a Jewish child whose parents had been deported.

Freeing people from the clutches of the Nazis – Jean was fascinated by the idea. But wasn't the undertaking too risky, if even the partisan army was frightened of the operation? He asked for some time to think.

23 Objections Overruled

The Grauwels tried desperately to get their adopted son Jacques out of Mechelen transit camp. They wrote to General von Falkenhausen and Queen Elisabeth, and visited an official in Brussels High Field Command. Like all of their Belgian fellow citizens, the couple assumed that the military administration was responsible for the arrest and transportation of the Jews. After all, it had passed all the laws for the stigmatization of the Jews and discrimination against them, and signed their labour deployment orders.

Wilhelm Baron von Hahn was responsible for requests of this kind in the military administration; the lawyer's tasks included applications for exemption from deportation. But Hahn, who showed a great deal of understanding for the Grauwels' case, could give them little hope. His hands were tied. The transit camp was, so to speak, SS sovereign territory. And all they cared about was that an internee was a 'full Jew' according to the National Socialist racial laws. Hahn knew only too well how the Judenreferent in Avenue Louise would react to this request from the Grauwels. Because every day the lawyer was swamped with requests and complaints concerning the coming transport from Mechelen, and which he – with additional observations of urgency and arguments – passed to SS officer Kurt Asche. The answer was always the same: objections overruled. Hahn would do nothing about the petition in favour of eighteen-year-old Jacques Grauwels, because for Asche and those like him, a Jew was a Jew and that was that, whether he was baptized, assimilated or adopted.

In the Security Service on Avenue Louise, there was only one problem during these April days: the fastest possible 'getting-rid' – as the NS bureaucrats called it – of the internees in Mechelen transit camp. Telegrams sped back and forth between SS headquarters in Brussels and the RSHA. By now almost 1,500 people were living in a very cramped space in the barracks. The danger of epidemics was rising. In order to prevent the outbreak of infectious diseases among the weakened and undernourished inmates, the prisoners were taken to Antwerp in groups to be disinfected.

With bags and rucksacks in which they had stowed their clothes, the members of a dormitory stepped out of the barracks gate and into the waiting tram. 'It seemed almost like a school outing,' Louis Micheels remembers in his book *A Holocaust Memoir*, writing about the special journey of the camp inmates to the harbour city. He had hoped to use this opportunity to make his getaway with his fiancée Nora. But the tram was strictly guarded. SS men with rifles were posted at the front and back entrances of both carriages.

Escorted by their guards, the prisoners entered a large building not far from the centre of Antwerp, which turned out to be a public baths with quarantine equipment. The men and women went to separate changing rooms and handed over all their clothes to be disinfected, and were instructed to clean themselves thoroughly with a pungent-smelling green soap. Warm water thundered out of the shower-heads, a luxury they had not experienced for ages, and which they were allowed to enjoy for half an hour. After that, back they went to the transit camp. For most of them the outing would prove to be a harmless trial run for the gas chambers of Auschwitz. 'We passed through the disinfectant shower, the real one,' writes Claire Prowizur, 'the ones in Auschwitz and the other concentration camps were called the same thing, but the results were different.'

In the RSHA in Berlin, meanwhile, the latest figures on the 'Final Solution of the European Jewish question' were already available. The inspector of statistics had reported that in the Old Reich, in the

Sudetenland, in the Ostmark, in Bohemia and Moravia, the Eastern Regions and the Polish General Government – within the 'extended Reich zone' – 'Jewry' had declined by '3.1 million' between 1933 and 1943. 'This drop is the result of the cumulative effect of emigration, mortality and evacuation'. To this were added 842,066 'evacuations' – deportations to the extermination camps – within the 'sphere of German power and influence beyond the borders of the Reich', or in the occupied European countries such as France, Holland, Bulgaria and Slovakia. In Belgium, according to these figures, a total of 18,492 Jews had been 'evacuated' by April 1943.

What had happened to the people who had been persecuted and deported by the occupying Germans? In Belgian government circles uncomfortable questions were asked about the purpose and aim of the deportations. General Secretary Gaston Schuind, who held the office of Minister of Justice under the supervision of the military administration, had been alerted by members of the Jewish Council. Among the Jews waiting in Mechelen to be deported there were infants and old people who could hardly constitute a workforce. Even the explanation that was repeatedly trotted out by the Nazis, that they didn't want to separate families during the evacuation, failed to convince, because many of the old people were on their own, and some of the children were without parents.

On 14 April 1943, General Secretary Schuind wrote to Councillor Thedick in the military administration, a letter in which he advocated that at least those children without parents should remain in Belgium:

> I have been informed that a transport with all the adult Jews
> who are in Mechelen will set off for Germany. In addition,
> three hundred children will accompany the transport.
> Sixty are below the age of three, sixty are between the ages
> of three and six, 180 are between six and fifteen. Among them
> there are many who are not accompanied by their parents.
> They are forced to make the journey in wagons without any
> comforts.
>   I do not know the nationality of the children, but I have

the honour of drawing your attention to the situation of
these children, who clearly bear no responsibility for current
events, and whose protection is dictated by the principle of
humanity.

Two days later Schuind dictated a further letter to Oberkriegsverwal-
tungsrat Thedick. This time he took up the case of the old people who
were waiting in Dossin barracks for their deportation:

Higher humanitarian reasons lead me to refer to the
problems involved in a transport of these people. I have
been informed that their numbers included people who
are over the age of eighty and even ninety…
    In all likelihood these people cannot be used for work in
Germany. Under such conditions there can be no point in
dispatching them to the East.

These two official appeals against the deportation of non-Belgian
Jews met the same fate as all other requests. Like all other petitioners,
the General Secretary of the military administration could not get
over the wall of non-responsibility. And the responsible Security
Service, to which the appeal was forwarded, did not even consider
itself obliged to reply to the letter from this member of the Belgian
government.

The committee members of the Belgian Jewish Council met on
that 15 April, as they did every Thursday, in the office of Judenreferent
Asche on Avenue Louise. They stood in front of the imposing desk of
the SS officer to receive the Obersturmführer's instructions and cau-
tions. That day Asche had a special announcement to make to them.
After more than three months, another transport train for the evacuation of the Jews from Mechelen was to set off. The date had been
given to him by the RSHA in Berlin. For the deportation of the prisoners, they planned to use freight and cattle trucks confiscated from
the Belgian railway.

A day later, on 16 April, Samuel Vanden Berg noted:

We are experiencing some more sad days. Yesterday we were informed that a new transport of Jews will leave the camp on Sunday or Monday. They have deliberately chosen the Monday evening of Seder. This time the transport train will consist of goods wagons, in which they will put benches, a few mattresses for the old people and straw for the rest. One bucket for drinking and one for the opposite. The doors will be sealed with barbed wire to prevent any attempts at escape similar to those on the last transport. We have intervened to ensure that children without parents and old people are left here. The Ministry is also intervening, but we are awaiting the decision from Herr Asche, who is dealing with the transport in place of Herr Erdmann, who is on leave. We cannot expect anything good from a man who would personally eat the Jews if he could. Let us hope that he and all the others suffer the fate they deserve.

The fate of the people in Dossin barracks was as good as sealed. Those who were still trying to avert it were running out of time. Hertz Jospa and Maurits Bolle learned about the planned date on the day of the announcement by Kurt Asche, and immediately contacted Youra. The action was scheduled for the following Monday.

24 The Penultimate Day

When Simon Gronowski was playing with his playmates on that spring Sunday afternoon, 18 April, he noticed a group of young men sitting together in a corner in the sun. They were wearing, he thought, beautiful green uniforms. They were talking and laughing with each other and making such a benign impression that he and his playmates dared to approach them. And when the children, becoming bolder by the minute, ran around them, the policemen even gave them friendly pats on the head. The children were already wearing the rectangular cardboard signs with their deportation numbers around their necks. Tomorrow was the day of departure.

The men came from the Rhineland, they were Schutzpolizei, or constabulary, who were to accompany the deportation train over the border to Germany as reinforcements for the SS guards. Some of the men in green had looked curiously around the courtyard and in the dormitories, in search of familiar faces. Some of the internees came from the nearby Rhineland, and had emigrated to Belgium before the German invasion. One of these policemen actually met a young man from his home town of Mönchengladbach. He was the son of the businessman who had employed him as an apprentice when he was a teenager.

There was great excitement among the internees, since Dagobert Meier, the Jewish camp elder, had announced the departure of the train for Monday. On the day of the Jewish spring festival, when the Hebrews celebrated the memory of the liberation of their people from Egyptian slavery, they would set off on their fateful journey, of which they feared the worst. Meier was barraged with questions about their destination. But he refused to discuss a thing, and would only repeat that there was no reason for alarm: 'You are going to a labour camp in the East.' The journey would last two days, and they would be amply supplied with food.

Among the silent rebels the conspiratorial preparations were in full flow. They had received reinforcements over the past few days. The Communist partisans Jacques Cyngiser (1366) and Abraham Fischel (1360) had been arrested in Brussels and transferred to Mechelen. Majer Tabakman (1381), a member of the Zionist workers' movement, who had described his escape from the nineteenth convoy in the newspaper *Le Flambeau*, had also fallen into the clutches of the Gestapo. He took advantage of the prevailing confusion in the reception office on the day of his arrival. With seventy newcomers the crowd was bigger than it had been for weeks, and the staff were hopelessly overstretched. So no one noticed that the cobbler Tabakman was actually a candidate for the special list of those who had already escaped in the past.

The Gestapo was finally emptying all the Belgian prisons. All the Jewish prisoners were taken to Mechelen. And so, on Saturday, two days before the departure of the twentieth convoy, the prisoners of the Liège Citadel climbed out of a truck in the courtyard. Among the new arrivals were several Jews from Arlon with their 78-year-old rabbi, a respected member of the haute-bourgeoisie from Liège, who had not been protected by his membership of the Jewish Council, and a young man who had been the victim of a traitor. Willy Berler, aged twenty-five, who had reached Liège from his Romanian homeland in the region of Bukovina and managed to scrape a living as a language teacher, was obsessed by a single thought: how he could escape the National Socialist extermination machine.

The sight of the oppressed prisoners and their warders, armed with whips and truncheons, shocked the young man. 'In Mechelen I was struck for the first time by that feeling of horror that would stay with me for the next two years,' reports Willy Berler, who set off for the hell of Auschwitz with the twentieth transport, and was one of the few to survive.

For the Resistance fighters and other unruly inmates who were preparing to escape from the transport train, the secretary Eva Fastag proved to be an invaluable help. The young woman was a good acquaintance of Jacques Cyngiser from before the war. The trained cobbler had barely arrived in Mechelen at the beginning of April when preparations began for the planned escape. He was able to persuade Eva Fastag, who was responsible for drawing up the deportation list in 'reception', to change the list. She ensured that the men and women of the Resistance were given consecutive numbers where possible, even if they had arrived in Mechelen on different days. Thanks to her manipulation, two groups of would-be escapees would be concentrated in two trucks when they set off.

Eva Fastag had also engineered for Cyngiser to be the 'chef de wagon'. For each truck holding about fifty people, a guard was appointed, who received a yellow armband and was to have one qualification above all: a knowledge of German. His role was to ensure calm among the deportees. At their destination, he would be made responsible for the orderly arrival of all inmates. On the journey, he was to signal with a yellow flag out of the barred window if there were any fatalities in the truck.

In Claire Prowizur's group, the tall, ginger-haired Dutchman had been chosen. He and his equally massive son were resolved to escape from the train.

A few days before, the secret rebels had received some promising news. In his macaroni – a favourite foodstuff that was chewed raw – one of them had found several written-upon scraps of cigarette paper. The puzzle that Abraham Bloder (1380), the recipient of the package, assembled, produced the information that members of the Resistance were going to stop or even attack the transport train. The message spread like wildfire. It encouraged the Resistance fighters and fired them on even more to prepare for the approaching day of reckoning.

They were all aware that they could not hope for a miracle, businessman Joseph Silber explained years later. 'We had to make the big effort ourselves.' He had emptied his case of all personal belongings, and instead filled it with knives, razors, small iron bars, stones and a hacksaw. 'Thus equipped, my comrades and I waited for the crucial moment.'

A few prisoners had come into the possession of knives and sharp razors through the food parcels that their friends and relations sent to them. But most of the tools hoarded by the Resistance fighters came from the camp workshops, or had been acquired from co-conspirators among the Jewish staff.

Albert Clément appeared with his tool-box in the dormitories. Minor repair jobs had brought the man from the maintenance service on to the scene. While he was making good any damage, there was ample opportunity to hide tools with one or other of the dormitory inmates. In that way each group managed to get hold of a precious hacksaw. Albert Clément pressed a 50-franc note into the hand of anyone who had ever confided that he was planning to escape, or whom he suspected of having enough of an unruly spirit.

That Sunday, Claire Prowizur had only one question in mind: how could she managed to slip her father, transport number 74, into her own truck? Chaskel Prowizur was seriously ill, lying on his straw mattress. Aspirin and poultices had not brought his fever down, and for three days he had had a temperature of 104, and serious diarrhoea. Under no circumstances did Claire want her father to travel in another truck. They only had a chance of his escaping from the train if they were together. She had to find someone with a transport number close to her own – 255 – who would be prepared to swap. 'That was easier said than done,' Claire Prowizur writes in her memoirs. The other party would have nothing to gain but a lot to lose if one of the guards happened to notice the wrong number. But 'Heaven looked down on us.' A young prisoner who was assigned to the same truck as herself said that he was willing to make the swap. Claire's wedding ring, the only valuable object she still possessed, switched from her ring finger to the mouth of its new owner.

Miserable as life in Mechelen was, during those last hours, many prisoners became aware of the advantages of being in a camp on Belgian soil. Their situation could only get worse in the East, particularly in Poland, where the Jews were almost universally hated. Here in Mechelen they had been able to receive letters, food parcels and sometimes even visitors. Mendelis and Henda Goldsteinas – numbers 779 and 780 – were simply devastated because they had to leave their little daughter Abela behind. They knew their child was safe with a Belgian family, but would they ever see each other again? Hena Wasyng, number 736, who was about to board the same truck as the Goldsteinas, felt much the same thing. Her sons, just three and nine years old, were hidden in a Belgian household. The two children had already lost their father. What would become of them when she could no longer take care of them? The doctor Louis Micheels and his fiancée Nora had hoped in vain that their names would be struck from the transport list at the last moment. This time Dr Bach didn't request the Dutchman as an assistant camp doctor as he had before. Instead, Micheels was employed as transport physician. It was explained to him that this would raise his chances of preferential treatment. But Micheels was sceptical. 'I did not believe it.'

Régine was also to assume a task on the transport, tending to those sick and old people who were not really fit to travel.

This was the first time that the new camp commandant, Hans Frank, had been responsible for the preparation of a deportation train. He wanted to avoid the chaos that had prevailed under his predecessor Schmitt on such occasions. Schmitt was now facing disciplinary proceedings for fraud and corruption. Like all demoted SS officers he would probably be sent to the Front as a private.

Frank was ambitious. If the deportation went smoothly, it would strengthen his authority in the camp and make an impression on his superiors in Avenue Louise. To inform the camp inmates in which sequence they were to line up the following day in the barracks yard, he organized a kind of dress rehearsal for the march past to the death train. Consecutive prisoner numbers were called out until finally several lines of fifty people were assembled in the yard – each line of people the human cargo for a single goods truck. Ita Gronowski's former classmate Jacques Grauwels was one of those who took part in the rehearsal.

When the eighteen-year-old – number 1314 on the list – looked around his group, he saw 'many elderly people and only one boy of about the same age'. At the time Jacques saw even a forty-year-old as an old person. The two boys started talking to each other, and each discovered that the other planned to take the next opportunity by the scruff of the neck, and make himself scarce. Try as he might, Dr Grauwels can't remember the young man's name. But the boy had a 50-franc note, and promised Jacques he would share the money with him. In return, Jacques was to try to get hold of a tool so as to escape from the railway car. The same evening, Jacques stole a small hacksaw from one of the workshops.

Nervous excitement had broken out in the dormitories in anticipation of the journey. People were getting their belongings together, packing their cases and bags, and saying their last farewells. Simon's mother used the remaining hours to write her husband a letter of farewell. To deceive the censors, she called her husband Léontine. Her husband had escaped arrest because of a stay in hospital, and was now hiding in Brussels:

> For Léontine. Four weeks have passed: now I am setting off with our Simkele, and I don't know where fate will take us. But my heart is strong, full of hope and courage; believe me, darling, I am not exaggerating, as I write you my letter my heart is overflowing with hope, yes, the hope of seeing you again, you, my love, that gives me the strength to bear anything. I imagine a happy future for us. I cling to you as a drowning man clings to a straw. Levynke, be strong and brave, so that you can see your family again, eat well, don't deprive yourself, you've earned it. I would like to come back to you, beaming with joy, and we will see each other again, I believe that and it gives me courage. My love, I embrace you. I will love you until I die. Your Ania.

And I will protect Simkele as my dearest possession; you can be quite sure of that; above all, be careful. Don't go running about if you don't have to. Goodbye again, Lova, my darling, until the lovely, bright day when the sun rises for us Jews, and I am with you and with our children once again. I give you a big hug. Goodbye. Ania.

That letter was to be the last sign of life that Léon Gronowski would ever receive from his beloved wife.

25 19 April 1943

When Youra passed the newspaper kiosk on his way to work at the Pharmacobel laboratory, he usually glanced at the headlines. There was no point in buying a newspaper, because the Belgian press had been brought into line with Nazi policy. They merely disseminated the victory reports and fairy-tales that they were fed each day by Goebbels's Ministry of Propaganda.

But on that Monday morning, for a change, the young doctor did buy the early edition of *Le Soir*. The newspaper opened at a report from Belgium. A new contingent of Flemish volunteers had left Brussels on Sunday, amidst fanfares and the applause of an enthusiastic crowd. The young boys, all of them Nazi supporters, wanted to go to the Eastern Front and fight – 'to the final victory' – against 'Bolshevism and its Anglo-American allies': cannon fodder for Hitler's army. Despite the fine weather, the farewell celebration for the Flemish volunteers had been moved from the Grande Place to the Palais des Sports, the newspaper observed without further comment. Clearly the organizers had feared the displeasure of the citizens of Brussels, who might not have accepted such a public demonstration of National Socialist war-mongering.

Django Reinhardt and Paul Meurisse had given a concert on Sunday evening in the Palais des Beaux-Arts. Every now and again there were such musical rarities, at which the '*zazous*' would meet.

The cinemas, a cheap leisure activity at three francs a ticket, showed almost nothing but German films. The Acropole was showing *Sergeant Berry* with Hans Albers, and at the Ambassador one could see *Annelise* with Luise Ullrich. The newspaper *Le Soir* praised the anti-Soviet exhibition *Voici les Soviets* as a great hit; 100,000 people were already supposed to have seen the show at the Cinquantenaire.

That morning Youra Livchitz was most concerned with one particular heading, the weather report, whose curt prognosis – 'rain after fine sunny days' – would have far-reaching consequences for him and many others. Youra devoutly hoped that it would at least stay dry for the coming night. On that evening of 19 April 1943 he, along with Robert Maistriau and Jean Franklemon, was going to ambush the twentieth transport train to Auschwitz.

Youra's quest for fellow combatants had proved to be extremely difficult. Amongst almost all the friends and acquaintances he had asked, anxiety had finally outweighed their initial enthusiasm. Only his two schoolmates had declared themselves willing to join in. Jean Franklemon and Robert Maistriau, four years Youra's junior, had one thing in common for all their differences: from childhood they had been members of the scouts. Having grown up with the motto of performing a good deed every day, they already had the altruism required for the rescue mission. And like Youra they were unconcerned enough to commit themselves to this life-endangering enterprise. 'We were perhaps a bit naive,' Maistriau reflects, looking back on his participation in the ambush. 'After all, for Jean and myself it was the first operation in which we had taken part. It was a trial by fire.'

Youra secretly hoped that Richard Altenhoff would also participate in the mission. He had agreed to come to the meeting-place and bring a pistol from the 'Groupe G' arsenal. Perhaps he would jettison his qualms at the last minute.

Youra had given Robert Maistriau the task of getting hold of four pairs of pliers and a hurricane lamp. During his lunch-break, Robert found the tools required in a shop in the centre of Brussels, not far from the offices of the company Fonofer, where he worked. The

German trademark 'Feuerhand' he thought he remembered later, was engraved into the lamp. In a stationery shop Robert Kleister bought some red tissue paper, which he glued around the glass of the lamp. From a distance the light would look like a red railway signal.

That Monday Robert kept remembering what he had agreed to do with Youra and Jean two days before. They had met in a patisserie, where Jean and Youra, unimpressed by the seriousness of what they were about to embark upon, indulged their appetite for cakes. Robert had been too excited to eat a thing. Wasn't there anything they'd forgotten? Were they equipped for all eventualities? His enthusiasm for the mission was undimmed. Robert could hardly wait until the evening. They planned to meet with their bicycles in the Place Meiser at seven-thirty. Robert had told his mother he was going to spend the night at a friend's house. She was not to worry about him.

For Belgium's governor general, Alexander von Falkenhausen, it was a largely uneventful day. After a peaceful weekend in the green and wonderful idyll of Seneffe, the general was back on duty. It would appear that he was having some problems with his teeth, because he had two dental appointments, one in the morning and one in the afternoon. And the name Elisa appears three times in his diary for that day. At nine-fifteen he dropped Princess Ruspoli off at her flat on the way back from Seneffe, at twelve o'clock Elisa appeared in his office on the Place Royale, this time probably in her function as his adviser on public work. And at seven-thirty in the evening the attractive aristocrat accompanied her general to his favourite restaurant, Au Filet de Boeuf on the Rue des Harengs, a side-street leading off the Grande Place.

It was the day when Samuel Vanden Berg, a committee member on the Jewish Council, noted in his diary: 'So now I am fifty-three years old.' And it was the day of the Jewish rebellion against the annihilation of their people. On 19 April the revolt in the Warsaw Ghetto broke out. The last survivors of the ghetto took up arms to die in their battle against Hitler's uniformed murderers. On the same day, many miles to the west, another extraordinary act of rebellion against the Holocaust was to take place: the raid on a deportation train to Auschwitz.

26 The Twentieth Convoy to Auschwitz

For Kurt Asche, duty on that 19 April began earlier than usual. He was driven to Mechelen at seven-thirty in the morning. There, apart from brief interruptions in the officers' mess for coffee-breaks and lunch, he would spend the whole day overseeing the orderly boarding of the prisoners on to the train. After more than three months it was high time for the camp to be emptied and disinfected. The RSHA had already sent instructions for the next stage of the 'Final Solution'. The period of grace for the Jews with Belgian nationality had run out. They were shortly to be 'evacuated' as well.

Obersturmführer Asche was proud to have contributed, with all his powers, to the elimination of Belgium's Jewry. Many prisoners were setting off on a journey to Auschwitz extermination camp thanks to his good works. A good dozen spies and informers whom he could bribe or blackmail to ever higher levels of productivity, had sought out the Israelites in their hiding places. He himself had been ruthless in ensuring that no one was struck off the deportation list. The Judenreferent had simply ignored all interventions, even those from high Belgian government offices. His hard work was sure to be rewarded by the RSHA in Berlin. Kurt Asche was still hoping for a promotion.

The results of his hard work were clearly to be seen. According to the records of the camp authorities, 1,631 Jews, including 262 children, were waiting to be transported. The oldest deportee, Jacob Blom, number 584, was ninety years old. The youngest inmate, Suzanne Kaminski, number 215, was not even six weeks old. Her mother Josephine Schütz had been in the camp since the end of January, and it was there that she had given birth to her daughter; a life that would end in the gas ovens of Auschwitz.

Early in the morning the goods train had drawn up on the old railway tracks in front of the barracks. The trucks blocked the view of the sad spectacle from the people who lived on the other side of the road. No one was able to watch the people being driven into the trucks like a herd of cattle.

At eight o'clock the internees bearing numbers 1 to 100 had come into the courtyard. They included prisoners on the special list such as Samuel Perl, the young diamond-grinder from Antwerp, and Rudolf Schmitz, from Cologne, who had already 'hopped off' one transport train. This time they would have no chance of escape. Their truck was right behind the truck of the armed sentries.

The line moved haltingly out of the courtyard. At a table that had been set up under the sheltered entrance portal sat a uniformed SS man who compared the transport numbers on the cardboard signs of the internees with the numbers on the list in front of him. Meanwhile the consecutive numbers on the deportation list were called out. Soon it was the turn of Claire, her father and her husband Philippe. Their names on the list were ticked off by the man at the desk. No one noticed that Chaskel Prowizur, with his raging fever, was wearing someone else's transport number around his neck.

In his dark blue suit, and with his left hand in his trouser pocket, Obersturmführer Asche stood at the point where the line of prisoners turned out of the barracks gate and towards the railway carriages. SS guards and policemen formed a dense barrier around the sadly bent figures who drifted slowly towards the railway. Every now and again Asche recognized an 'old friend'. The emaciated figure bearing transport number 221 struck him as familiar. It was the Austrian Ernst Landau, who had been presented to him on one of his visits to Breendonk concentration camp by Commandant Philipp Schmitt as a particularly troublesome character. Landau had stirred up feelings against the SS.

Asche walked towards the journalist who, after many months in the hell of Breendonk, was now preparing to acquaint himself with the hell of Auschwitz, and spoke to him. Hunger and hard labour in the camp had turned the man into a wreck. He had spent the weeks in the waiting room for the Holocaust in a state of gloom. But Ernst Landau has never until this day forgotten the scornful words that the Obersturmführer spoke to him before he climbed aboard the deportation train. 'So far you've had it easy,' said the Judenreferent, 'and where you're headed now you're in for a very nasty surprise.' And after a short pause: 'That is, if any of you have time.'

Asche steadfastly tried to ignore the elderly gentleman with the number 522 on his cardboard sign. But the bank director Fritz Wallach from Berlin discovered the Judenreferent, who had quickly turned away. Wallach broke away from the line, made for Asche and raised himself to his full height, trembling with fury, in front of the Obersturmführer. The prisoner had nothing more to lose, the die was cast. He had paid Asche 25,000 marks in February upon his arrest, to ensure that he was struck from the list. The Judenreferent had taken the money and then not lifted a finger. 'You dishonourable wretch,' shouted the banker, 'you will get the punishment you deserve.' After that Fritz Wallach seemed to collapse, as though deflated. He silently rejoined the line.

The convoy was so long that the deportees could not see the beginning or the end of the train. With the help of a small step-ladder, the prisoners climbed the four feet or so into the trucks. Inside, straw was piled up. The fifty or even sixty inmates of a railway truck jostled into the tiny space. At first they simply stood there. Once the last passenger was on board, the heavy sliding door was pushed shut with a squeak, and with a loud metallic rattle the key was turned in the padlock. It was dark. A faint light fell through the barred hatch. The air quickly turned stale. In one corner stood a bucket, which all the prisoners were to use as a toilet. But how was it to be emptied? The train jolted a few yards forwards and then stopped so that the next truck could be filled.

'The fear of the people,' Régine Krochmal remembers, 'was almost physically tangible on that 19 April. We didn't know what to expect. Would things get better? Perhaps we really were going to a work camp. Or would things be even worse? The nurse planned to escape, and Simon Brauner, the partisan leader, had encouraged her in this idea. Of the other Resistance fighters who had been preparing their break-out for days and weeks, however, no one had spoken to her. When she passed the controller's desk, bearing number 263 around her neck, the SS man sent her to the medical car. There the sick and the bedridden lay pressed tightly together on the straw. A young doctor was supposed to be tending the patients with her. But how could she have helped them? There was no water, no food, no medicine, not even so much as a lamp.

Dr Bach, the director of the medical wing, appeared at the open sliding door of the railway truck and called Régine out. He was visibly nervous. From a distance it must have looked as though the doctor were giving the nurse some additional instructions. But in fact he was telling the young woman to flee the train. 'When you get to Auschwitz with the patients, you will all be gassed and burnt.' As inconspicuously as possible he slipped Régine a long knife, which she quickly hid in the inside pocket of her nurse's cloak. She was to use it to open the wooden bars over the hatch. For the first time Régine heard of the fate that the Nazis had prepared for them all. Although, as a member of the 'Austrian Freedom Front' she was better informed than most, she didn't want to believe the doctor. Certainly, the old and the sick would barely survive the harsh conditions in the labour camp, but it seemed 'unthinkable, unimaginable' that all of them, the young, the healthy, the women and children, would be murdered. Gassed and burnt – for her that was not the warning of a reality, but a metaphorical description of the shocking living conditions that awaited her at her destination.

The turn of Simon and his mother did not come until the afternoon. From the window of their dormitory they watched the line of people slowly disappearing through the barracks gate. Ita Gronowski stood at the window of the dormitory of the Belgian Jews looking out at them. The previous evening she had bidden a tearful farewell to her little brother and their mother. The young girl was staying behind in the transit camp because she had had Belgian nationality since the age of sixteen.

The numbers 1200 to 1250 were called out. Simon and his mother got ready, with their luggage beside them. They edged slowly forwards. They moved further and further away from Ita, who watched them with infinite sadness. 'We gave her encouraging signs, we waved her goodbye,' remembers Simon. 'Before I passed through the gate, I turned around once more. It was the last time I ever saw her.'

At some point towards evening, when the deportees had already disappeared into the trucks, all the young men were ordered to get out and stand in a row in front of the train. From the barracks entrance, a group of uniformed SS men and Gestapo agents in long coats approached, along with a boy in civilian clothes. His face was swollen, red and blue, and one eye was bloodshot. It was nineteen-year-old Resistance fighter Henry Dobrzynski, a member of the partisan army. His escorts from SS headquarters in Brussels studied the reaction of the lined-up camp inmates and the face of their own prisoner, as they passed the dense crowd. The Gestapo hoped the confrontation might bring other partisans to light. But the faces of those who knew Dobrzynski – including Abraham Bloder, number 1380, Jacques Cyngiser, number 1366 and Léon Kutnowski, number 383 – remained impassive. Only Henri Silbersztejn, number 338, had failed to work out what was going on. When Dobrzynski was led past him, he made as though to greet him. The partisan had noticed his comrade's spontaneous movement. He raised his arm, as though unintentionally, to show his handcuffs. Now Silbersztejn understood, and stiffened. He had almost given himself away.

Only after the war did Silbersztejn learn what had happened. Dobrzynski had been arrested on 14 April during an attempted assassination. The SS thugs on Avenue Louise tortured him day and night to find out the names of his fellows. But the young boy, who had been involved in thirteen bomb attacks and several attempted assassinations of collaborators, did not betray anyone. He doggedly explained:

'They're all in Mechelen.' So, shortly before the departure of the deportation train, they had brought him to the transit camp to confront him with his comrades. The confrontation gave the SS no clues of any kind. Three months later Dobrzynski, the son of Polish immigrants, was shot by the Germans in Breendonk concentration camp.

Among the last to board the convoy were the Dutch doctor Louis Micheels and his fiancée Nora. Micheels – number 33 on the list – was assigned as escort to a medical car with about twenty severely ill women and their children. One of the sick women lay motionless, groaning on the straw-covered floor. She would not last the night. Some women cowered against the board wall with their little children, their big, fearful eyes fixed optimistically on Louis and Nora. The two young people could only watch the torments of the inmates. Louis says, 'there was nothing I could do in my role as doctor. I had a few medical textbooks and a stethoscope with me, but no medicine. I did not know how I could possibly give medical care.'

27 The Raid

Youra was at Place Meiser with his bicycle at a quarter past seven. He was waiting for Richard Altenhoff. Even up until the last moment he didn't want to give up hope that this cautious yet courageous activist from 'Groupe G' would be part of their team. He had not yet been able even to say goodbye to his brother Alexandre, who had so much wanted to take part in the action. It was too risky, because Choura was lying under a false name in the Edith Cavell Hospital, where the bullet had at last been removed from his leg.

And finally, just before half past seven, Richard appeared around the corner. Even before the engineer had said a word, Youra knew that he could not rely on him. He could see it in his eyes. But Altenhoff had brought him a small-calibre pistol, just in case. It wasn't much, but it was better than nothing at all. The young medic quickly slipped the revolver and the cartridges into his pocket.

Jean Franklemon and Robert Maistriau arrived on their bicycles at the same time. Robert's cycling bag was crammed full. He had stowed a hurricane lamp and pliers in it. Youra and Richard nodded brief greetings to them, and then continued with their quiet, intense conversation. All of a sudden Altenhoff took his leave. Robert watched him shaking hands with Youra for a long time. Then Richard jumped on to his bicycle and called '*bonne chance*' to the others. So three school-friends would be carrying out the action that organized

Resistance considered too dangerous: stopping the train to Auschwitz in the Flemish provinces. And they were, as Maistriau acknowledged in retrospect, 'badly equipped and badly prepared'. We do not know why Richard Altenhoff decided not to take part in the ambush. And we can only guess at the combination of fear and heroism, of scruples and the urge to act that Jean and Youra were feeling. Robert Maistriau, the only living witness of this stirring mission, describes his state of mind: 'It was a mixture of adventurousness, a desire to help and a wish to harm the Germans. At that moment no one could have held me back. We fully believed in what we were doing.'

Youra had already travelled this stretch of track over the previous week. The boys would have covered much of the twenty-five kilometres before darkness fell. And he had also reconnoitred the place where they would stop the convoy. His brother had found the spot on the map: it would have to be as close to Brussels as possible, so that they could reach it easily by bicycle. It could not be far from a public means of transport, so that anyone who escaped had the chance of getting back to Brussels, Antwerp or Charleroi, where they could seek shelter with friends or relations. It had to be on a bend in the track, so that the train would be travelling at reduced speed. And it had to be in an uninhabited area, so that the prisoners could disappear into a nearby forest or into the bushes.

The area just after Boortmeerbeek fitted the bill. There was a forest there, and the tram for Brussels set off at regular intervals from the station in Haacht, only a few miles away. Taking a closer look around, Youra then discovered the ideal place for the attack: just past a bend in the track, a mile and a half after the station of Boortmeerbeek.

The three young men must have reached the spot by about ten o'clock in the evening. That was the time of the departure of the train in Mechelen. Hertz Jospa had received this information from someone he trusted on the Jewish Council. So far all deportation trains had travelled according to this fixed timetable. The Germans thought it important for the transports to travel at night, so that they could cross Belgium unnoticed.

There had been some rain showers during the day. But now the clouds parted every now and again. The moon was full. The wind drove the clouds scudding across the sky, and made things hard for the three cyclists. They had to pedal furiously. From broad Avenue Léopold, which led to Melsbrock airport, they turned left into the Chaussée de Haacht. They were soon out in the countryside. A few more miles and they had crossed the cultural and linguistic border into Flanders. Brick houses alternated with fields, vegetable gardens and smallholdings. Poplar trees lined the cobbled country road, which stretched in a straight line via Diegem, past Steenokkerzeel to Kampenhout and finally to Haacht. Jean Franklemon, the son of a teacher from Flanders and a fluent Flemish-speaker, told his friends that it was no coincidence that the province was called '*het platte land*'. The region really was as flat as a pancake.

It grew dark. The dynamos of the bicycle lights whirred, and the faint beam from their headlights danced in front of them on the cobbles. Because of the war a blackout was imposed. Only a few days previously, an area of Antwerp had been seriously damaged by an Allied raid. The streetlights were switched off, and only a little light peeped out from between the narrow cracks of the closed curtains. But when the clouds parted, it was almost as bright as day.

As they cycled along the forest path between Haacht and Boortmeerbeek, parallel to the railway tracks, they heard a train coming from Mechelen. In horror they leapt off their bicycles. The puffing train came level with them, emitted a few whistles and fell back again. It was only pulling the tender. False alarm. Relieved, they cycled to the place that Youra had chosen. They hid their bicycles in the embankment. Here, when the coast was clear, or about an hour after the action, they would meet up again.

Youra pressed into their hands the 50-franc notes that were to be distributed to the refugees. It had been agreed that he would post himself at the front of the train, to keep the German guards in check with his gun. They assumed that the German armed guards were in a passenger carriage just behind the tender. Meanwhile Robert and Jean were to attempt to open the truck doors at two different places on the train with their pliers.

By the time they parted it was a quarter past ten. Youra set off in the direction of the expected train, while Robert and Jean ran off in the opposite direction. At the point where the train would emerge from its bend on to a straight stretch of track, Maistriau set up the hurricane lamp in the middle of the track. When they had lit it, it really did look like a red signal. Jean went a little further towards the train. By their estimate it would be more than six hundred feet long. They had agreed that 'Pamplemousse' would operate at the end of the transport. Youra had heard that on all previous transports from Mechelen there was only one armed sentry at the head of the train. Towards the rear of the long convoy the risk of being surprised by the Germans in their mission would therefore be smaller. The three hid and waited for the train, each in his place in the bushes. 'It was a bit like the feeling that I knew from my adventures with the scouts,' Maistriau remembers, 'but at the same time I was aware that this wasn't a game, but a matter of life and death.'

Train 801 had left Dossin barracks at precisely ten o'clock. A steam locomotive pulled the thirty trucks. It was travelling at about thirty miles an hour, and on crossings the speed fell to about six miles an hour.

Jacques Grauwels and his companion had used the long waiting time in Mechelen to saw through the bars in one of the four hatches with their little hacksaws until they could simply be broken by hand. They had chosen the hatch to the rear on the right-hand side of the truck so that, when they jumped, they would land not on the hard gravel of the parallel track, but in the embankment. The other prisoners watched the two men working away with a mixture of fear and displeasure. After all, it had been instilled into them that every single one of them was to reach their destination. If any deportees were missing, their fellow passengers would pay for it in blood. They would be shot on arrival.

But the two boys would not be deterred from their plan. The train had just set off from Mechelen when the first of them climbed up to the hatch and twisted himself into the narrow opening so that he could slide out backwards. Clinging to the frame, he dangled his feet around the corner of the truck until they finally found purchase on the buffer. When the train had passed at a walking pace through the little station of Muizen, they jumped out in quick succession. Jacques fell on to a grass-covered slope. The dark trucks thundered past him. At regular intervals a floodlight mounted on the roof of a railway carriage would flash to life and run its beam along the train. Jacques saw uniformed men sitting at the end of the convoy.

His mate had also landed relatively softly, safe and sound and not far from him. They laughed with relief. But their joy only lasted a moment. They had to get to safety. 'We ran, ran, ran…', remembers Jacques.

A few moments later another figure leapt out of the shadow of the moving train. Régine Krochmal had taken to heart the warning of the Jewish Dr Bach, that they would all perish in Auschwitz. She also tried to persuade the young doctor who had been assigned as a medical escort to the so-called medical car to do the same. With no medicine, how were they to help the patients who lay there on the piled-up straw? She had no way of treating the sick people and making their journey any easier. 'I explained to him that I was a member of the Resistance, and that I wanted to get back to my group to continue our work.' But the doctor was deaf to her arguments. As a physician it was his duty to stand by his patients. 'He argued,' eighty-year-old Régine marvelled, 'as though we were entirely at peace.' Only with difficulty did Régine manage to keep him from preventing their escape preparations.

She was lucky. The little openings of the medical car were only nailed shut with pine slats. It had probably been assumed that the inmates of this truck were too feeble to risk escape. Shortly after the train set off, Régine, who was just 5ft 3in, clambered on to a suitcase and cut the struts over the hatch with her big knife. Then she heaved herself up to the opening. For such a nimble little person it was easy to slip out of the hatch feet first. For a moment she crouched like a half-open penknife, her head and torso bent forwards, in the window opening. She clutched the upper edge of the hatch with her fingers. When the train slowed down, she pressed her feet against the outside wall of the truck, loosened her grip and fell forwards.

She landed on the embankment at the edge of the track. 'At that moment it was as bright as day,' she remembers. 'The moon had emerged from behind the clouds.' She had survived her fall unharmed. She lay there motionless, pressing herself against the ground as though she wished to be one with it. 'I tried to make myself invisible.' The trucks clattered past. After a few moments she heard the train suddenly stopping. A little while later shots rang out. Only years later did she discover what was going on: 'It was our transport being attacked.'

Robert Maistriau had heard the whistles of the locomotive in the distance. The sounds carried a long way in the silence of the night. Hidden behind a tree, he uttered a few prayers to heaven: with any luck everything was all right. Before the train rounded the corner, he saw the clouds of steam and heard the heavy pounding of the engine. Seconds later the train thundered towards the hurricane lamp. As the lamp on the track was at the end of the curve, the train driver clearly saw the red signal only at the last minute. Although he immediately throttled back the engine, the first few trucks rolled over the lamp. Robert held his breath. Finally the train came to a standstill. The brakes, he remembered many years later, 'made a hellish noise. At first I was petrified. But then I gave myself a jolt on the basis that if you've started something you should go through with it.'

Robert dashed to the nearest railway truck. 'I held my torch in my left hand, and with my right I had to busy myself with the pliers. I was very excited, and it took far too long until I had cut through the wire that secured the bolts of the sliding door.'

Finally Robert was able to push open the heavy door of the cattle truck. He pointed his torch into the truck. Pale, frightened faces stared out at him. '*Sortez, sortez!*' he shouted, and then, in an unmistakably French accent, ordered the hesitating prisoners in German, '*Schnell, schnell, flehen Sie!*' Youra had taught him that sentence because he assumed that many of the deportees, who came from Eastern and Central Europe, were more likely to understand German than French. There was a lot of pushing and shoving in the truck. Some of the prisoners tried to keep their companions from complying with his orders. 'It's forbidden. The Germans will shoot us all as a punishment.'

For a moment thirty-year-old Hena Wasyng didn't understand what was going on. Years later the deportee registered as number 736 described the dramatic rescue mission and the hours leading up to it, which she and her fellows had spent perched in the cattle truck:

> It was Pessach. We wept and thought of the Jewish festival, and above all of our hidden children, whom we had to leave in Belgium. One young man stood close by the hatch and stared out into the distance. He was probably dreaming of escape. Suddenly the train stopped. We didn't know what had happened, or where we were. There was shouting, pushing and shoving in the truck. The boy by the window suddenly shouts, 'Over here, over here.' A young man from the Resistance opens the door and gives money to the people at the front, and orders us: 'Get out, save yourselves!' I was frightened, and didn't dare to jump, but then I realised that my two sons would be alone for ever if I didn't have the courage now. So I jumped.

The thought of their daughter Abela also helped Mendelis and Henda Goldsteinas get over their fear. They wanted to see her again. So Abela's parents didn't waste a moment when the young man yelled, '*Sortez!*' Unlike most of the prisoners, who were petrified with fear, the Goldsteinas weren't intimidated by the shouts of the '*chef de wagon*', the man whose role it was to ensure order during the journey in their truck, and who tried to prevent their escape.

'We jumped,' Henda Goldsteinas related thirty-three years later in a newspaper interview, 'in spite of the fact that the first shots were already ringing out.' But their truck was in the middle of the train and thus, for the time being at least, far from the SS and the police who were posted in the railway carriages at the front and the rear of the transport. The German policemen were completely thrown by the attack. At first they held back because they believed they were dealing with a well-organized and reckless group of armed partisans. That was exactly the impression that Youra had wanted to create in the Germans by firing a few bullets from his hiding place. At first the German guards shot randomly, taking cover behind the train, and only after that did they comb the immediate surroundings.

Along with other refugees, the Goldsteinas and Hena Wasyng ran the few feet across the strip of grass to the little wood, where they waited excitedly for the young man who had led them out of the convoy. Others, who had jumped out of the train as well, immediately disappeared into the undergrowth so as to give their pursuers no chance. Suddenly Wendelis Goldsteinas noticed that his wife wasn't wearing her white scarf. She had lost it on the short journey from the truck to the wood. It had caught on the branches of a bush, and now gleamed white in the moonlight. Without thinking, the chemical engineer ran back to retrieve the precious object.

Robert tried to open the lock of the next truck along. He had put his torch in his trouser pocket so that he had both hands free to busy himself with the pliers. But he hadn't time, the gunfire was getting closer and closer.

In the meantime the Germans had understood that they were not facing superior forces. The other side hadn't returned their random fire. For Robert the situation was a dicey one. In the bright moonlight he presented an easy target. With his head held low he ran to the wood where the little crowd of rescued people were waiting. He called to them to throw themselves on the ground. They stayed there. 'I can't remember how much time passed. Was it ten or twenty minutes?'

At some point silence fell. Then the train drove on. None of the guards had patrolled the vehicle to check the trucks. The Germans were probably afraid of sniper fire. When he saw the red tail-lights of the convoy, Robert rose to his feet. His protégés, about seven in number, followed him, and gathered around him. He gave each of them a 50-franc note and advised them to scatter and hide. In Haacht they would be able to take the tram to Brussels early in the morning. 'One woman,' he remembers, 'hugged me effusively and said she didn't know how to thank me. Another asked my name and address so that she could give me a present when the war was over. That struck me as rather naive.' The first lesson you learned in the Resistance was that names and addresses were taboo.

Shortly afterwards the wood swallowed up the refugees. Robert returned to the hidden bicycles. And shortly afterwards Jean turned up. 'Pamplemousse' was glad to have got away with his life. At the rear of the train, where he had taken up his position, it had been far more dangerous than they had expected, because this time there was another group of police at the very end of the convoy.

When the train stopped, Franklemon had stalked up to the trucks at the back. The bolt of the heavy sliding door, he saw, was additionally secured with wire. He pulled out his pliers and started cutting through the wire. He was about to open the bolt when he suddenly heard the words, 'Hände hoch'. About thirty metres away, round about where the engine was, stood a uniformed man. He was aiming his rifle straight at him. Jean ran sideways into the bushes. The German came after him. Many years later Franklemon was to tell his daughter how in that life-threatening situation he suddenly remembered an episode he remembered from a comic. The idea might even have saved his life. Like the hero in the comic, Jean started running in a zigzag so that his pursuer wouldn't be able to aim at him. But his adversary was quick and seemed to be in good shape. When Jean looked around he saw the German with the rifle in his hand close behind him. The policeman raised his gun and tried to strike Jean on the head with it, but Jean parried the blow with his left fist. The fear of death gave him strength he had never dreamed of, and his opponent stumbled and fell.

Franklemon charged on. For a long time he thought he could hear his hunter's footsteps. But when he finally stopped to catch his breath, he was on his own. He could hear the loud thumping of his heart, the roaring in his ears that he had mistaken for the policeman's footsteps. He hid in a ditch and waited. Only now did he feel the sharp pain in the hand with which he had defended himself against the rifle-butt. In the distance he heard gunfire and the loud shouting of the guards. About a quarter of an hour later he was relieved to hear the train finally setting off again.

But where was Youra? Robert and Jean had lost sight of him. They didn't dare call out to him. They would only give themselves away. Police might have got out to search the surroundings for refugees. They waited another half-hour and then set off towards home. Youra's bicycle was still in the embankment. Travelling along paths through fields and side roads, they arrived in Brussels at about two o'clock in the morning.

Somewhere around the Avenue de Tervuren they rang at a house door. A drowsy young woman opened the door and let the two exhausted heroes in without wasting too many words. She was a member of Jean's circle of theatrical devotees. While Jean and Robert talked about their happily survived adventure, their host served coffee and made them a bed on the sofa in the living room. What Robert Maistriau is still unable to forget, even today, is the taste of that reviving drink, which they sipped out of thick cups. 'Never again have I drunk such good coffee.'

They were worried about Youra. Had he been injured? Or had he fled on foot because the Germans were after him? It was almost four o'clock in the morning when Jean and Robert fell into a troubled sleep.

At the same time Youra had covered most of the return journey to Brussels. It was hard going. Whenever he saw the headlights of a car in the distance he escaped into the ditch lest he be seen. When he reached Steenokkerzeel, a military truck coming from Brussels roared past him. The Germans had probably called for reinforcements, to search for escapees from the deportation train. Youra had no idea how many had been able to escape from the convoy.

Hidden in a bush, he had fired several shots from his pistol when the train had stopped. As he came level with the lit passenger compartment, where the armed sentries sat, he was able to observe the uniformed men stiffening with fear. Only after a few minutes did it occur to them to put out the light in the compartment And more minutes passed before the first sentries dared to leave their car. Youra fired twice more. But that was probably a mistake. Two guards came towards him, pistols raised. By now the moonlight was so bright that he was able to make out the pale faces of the Germans.

He broke backwards out of the thick bushes and dashed into the forest. The two policemen came after him. One of them was so fast that he stayed hot on Youra's heels, while the other one fell far behind. Youra was running for his life. Now he had only one chance: he had to fire at his pursuer. The young physician had never taken aim at a human being, and he was a completely inexperienced marksman. But there was no other solution: he stopped behind a thick tree-trunk, raised his gun, aimed at his pursuer and fired twice. The man stopped and moved carefully back, taking cover behind bushes and trees. The policeman probably found the night-time duel just as strange as his inexperienced adversary.

Youra held out for a while. Some distance away he heard loud shouting. The two Germans were clearly looking for him. Then the voices faded away. He heard shots coming from the direction of the train. Getting back to his bicycle struck him as too risky. He would have to get home on foot. Only at dawn did Youra reach Brussels, thoroughly exhausted. It was about six o'clock in the morning when he rang at the doorbell of a friend who lived near the Place Meiser. All Youra wanted to do was sleep.

Seventeen deportees, according to the Belgian historian Maxime Steinberg in his book *La Traque des Juifs*, escaped that night from the compartment opened by Maistriau. Seventeen people, barely any of whom had thought of escaping from the convoy, were saved from certain death in Auschwitz by the three schoolmates. And possibly even more found their way out of the convoy thanks to the foolhardy amateurs. After all, Robert had started work on another lock. And Jean Franklemon had practically unbolted the sliding door of his truck before fleeing from the armed policemen. Perhaps thanks to this preparation the inmates of these two trucks were able to free themselves with their own tools.

One would have had to be young, fearless and filled with sympathy for the plight of the Jews to take part in this life-endangering adventure. An act of heroism in the face of all reason.

28 The Breakout of the Silent Rebels

In the medical truck at the very rear of the train, the young Dutch doctor Louis Micheels and Nora van Esso sat huddled together in a corner. They heard the moaning and groaning of the sick women, and the quiet whimpering of the children, whom they were unable to help. 'We were surrounded by nameless death,' the American psychiatric professor Micheels remembers, decades after this wretched scene in the gloomy railway carriage. Thoughts of escape ran through his head. 'We did not know our companions, had never seen them before... Perhaps the wooden bars across the windows could be yanked off. But SS guards were all around us... What if I got out and Nora did not?... The best we could do was to save our strength and sleep as much as we could.'

Suddenly the train stopped. Louis gave a start. He thought he had been asleep for hours. Presumably they had passed the border long ago, and were already in Germany. Could it be the partisan attack that had been rumoured in Mechelen? Light fell through the hatch, and Micheels heard gunfire. When he looked out through the opening he saw people running some distance away. It was impossible to tell whether they were hunters or their prey. Louis tried to yank the wooden bars out of the window, but he was too weak. So their fate was sealed. Nora and Louis would not leave the truck until Auschwitz.

The Viennese Ernst Landau, number 221, was dozing in a carriage towards the front of the train. His long stay in the hell that was Breendonk had left the twenty-six-year-old so enfeebled and emaciated that he barely knew what was going on. 'I was a *Muselmann*,' the journalist, who miraculously survived Auschwitz, said in an interview. '*Muselmann*' was the term used in the concentration camps for the gaunt, bent figures who had completely given up on their lives.

Extremely tense, Willy Berler was waiting in another carriage for the chance to make his getaway. He didn't know any of the prisoners. Although he had been one of the last to arrive in Mechelen, on the prisoner transport from Liège, he was given transport number 1058. Among his companions in the carriage he noticed two who were about the same age as himself. One of them was called Friedel. 'They were the only ones with a vague idea of what awaited us in Auschwitz,' remembers Berler, now a retired Brussels businessman. The group of potential escapees had quickly reached an agreement. Together they managed to break out the bars of the air-hatch. Now they only needed to wait for a good opportunity to jump out of the truck. All of a sudden the train stopped. Shots rang out: 'At the time I had no idea what was happening out there. Only later did I learn that this was the attack on our transport.'

When the convoy set off again, the prisoners in the truck who had decided to escape agreed on the sequence in which they would jump. Six of the fifty-or-so prisoners wanted to break out. Willy Berler was to be the last of these. In the endless months that followed he would run through those minutes in his mind's eye, time and again.

> At the peak of the excitement I watch the boy just ahead of me vanishing through the opening. I quickly haul myself up to the hatch and lean my torso out to drop into the void, when something terrible catches my eye: the unfortunate fellow ahead of me got his jump wrong and got stuck on the train. His head split open like a watermelon. It's the first time I've ever seen a dead body... I feel dizzy, I'm sure I'm going to jump into thin air. I don't jump. I pull back, roll back into the truck and decide to keep on with the journey, the long

journey. After all, I tell myself, we're going to a labour camp; and I'm young and strong. If only I'd known! A hundredth, a thousandth of the truth about Auschwitz would have been enough to make me jump.

In 1964 the businessman Joseph Silber – transport number 848 – prepared a personal account as an eyewitness of 'this Jewish revolt against deportation', which is to be found in the files of Kurt Asche's trial. In his suitcase, Silber had smuggled along every possible tool that seemed to him to be useful for the breakout. He had a little hacksaw, an iron bar, a big hook, a wooden handle and stones that were to substitute for a hammer. Hardly had the sliding door been locked in Mechelen when the businessman started sawing an opening in the side wall. Not all the prisoners agreed with that. The '*chef de wagon*' tried to stop him. Without even thinking, Silber, a powerful man in his mid-thirties, knocked him to the floor. After that the man with the armband didn't dare go near him. Silber tried to enlarge the opening, but to no avail. Then he decided to transfer his attention to the hatch. He removed the bars and pulled himself up. Using the wooden handle, to which he had attached the iron hook, he tried to open the bolts on the side door through the hatch. Not a chance. Bent double, he crouched in the low hatch. He could hear rifle-fire. And he saw people jumping, one after another, out of the other trucks. As the train slowed down, he jumped out as well. He landed in the bushes. Once again he heard shotgun salvos. When the train had disappeared, he stood up.

'The ones who jumped out on the left-hand side,' Silber remembered twenty-one years after the event, 'paid harshly for their mistake.' He dragged away a wounded man lying on the neighbouring track. He helped a man from Antwerp, who had been injured in the fall, back on his feet. Together the two of them set off for the nearest village, where they would find help.

Beyond Leuven, around about Boutersem, it was time for the group of partisans and Resistance fighters who were concentrated in a single car to make their getaway. Their '*chef de wagon*', Jacques Cyngiser (1366), was among the initiators of the breakout, which included, among others, Symcha Weberman (1379), Icek Wolman (1369), Abraham Fischel (1360), Abraham Bloder (1380) and Nathan Mitelsbach (1362). They had drilled a hole in the sidewall. With his arm, one of them reached the lock on the sliding door to open it. While the Germans were firing on the escapees from the window of the sentry-carriage to the rear of the train, they jumped out of the truck one after the other. The militant members of the Resistance were not intimidated by the gunfire. Only after the end of the war would they learn how many had been wounded or even killed.

At eleven o'clock in the evening the railwayman Albert Dumon turned up punctually for work on the platform at Tienen. He was waiting for train number 801 from Mechelen. Dumon was to replace the train driver and take the transport on to Tongeren. He knew what freight was being transported in the cattle trucks. And he was not indifferent to his knowledge. His family had taken in a little Jewish boy. Albert Dumon was no militant Resistance member, he was simply one of those fine Belgians who helped the Jews because he was furious about the ruthless manhunt that the occupying forces were carrying out. Terrible stories were told about the fate of the deportees. The train driver would do everything within his power to make it easier for them to flee from the train.

The convoy was unusually late. The familiar whistle of the locomotive wasn't heard until about eleven-thirty. As the train approached, Dumon heard gunfire. Something dramatic had happened. This clearly wasn't a normal delay.

Dumon, the only railwayman later questioned about the twentieth convoy, took on the engine from his colleague in Tienen, tested the brakes and then drove the train on towards the East. They throttled the engine down as often as possible, and passed the crossings at a walking pace of only two or three miles an hour: 'It was clear that many Israelites were trying to escape the trucks. But to their bad luck there was a full moon, which meant the Germans were able to fire on the escaping people.'

The SS had placed all the particularly dangerous subjects in the truck at the very head of the convoy – all those who had already escaped in the past. The truck was specially secured, with barbed wire over the sliding door and metal plates over the window hatches. They were eighteen men and one woman, Samuel Perl remembers, all fully resolved to risk their leap into freedom. Led by a man from Vienna, they combined their forces to address a side wall. Shortly before St Truiden they had done it: a big rectangle had been sawn out. Then they established the sequence in which they were going to jump. The comrade who was to leap out ahead of Samuel Perl was hesitant: 'You go first,' he suggested. The Antwerp diamond-grinder wasted no time and hurled himself out. He landed safely on the ground. As he lay there he heard shots.

Only after liberation would Perl learn that this man, Benjamin Zweig, who had allowed him to jump first, was found by villagers, riddled with bullets, and died three days later in hospital.

Rudolf Schmitz, number 4 on the special list, took the shots as a warning. He decided against escaping from the truck. 'I said to myself, I've got plenty of time to risk my life.' He travelled on to Auschwitz and survived.

Nestling up against his mother, little Simon had gone to sleep. He had heard something of the attack on the train, the sudden stop, the shouting and the gunshots. Before his eyes closed, he saw a few men working busily away at the door of the truck.

How long had he slept? Simon woke up in his mother's arms. A cool breeze swept through the open truck door, and that was probably what had woken him. A cluster of people stood by the opening. Simon, who had practised jumping from his bunk in the transit camp, saw them jumping out in turn, and thought to himself: 'It's the right-hand side that faces the embankment, the right-hand side where you don't fall on the neighbouring track.'

Then Chana Gronowski took her son by the hand and went to stand with him by the door. The sixty-seven-year-old lawyer's eyes still fill with tears as he remembers that fateful moment:

She walked me to the door as though leading me to freedom and to life. She fulfilled the promise that she had made to my father in a letter: 'I will look after him as my dearest possession, you can be sure of that.' I had to wait till it was my turn. My mother told me to lie with my belly on the floor and try to find purchase with my feet. The footplate is about seventy centimetres below the door frame. But my feet are dangling in the air. My legs are too short to reach the step. With my left hand I cling to an iron handle, and with my right the bottom rim of the door. My mother holds me by the shoulder and the jacket, and lets me slowly slide down. Finally my feet touch the footplate, and I find my balance, standing on the step. '*Geyt tsu schnel der tsug* – the train's going too fast,' said my mother in Yiddish. They were to be the last words I heard her say. When the train slowed down, I told her, 'I'm jumping now!' Without falling over, I land four square on the gravel. At first I stand there without moving, and clearly see the train passing me on my right, a great black mass, spitting white steam into the night sky and whistling shrilly.

Simon stood there and waited for his mother to come after him. But the train stopped again. Simon saw men in uniform running along the train. If Chana Gronowski had risked jumping at that point, she would have fallen into the hands of the Germans. Simon stood there transfixed. Instinctively, the eleven-year-old wanted to go back where he had come from, back into the truck, back to his mother. But then he would have run straight into the arms of the police. Following a sudden inspiration, he turned around and ran away. He ran into the forest and left the death-train behind. Simon, the little scout, ran evenly and surely through bushes and forests, over meadows and fields as he had when playing with the scouts. A tune defined the rhythm of his footsteps and drowned out his fear: Glenn Miller's 'In the Mood', one of his sister Ita's favourite songs.

In the truck where Claire Prowizur, her husband Philippe and her seriously ill father were sitting, the people who planned to escape first had to put their '*chef de wagon*' out of action. The man the SS had put in charge was the heavily-built man from Amsterdam, in his mid-forties. From the very first, the tall, sandy-haired Dutch Jew and his son had been among the initiators of the escape. The father had repeatedly stressed that he would jump first to encourage the others. But now he would hear nothing of it. He was wearing a yellow armband, and had to ensure that everyone turned up safe and sound at their destination. When someone started sawing away at the bars of the hatch, the Dutchman ripped the tool from his hand. He wouldn't let anyone escape from the train. He was in charge, and they had to obey him. The man, who had always seemed tranquil and solid as a rock, flew into a rage. He was clearly going mad. He lashed out at anyone who came near him. Finally several prisoners managed to overwhelm the muscular man. His son tied him in a blanket as though in a straitjacket, so that he couldn't stop the others from escaping. The young man abandoned his planned escape to accompany his father to Auschwitz.

Claire was only dimly aware of the fight in the truck, the stopping of the train shortly before Haacht and the gunfire outside. All her attention was focused on her father, who was suffering from a serious fever. Would he be able to escape in such a state? Hard to imagine. He lay there feebly on the straw, and could no longer be spoken to. He wasn't capable of taking a step. Years later, she described those crucial moments before the escape in her autobiography.

'I'm not going to jump out of the train,' she told Philippe, 'I can't just abandon my father.' Her husband was shaken. He talked to her gently: 'Clairette, what good will it do anyone if you sacrifice yourself? Come and look the facts in the eye. Your father is in a coma. Once we get to Auschwitz, and you know this, you'll be separated. They'll take you to one side and him to another.'

The train rolled through the moonlit night, and each beat brought them closer to the German border. On German soil they would have no chance of escaping the Nazis. Who could they turn to in that hostile country? Who would help them there?

Philippe's entreaties became more pressing: 'You're going to your death with your eyes wide open. Your father isn't even reacting now.

Our life together has just begun. We've been married for a year.'

'I'll come back from Auschwitz, Philippe,' Claire promised.

'Maybe you'll manage to get back, Clairette, but it's sure to be without your father. Try to see reason, Clairette. I'm begging you, because I love you. I want you alive.'

That was the key sentence. She would not stay with her dying father, she would flee.

'And I love you, Philippe. I will jump from the train. I want to spend my whole life with you. I want to live.'

She bent down to her father and bade him farewell. He didn't seem to be aware of her.

Only twenty years later did Claire discover that her father had approved of his daughter's escape. In Tel Aviv, on the main shopping street, Dizengoff, she met a woman from her truck who had survived Auschwitz. She had been at Chaskel Prowizur's side when he died. Shortly before Auschwitz her father had awoken once again from his dazed state, and asked for 'Klärchen'. When the dying man heard that his daughter and her husband had jumped from the train on Belgian soil, he seemed to take comfort, and asked her to look for his daughter afterwards, and tell her that he was happy she had escaped. Claire should live in peace.

Claire and Philippe left their bag behind. It would only hinder their escape. And the two 50-franc notes that Albert Clément had given them in the camp were still in the bundle. But there was no time now to look for the money. They had to get a move on. The border was getting closer and closer. Philippe was afraid that Claire might change her mind again.

He lifted his wife up to the hatch so that she could perch on the little ledge with her legs outside, and her upper body inside the truck. Then Claire turned in the opening, held on tight to the edge, and slowly let herself down the outside wall. About half a metre to the right of the hatch was the end of the truck. She dangled her feet around the corner until they found the buffer between the railway carriages. She let herself down there, clung on to the vertical board and waited:

Did I have some special factor that protected me against danger? Was my brow so radiant that it put danger in the shade? I know I felt astonishingly certain, crouching there between the two trucks. The tracks slid past underneath me, flashing before my eyes, which were looking for a dip in the landscape that might catch me when I jumped. It was a strange feeling, being alone and free, responsible for each coming second. I had only one problem: choosing my moment. Beneath a glittering, starry sky, a cold, bright moon, I hurled myself into the void, both arms over my ears, my hands behind my head to protect it.

Claire survived the jump unscathed. Lying on the ground, she saw an endlessly long train thundering past her. A floodlight lit the front of the train. And she saw someone jumping out of a carriage, heard shots ringing out. Had the bullets hit Philippe? When the rear lights of the convoy were nothing but little red dots, Claire ran to where she had seen the man escaping. She called out and ran. Someone came towards her. It was Philippe, who had jumped shortly after she had. 'We fall into each other's arms. We laugh and cry. How happy we are, oh God, we're so happy.' After a few steps they bumped into a lifeless body. Someone who had tried to escape, drenched in blood, riddled with bullets from the German machine-guns.

Philippe had already hatched a plan. They would walk until they reached a village with a church. They would then ask the priest for help. It was rumoured among the Jews in Belgium that the clergy sympathized with their cause.

29 We are Good Belgians

At Haacht station the commuters were waiting for the first tram to Brussels. They were manual labourers and office workers whose shifts began at seven o'clock. On that Tuesday morning, several people who were clearly strangers to the area, were among those waiting. An exhausted-looking couple of about forty stood close together as though supporting one another. The woman wore a white scarf over her winter coat. Hinda and Mendelis Goldsteinas had spent the night in a little wood, and now hoped to make it home safe and sound to Brussels. Hena Wasyng was standing at the same tram stop. After the young Resistance fighter had told her to make her way back on her own, she had run into the forest. She had rested in a barn for a few hours, before going in search of a tram stop. At a crossing, the station-master had spoken to the woman who was wandering about on her own. He knew that the train had been stopped by the Resistance. 'Don't worry,' he assured her, 'I won't give you away.' He pointed towards Haacht station.

Hena Wasyng described that unforgettable scene years later:

> A number of us met up at the little station. I recognized some people from the convoy, but everyone immediately looked in the other direction. We didn't dare look at one another, let alone speak to each other. The young man who had been

standing so longingly by the hatch in our truck was also waiting for the tram. He was wearing a different jacket and looked like a Fleming.

Presumably this refugee would have been Hubert Lindner. The deportation number of the man from Vienna, who had turned eighteen seven days previously, was 762. Like many of his fellows he had clearly happened upon helpful people that night, who had supplied him with what he needed for the rest of his escape route.

A pretty, dark-haired nurse stood somewhat apart from the rest. Her uniform was tattered. Régine Krochmal had walked parallel to the tracks after her escape, lest she lose her bearings. At some point she had reached the stationmaster's hut. Régine carefully opened the door. The young railwayman gave a start and turned around, but immediately calmed down when he saw the dainty little person. 'I jumped out of the convoy,' she explained to him, 'please help me.'

Without wasting a word, the young man took Régine's hand and drew her through the door behind him. To the rear of the stationmaster's hut he pointed to a little hayrick, put his finger to his lips and pushed her in.

Later she heard loud knocking on the door of the hut. A man asked in German whether he had seen anyone who had escaped from a train. The railwayman let the military policemen in and offered them a drink. For a long time no voices were heard. Then Régine heard the men saying goodbye. That danger had passed. She nodded off. Before dawn the stationmaster woke her up and explained to her how to get to the tram for Brussels.

At six o'clock on the dot the tram left the depot and picked up the passengers at the tram stop. At the last moment two young men climbed on. Jacques Grauwels and his friend's shoes and trousers were completely drenched and filthy. After they had jumped from the train just after Muizen station, they had travelled across country until they had reached a barn just before Haacht. 'We probably passed close by the spot where the attack happened,' Dr Grauwels later realized. 'It's a miracle they didn't catch us.'

They were afraid they would stand out with their dirty clothes. After all, the German military police regularly checked the passengers on public transport in search of people refusing labour service. So Jacques and his mate stood on the stairs, so that they could jump down at any time. And then something happened that Jacques Grauwels would never forget as long as he lived: 'The workers had probably noticed that there was something up with us both, that we had some sort of problems. As though in response to a silent order, they circled us both on the platform so that we were protected against prying eyes.'

At some point in the early morning Claire and Philippe had reached a little country village with a church. Claire was limping. She had lost a heel of one of her shoes. The exhausted couple waited outside the porch until early-morning mass was over. When the congregation had dispersed, they entered the silent church. The priest was just locking up the building. They were Jews, they said, who had escaped from the train to Auschwitz. And they had no money to travel on. The cleric was astonishingly composed, and didn't seem to be particularly surprised. 'God bless you,' he said, reached into his black habit and pressed 50-franc notes into Philippe's hand. Then he explained to them how to get to Liège. There was a tram stop nearby. In Liège the two refugees knew the address of a woman who was married to a cousin of Claire's. A non-Jew, who would certainly help them travel onwards.

Simon had walked all night. The thought that he might once again see his father, his little dog Bobby and his friends in the scouts, spurred him onwards. He kept on whistling the tune 'In the Mood', a tune that would always – even later, when he became a jazz pianist – be linked with that night. Once he saw a big, gleaming house, a castle surrounded by a park. Because it looked so majestic, Simon didn't dare to approach it. There might be Germans in it.

At dawn he reached a village. The boy rang at the first door he came to. A woman opened up, and looked in astonishment at the dirty, ragged boy. He had been playing with his pals near the village and had got lost, Simon stammered. He had been wandering about all night.

The woman, a Fleming, took him by the hand and brought the little boy, who didn't speak a word of Dutch, into the home of the village policeman of Borgloon. Simon repeated his story about his lost playmates once again. Although he was aware that the man didn't believe him, he insisted on his version of events. He was worried that they might hand him over to the Germans.

The policeman left the house, and returned a little while later with the latest news from the village: three corpses had been found near Borgloon. They were the inmates of a deportation train, who had been shot by German guards while they were escaping, or who had suffered fatal injuries while jumping out of the train. Turning to Simon, the policeman said: 'I know everything. You were in the Jewish train and you escaped. You don't need to worry. We are good Belgians, we won't betray you.'

Finally Simon was able to summon the courage to tell them what had really happened to him. When he talked about his mother he started crying. The policeman lovingly comforted the little boy. His wife washed him, gave him something to eat and drink and stitched up his clothes. At lunchtime one of the policeman's colleagues drove Simon along secret paths to Ordingen station on the luggage-rack of his bicycle because German military policemen had been seen on the station at Borgloon. For Simon Gronowski this journey was like coming home to the freedom that he had been denied for so long. 'Once again I see the blue sky again, the sun, the fields, the trees, the forest I knew so well; I rediscovered the cheerful song of the birds, the scent of nature. Again I breathed the air of spring and freedom. A world without the SS – was it possible?'

With the 50-franc note that Simon's mother had hidden in his knee-sock, the policeman bought him his ticket to Brussels. On the journey back to Brussels, the train stopped at every little station. Simon saw German uniforms everywhere. But no one checked the compartment in which he was sitting, vigorously staring out of the window. All around him he heard people saying, 'Apparently there was some trouble with the Jewish train last night.' He got out in Schaerbeek and took tram number 5 to the home of the

Rouffaerts, the parents of his best friend, who had always helped his family in the past.

In total, 231 deportees fled the convoy on 19 April 1943, before the German border. Twenty-three Jews died in the attempt, either under the hail of bullets from the sentries or by falling badly. Every escapee from the death train to Auschwitz could count on the help of the Belgian population. No one was betrayed. '*L'honneur des Belges.*'

12. Henda and Mendelis Goldsteinas on Avenue Louise before the war. During the war they were forced to change their names to Yvonne and Marcel Poncelet to avoid detection by the Nazis.

13. Avenue Louise today: the former Gestapo Headquarters with a memorial to the RAF pilot who attacked the building on 20 January 1943.

14. Claire Prowizur and her husband Philippe, 1951. They were both sent to Mechelen but escaped from the train on its way to Auschwitz.

15. Labour Deployment Order for Mechelen transit camp.

16. Ita Gronowski was made to wear the Star of David on her clothes and resented 'being stared at like a rare animal. I force myself to laugh, but deep inside I'm filled with bitterness.'

17. Simon Gronowski with his parents in Brussels. His mother failed to escape the transport. 'The train's going too fast' were the last words Simon heard her say.

18. Detail from the list of deportees, noting that Simon's method of escape was his jump from the train (a sauté du train).

19. Régine Krochmal (centre) with two comrades from the Austrian Liberation Front, September 1944. She survived Mechelen.

20. Survivors: (from l to r) Philippe Franklemon, Jacques Grauwels, Régine Krochmal, the author, Robert Maistriau, Simon Gronowski.

30 The Betrayal

Even today Jacqueline Mondo can still hear the quiet, hesitant ring on the door that so startled her and her parents on that night in mid-May 1943 and that would have such fateful consequences for herself and her family. Her father went downstairs to open the front door. He found himself looking at a man in an SS uniform with untidy dark hair and a swollen, bloody face. Only when the man raised his left hand, with a handcuff dangling from it, did Octave Mondo recognize who he was looking at: it was his daughter's boyfriend, the young doctor Livchitz.

Youra had escaped from SS headquarters on Avenue Louise. He had done it with incredible style. In the morning, Gestapo agents had arrested him near a garage in Ixelles, where he had laid down an arms dump with Pierre Romanovitch.

The 'White Russian', who was very active in the black market, seemed to have excellent contacts. He had been arrested for currency smuggling in mid-June, but was released again after only three days. Youra Livchitz had no suspicions about his new friend. A terrible misjudgement. Normally the only criminals who saw the prison walls again from outside were those that the military police or the Gestapo considered useful: people who were prepared to betray others.

Romanovitch was clearly well equipped by his clients on the Avenue Louise to create the impression that he had a mighty

Resistance group behind him. He himself had put it about that he was working with the 'White Army'. And Youra, without any suspicion, had been taken in by the plausible rogue. The successful attack on the twentieth transport had even strengthened his combative idealism. Along with his new friend Romanovitch, who had not only a car but also a secret arms dump, he planned a further coup against the Nazis.

When the 'White Russian' asked him to help him to move rifles and revolvers from a hiding place to a garage on the Rue Vanderkindere, he was there in a flash. After they had loaded the weapons from Romanovitch's car to the new depot, the 'Count' generously offered Youra a pistol of his own. They had only just parted when Livchitz was stopped in the street by Gestapo agents, searched and arrested for possession of a weapon.

For hours he was questioned by the SS police in the sixth floor of the building. They beat and pistol-whipped Youra to make him speak. Then, when they left him alone in the evening, handcuffed in a one-man cell, he managed to open one of his handcuffs, with the help of a safety pin, which he, like many Belgian Resistance fighters, wore as a secret identification on the back of the lapel of his jacket. Then he yelled for help. When the guard opened the door, he saw the prisoner lying on the floor, bent double and roaring with pain. He had serious stomach pains, Youra groaned, and urgently needed to go to the lavatory. Along the cellar corridor to the toilet, the tall athlete struck the smaller SS man from behind, took his gun and hit him over the head with it. Then he stripped the lifeless German, and pulled on his uniform jacket and trousers. At an even pace he left the notorious SS headquarters and called to the two guards, '*Gute Nacht*'. Hardly was he out of sight than he ran as fast as he could to nearby Rue Guillaume Stocq. Jacqueline's parents lived at number 56.

The Mondos generously took in the young hero, who had managed to escape from the cellars of Avenue Louise. The tax and accounts assessor Octave Mondo and his wife Angèle were members of the Belgian Resistance organization 'Armée Secrète'. When the rumour spread among friends about who the Mondos were looking after, they brought food to give the young man his strength back. They were all aware that it was extremely dangerous to have Youra Livchitz in the house. On all advertising columns there were wanted posters bearing the photograph of the 'Communist terrorist'.

Rachel Livchitz had to go into hiding now as well. At first she was able to live with Minnie Minet, and then – until the end of the German occupation – she took refuge with various Theosophical friends.

The Mondos urged young Livchitz to get out of Brussels as quickly as possible. They had organized a safe house for him near Antwerp. But Youra didn't want to leave the city yet. Above all he wanted to contact Pierre Romanovitch to warn him. The Gestapo might be on his tail if he drove his car to the arms depot in the garage.

Jacqueline finally declared herself willing to talk to Romanovitch. She found 'the good-looking, elegantly dressed man in his mid-thirties' at the agreed meeting-place by the Porte de Namur. He introduced himself to the pretty medical student as 'Comte Romanovitch'. She remembered above all his message to Youra Livchitz: on no account was he to stay with the Mondos, it was too dangerous.

And Youra really did leave his host family when he had somewhat recovered from the horrors of his treatment in Avenue Louise. He went into hiding at the home of the niece of a cleric who had worked with the Resistance.

Young Livchitz's escape from the Gestapo cellars had done the rounds of the Resistance. Hertz Jospa was given the task of contacting his young friend. After they had shadowed Romanovitch and his girl-friend for several days, the comrades had reached the conclusion that the 'White Russian' was playing a treacherous double game. Although he was supposed to be a militant Resistance fighter, he was constantly going in and out of Gestapo headquarters.

'The events leading up to his arrest finally opened Youra's eyes,' says Hertz Jospa in his eyewitness account for the Wiener Library:

> I no longer had to bother about explanations. Youra was convinced. Furious at having been tricked in this way, he wanted to avenge himself with all his powers. 'My life no longer has much value,' he said. It no longer had a meaning

for him if he could not take his revenge. Nonetheless, he promised to be disciplined, and as a final request asked to be able to kill the male whore who had betrayed him. After that, they could do what they wanted with him.

I energetically resisted this nonsensical plan, because Youra had been exposed and was in danger. We could have found him a hiding place in a monastery in the Ardennes, where he could have lived as a monk until liberation. Youra categorically refused. He wanted to continue his struggle. If his presence in Belgium was too risky, he wanted to go to England. If the Resistance refused to send him there, he would be able to make use of the escape organization of the priest who had got hold of that hiding place for him. I conveyed our answer to him. The Resistance didn't recommend that he head for England, but it didn't stand in his way either.

The brothers Youra and Alexandre Livchitz were now in the same hopeless situation. They were isolated from their friends, useless to the Resistance. They felt superfluous. And even worse than that, they represented a threat to everyone who came in contact with them. Flight to England seemed the only way out. A delivery truck was to bring them to France, and from there they were to be smuggled on to England.

But their escape route was betrayed. On 26 June, German Field Police checked delivery trucks on a road leading out of Brussels, shortly after the Livchitz brothers and other refugees had climbed on board. The German police had clearly received a tip. Alexandre and Youra were transferred to the Belgian concentration camp in Breendonk, the notorious punishment camp. In the vaulting of this old fortress not far from Mechelen, the torture cell, with tools such as thumb-screws and ceiling hooks, can still be seen. In one corner there is a desk behind which their interrogators sat. And there is still a little, harmless-looking wood-burning stove in which the SS men heated up the iron pincers with which they tortured their prisoners.

The only chink of light in this gloomy castle, where a horde of brutal and sadistic Nazi thugs ruled, was the Austrian army chaplain. Monsignore Otto Gramann watched with horror what was going on around him, and tried as best he could to ease the suffering of the internees. The former cavalry officer smuggled out information written on scraps of cigarette paper in the communion chalice, in his prayer-book and under his robe. He comforted the prisoners and accompanied those sentenced to death in Breendonk and in St Gilles prison during their final hours.

And one of these was Alexandre Livchitz: 'Every so often I have visits from the extraordinarily kind army chaplain who looks after me as best he can. This afternoon we talked together, and I was moved to tears,' writes Choura in his letter of farewell. The partisan commander had been condemned to death after a short trial in January 1944. In a cell in the Brussels prison of St Gilles, he waited for his execution on 9 February 1944. He had asked – as his last request – to be able to see Willy Baudoux once more. His lover was paying, in the women's section of the same prison, for the fact that she had harboured the armed partisan. The Gestapo had got their hands on a notebook of Alexandre's while searching the house, and that had put them on to his girlfriend's trail.

Willy's 'wonderful visit' to the cell had been far too short. Now all that Youra's brother could expect that evening was his last meal. Coffee, a jar of fish paste and biscuits. His right hand had been freed from its handcuff so that – under the watchful eye of two warders – he could write.

'Saps, friends, little brother,' he began his letter of farewell:

> For two hours now I have known for certain that I will be executed tomorrow morning at eight o'clock. One more rotation of the hands of the clock, and at last I will be free. I am calm, and when I was read the confirmation of the sentence as well as the rejection of my request for mercy, I didn't bat an eyelid. And I even believe that in the room where this ceremony took place the gentlemen present felt

that they themselves were the true guilty parties… I am not at all depressed, perhaps a little moved; I certainly was more so on that day when I was fetched from my room in Breendonk at half past seven in the morning and was not even able to say goodbye to Youra… I may say, and this stereotypical sentence is not in the slightest bit false, that I will go to the firing post (for I am being shot – at least it's better than being hanged) with my head held high, without regret, without pangs of conscience at having led to the arrest of other people, and with a sense of having tried to do my best to fight for a better life and for the beginning of a new world. I shall not end this letter without saying to you – and that as someone who is not at all a believer – that emotionally I do not believe in the absolute nothing; I have no particular love of anything hypothetical, but it is hard for me to admit that I will fall into the black hole that has appeared to me in my feverish dreams… That is all to tell you that my life will go on existing apart from my earthly body, perhaps in someone else or somewhere else. Who knows? In the end I will walk through the great portal with or without this idea – we'll see…

A week after Alexandre Livchitz died on the National Shooting Range under the bullets of the firing squad, his younger brother Youra was waiting for his coming death in a cell in Fort Breendonk. In retaliation for two bomb attacks on German offices in Brussels, military commander Alexander von Falkenhausen had ordered the shooting of hostages. From the list of those imprisoned in Breendonk, the general chose six 'Communist terrorists' for the execution date on 17 February 1944, among them the physician Youra Livchitz, resident at number 247 Avenue Brugmann.

A few days later Lily Allègre, Youra's shy little girlfriend from the Theosophical Society, received a message from the military administration. She was to make her way on a particular day and at a particular time to the Command on the Place Royale. There a kind, elderly uniformed man received the young girl. It was the army chaplain Graman, holding the letters of farewell from Youra and Alexandre in his hands. 'They both died as heroes,' he said. He had been present at their executions. Youra had refused to wear a blindfold. He wanted to be shot with his face towards the rising sun, as a symbol of life.

Youra had chosen Lily for this difficult errand because she was beyond suspicion, neither a Jew nor a member of the Resistance; and her parents would know his mother's hiding place so that they could pass his letter on to her.

At this time Rachel Livchitz was living with the Vander Hechts, close friends from the Theosophical community. The daughter of the house, Henriette, or 'Riquet', knew Youra from the 'Monada' commune, where he had caught her out with philosophical questions as they did the washing-up together. Together they had later hitch-hiked with Marcel Hastir to the holiday camp in Ommen. The news that Youra, the hero of her childhood and teenage years, had been shot by the Germans as a 'Communist terrorist' seemed so unimaginable to the medical student that she couldn't believe it.

'Saps' looked composed as Lily handed the letters to her. But her pain at the death of her sons was to be etched deep in the woman's soul. Throughout her long life – she died at the age of ninety-three – Youra and Alexandre would always be with her. Her sons' friends stayed in close contact with this extraordinary woman, whose enthusiasm for the beauty of nature and music was so infectious, until well into her old age.

Even today Lily Allègre remembers the tearless, sad voice of Rachel Livchitz, as she read her Youra's letter of farewell. It was the letter of someone disappointed and deceived:

> Dear Mama, even if words cannot express all my feelings, I
> am leaving this cell to make my way calmly to the other side
> of life – a calm that is also resignation to the inevitable. To tell
> you that I regret everything that has happened would be
> useless. I regret much more that I am no longer there to help

you in the first test that you have suffered: Choura. I would so much like to be there so that we could both work towards a future world.

Dear Mama, do not weep too much when you think of your children. My life hitherto has been very full, full of everything and above all with errors. I think of all my friends who are in prison, and ask their forgiveness. Remember me without pain. I have had good, excellent comrades until the end, and even now I do not feel alone. My greetings to everyone.

Dear mother, I must say goodbye to you, time is running out. Once again, it is not the last moments that were the hardest. Maintain your confidence and courage in life, time erases all things. Think that we died at the Front, think of all the families, all the mothers, hit hard by the war, a war that we all thought would have come to an end much sooner.

Your son, who loves you, Saps,

Youra.

He sent greetings to his friends, to Minnie Minet, Riquet and her family, Robert Leclercq, Marcel Hastir, the Mondos and Lily.

Clearly the news had not filtered through to him in the Breendonk camp that the Mondo family had also fallen victim to the traitor Romanovitch. Five days after Youra's arrest, on 1 July 1943, Octave Mondo, his wife Angèle, their twenty-year-old daughter Jacqueline and their seventeen-year-old son Walter had been arrested in their house at 56 Rue Guillaume Stocq. In file note 323/43SK of the Brussels Security Police and the Security Service it says:

Mondo is suspected of harbouring members of a terrorist organization in his flat – including the known terrorist Youra Livchitz who, after escaping from the building of the named service on 15.5.43, sought refuge with him for three days. The revolver that he had on him was hidden there, and the handcuffs had been filed open.

Jacqueline's parents disappeared into St Gilles prison. In March 1944, in a suite of the Brussels Palace Hotel, the family's court martial took place. The hearing lasted fifteen minutes. Octave and Angèle Mondo were condemned to death for supporting the enemy, their daughter was given a year's probation and their son Walter was acquitted. In the bathroom the parents and children were allowed to talk to each other once more. Octave Mondo was executed in Germany, and his wife died in Ravensbrück concentration camp.

On 3 July 1943, two days after the arrest of the Mondos, Richard Altenhoff was arrested. He too had been denounced by the 'White Russian Count'. The leading member of 'Groupe G' was accused of involvement in the twentieth transport. Nine months later, on 30 March 1944, the engineer was executed in the National Shooting Range in Brussels. In a letter, thirty-year-old Altenhoff says goodbye to his mother and his younger brothers and sisters.

> Now, at last, it is clear, I've been defeated – but not
> suppressed. And don't worry, they won't have the satisfaction
> of seeing me tremble. In the past I've always thought that
> the encroachment of death must be something terrible and
> frightening. But experience shows me that it is not so; I am
> relaxed, calm. But something weighs heavily upon my soul:
> the thought of the pain that I am causing you. Mama,
> hundreds of thousands of soldiers have died in this war, and
> I am one of them. I can easily bear the hours here because I
> know that you are brave and will stay in good humour. And
> my wish is that you will feel joy with all your heart on the
> day of victory.

On 7 August the Gestapo arrested Jean Franklemon at a tram stop. He too had been betrayed by the spy Romanovitch. Like many other political prisoners, Franklemon was sent to Breendonk, where he met Youra again. The friends had last met two days after the attack on the twentieth transport in Jean's local. Relieved at the success of that delicate operation they had drunk a glass together. Now they saw each other again within the dark walls of the fortress during exercise. And Youra admitted his fatal mistake to his old classmate: he had trusted Romanovitch, and given him and his lover Malka Cymring the names of everyone involved in the liberation action in Boortmeerbeek. Jean Franklemon was sent as a prisoner to Oranienburg and Sachsenhausen concentration camps. As though by a miracle he survived the death march on which the SS had sent the nearly starving and utterly weakened concentration camp inmates.

Only by chance did Robert Maistriau escape the wave of arrests after his betrayal by Romanovitch. The twenty-two-year-old had become a member of 'Groupe G' central office after his apprenticeship in the attack on the deportation train. He was responsible for organization and recruitment within the leading circle. Seven months later, in March 1944, he was arrested at a meeting. He was interned as a political prisoner in Breendonk concentration camp, and then deported to Buchenwald. Then he worked at the Dora labour camp, until he was sent to Harzungen hospital with pneumonia. He was finally freed by the Americans in Bergen-Belsen.

Jacqueline Mondo was to see Pierre Romanovitch again in 1947, before the military tribunal in Brussels. She testified as a witness against the traitor who had been responsible for the death of her parents. The 'White Russian''s beautiful lover, Malka Cymring, was heavily pregnant, and thus unfit for trial. Romanovitch was condemned to death, but the sentence was not imposed. His trail goes cold after the war, like that of 'fat Jacques', the spy, of whose fate there are different versions. Some say that Icek Glogowski was liquidated by the Gestapo for knowing too much, while others think he got away to Germany with the Nazis.

31 The Liberation

Simon Gronowski's favourite place to sit was right by the window. In the daytime, when the other children were at school, he sat there and watched the activity down below on the Chaussée de Waterloo through the chink in the curtains; he saw the women with their big shopping bags on their daily pursuit of food, busy and idle people, peering after the few cars that were allowed to drive in spite of petrol rationing.

Since his escape from the deportation train Simon had lived hidden with a Belgian family. The days passed slowly for the twelve-year-old. He longed for his scout troop, he was consumed with yearning for his mother's tender care. It was now a year since he had last received a letter from his sister Ita in Mechelen transit camp. As he knew from his father, with whom he assiduously corresponded, she had been deported the previous September. He had only seen his father once throughout those long months. It had been too dangerous for Léon Gronowski to leave his hiding place. Simon had had to promise his father to be sensible and on no account to yield to his urge for freedom. For three hours on weekdays he studied French and Dutch from the schoolbooks of the son of his host family.

It was 3 September when little Simon saw something unusual happening in the street; groups of young people passed laughing and singing under his window. People who met on the footpath fell into each others' arms. The car horns joined in for a rhythmical concert. Girls with flowers in their hands dashed past. Simon would learn a little later that they were on their way to greet the American and British soldiers who had taken Brussels.

Only the next day did Simon dare to go down into the street with Guy, the son of his guest family. The two boys ran to Porte de Hal to admire the arriving British army. The wide boulevard was lined with cheering *Bruxellois*. Flowers were held up to the soldiers in the tanks, and girls climbed up the monstrous vehicles to hitch a ride for a while. 'Half expecting the jubilant crowd to carry me along above their heads, I reached Avenue Louise,' writes Simon in his memoirs. 'There I saw the dome of the Palace of Justice burning. The Germans had set it on fire. In the Place Poelaert the people formed a chain to rescue the valuable books from the burning library, and I joined in. That was to be my first contact with justice.'

Claire Prowizur dashed into the street when the Allied tanks rolled into Charleroi. She had gone into hiding there with her husband Philippe, in the little suburb of Gilly, under a false name. Hiding and being quiet were finally over. Her jubilation was boundless. After keeping her true identity hushed up over the past few years, she now called out so all the neighbours could hear: 'We're Jews. We're free!' The citizens of Charleroi danced uninterruptedly for a day and a night.

The Nazis had pursued their murderous policies up until the end. And no one had stopped them. Military commander Falkenhausen had been recalled on 26 July, and summoned to Berlin where he was arrested by the SS. With his objections to the compulsory recruitment of the Belgian workers he had drawn the wrath of SS deputy Fritz Sauckel, who was pressing the Führer to recall insubordinate military staff. After the failed assassination attempt on Hitler on 20 July, the general was suspected of being a member of the circle of the conspirators.

When Belgium was liberated, the former military governor was imprisoned in Drögen SS police school near Ravensbrück. The Gestapo couldn't prove any of the accusations against him, because

Falkenhausen had always avoided recording delicate information in writing, in the form of letters or records of conversations. In Ravensbrück began the six years and eight months of the German general's wanderings through a great variety of camps and prisons. After Germany's capitulation the British and the Americans interned him, although they did acquit him from the accusation of being a war criminal. In October 1948 the seventy-year-old was brought before the Belgian war court, which sentenced him to twelve years' hard labour on 9 March 1951 for ordering the shooting of hostages. His head of administration, Eggert Reeder, received the same punishment in the same trial. They were both driven to the German border on the day of sentencing and set free. The general bitterly turned his back on the country that had been so unjust in its treatment of its fair-minded governor.

After the recall of the military governor in July 1944, SS general Richard Jungclaus governed in Belgium. But his days as a commander were numbered after the Americans landed in Normandy. By now petrol and coal were in such short supply that there were hardly any trains for the transport of the wounded German Front soldiers to the military hospitals in their homeland. Horses were hitched up to lorries to transport the invalids. However, for the Final Solution of the Jewish question, and the extermination of their opponents, the SS mobilized their last reserves.

On 31 July 1944, the twenty-sixth transport left Mechelen transit camp for Auschwitz. In all, 25,257 Jews had been deported from Belgium, including 5,093 children. Kurt Asche was no longer involved in the organization of the transports. The corrupt SS functionary was at first punished and sent elsewhere, and then in May 1944, for continued military disobedience and receiving stolen goods, sentenced to eighteen months' imprisonment. When Belgium was finally released from the yoke of the Nazis in September 1944, Asche served his sentence in the punishment camp of Mauthausen. Only in the late seventies was the fanatical anti-Semite brought to court as an accessory to murder. Until the amnesty for so-called fellow-travellers in 1955, Asche had lived under the assumed name of Kurt Klein.

Taking into account his advanced age of seventy-two, the former camp administrator with the German sleeping-car and dining-car company was sentenced to only seven years' imprisonment in 1981 by the regional court in Kiel. The spry pensioner lived to the age of eighty-eight.

When the Allies edged closer, the German SS teams in Mechelen transit camp tried to get away in secret. In the last week of August, Commandant Hans Frank called the Jewish staff together and explained that he and his colleagues had to go temporarily to Germany. The Flemish guards would stay behind and ensure that no one infringed the camp order. On their return, any offences would be severely punished. Frank gave the order to burn all the documents from the reception office. The traces of the Holocaust were to be erased. But the Jewish staff refused to obey. And so the lists of all Jews deported from Belgium have been preserved in the Deportation Museum in Mechelen.

Among the last prisoners in the transit camp was Régine Krochmal. She was under strict guard, in solitary confinement. The SS had put female members of the Resistance in the police cells at the Habsburg barracks, because Breendonk concentration camp was exclusively for men. After weeks of isolation and cruel torture, Régine railed against her fate. How long would she be able to bear this miserable existence, this loneliness in that gloomy dungeon? Immediately after breaking out of the twentieth convoy she had returned to her Resistance group. Instead of hiding, she went on distributing flysheets and underground newspapers of the 'Austrian Liberation Front'. She felt happier than she had been for ages: 'I was finally able to be useful again, and to feel the solidarity of the comrades.'

But then she was arrested with a stack of newspapers. As a member of the Resistance she encountered the terrible tortures of the Gestapo. Even today Régine Krochmal can't talk about what the Nazi thugs did to her when they tried to get her to talk in the windowless cell of the barracks. 'The thick walls swallowed up my cries.'

Régine only knew that everything was over when, on the evening of 3 September, two young SS-uniformed Belgians with machine-guns over their shoulders appeared in her cell. With tears in their eyes, they begged their prisoner to give them the address of her apartment. They wanted to hide there. The Americans were at the door.

In the same night, fellow prisoners opened the door to her cell. Régine was free.

I have often been asked how a German journalist ended up research-ing this almost unknown episode from the resistance against the German occupation and the Nazi extermination policy. While working as a correspondent for the news magazine *Der Spiegel* I met the lawyer Simon Gronowski. He told me that as an eleven-year-old he had jumped from a transport train that was supposed to be taking more than 1,600 people from Mechelen transit camp in Belgium to Auschwitz. And from that same Simon Gronowski I learned for the first time that on 19 April 1943, the twentieth death convoy was stopped by three young men to free deportees, an event that was quite unique in the history of the Holocaust.

I was immediately gripped by the subject. Journalistic curiosity combined with admiration and respect for the wider Resistance movement in Belgium and for the three young heroes, only one of whom is still alive: Robert Maistriau, now eighty-three years old, wasn't just the star witness to the attack, he also helped me to track down other eyewitnesses. I was able to reconstruct the story of the twentieth convoy to Auschwitz from archive material, trial files, con-versations with survivors and autobiographies. I often had the feeling that the eyewitnesses were glad to be asked about their story – even by a German. 'Come quickly, tomorrow if you can, who knows how long I have to live.' That was what Yvonne Jospa, the former Resistance fighter who helped to hide 4,000 Jewish children during the German occupation, said on the phone when she asked to set up a meeting. She died in January 2000, shortly before her ninetieth birthday. The openness and kindness of these people, who suffered unimaginably under Nazi rule in occupied Belgium, was probably my most astonishing experience. Things snowballed, as I kept getting new references to documents, people and events.

Since the publication of the German edition of *Silent Rebels*, the incredible story of the twentieth transport has been constantly acquiring new facets. The reviewer in a newspaper in southern Germany phoned me. From my book he had learned why his grandmother, who had worked as an interpreter in Brussels Gestapo headquarters during the German occupation, had her arm in plaster when she turned up at his parents' house early in 1943. She had been injured in Belgian pilot Jean de Sélys Longchamp's attack on SS headquarters.

At the launch of my book in Berlin a woman came up and spoke to me. She was crying. Her mother, Haja Roter, had been deported on that twentieth convoy to Auschwitz, and she was not one of the lucky ones who were able to escape from the train. In Brussels I met – once again, through the book – a psychoanalyst who told me about her father. His fate was also linked with that twentieth transport. Egon Markus comes from a bourgeois Jewish Berlin family, and his forefathers on his father's side had been decorated for their courage as members of the German army. Rather than entering the parental business, a glass-making company, he had to escape to Germany at the age of seventeen; he managed to get by in Belgium until he was arrested and taken from Mechelen transit camp on the twentieth transport to Auschwitz. He escaped from the train. Later in life, Egon Markus devoted himself to the reconciliation of Jews and Germans in Belgium.

At a reading at the Université Libre de Bruxelles a professor thanked me for the fact that the list of the 1,621 deportees is added at the end of the book. It meant that his father, the deportee Charles Weinstein from Czernowitz, finally had a monument. Jacky Barkan got in touch from Tel Aviv. The parents of the senior television director were also deported to Auschwitz extermination camp as numbers 190 and 1061. He himself survived the Holocaust as a hidden child.

When I was invited to a reading at the Goethe Institute in Los Angeles, a Mrs Schwartz called me a few hours before the event. She had seen the listing in *Jewish Weekly*, and just wanted to tell me that she too had escaped the twentieth transport. Unfortunately she couldn't come to the evening because she was ill. She could still remember her deportation number: 1152. At the time she had been called Lily Wolkenfeld. At the end of the phone call she said: 'It's the first time since then that I've spoken to a German.' When the book was published in French, I sent her a copy. She couldn't bear to read it in German. 'I am now on chapter eleven and I can't put it down. It brought back lots of memories as you can imagine,' she wrote. 'I also received a letter to present myself in 1942 to go to Mechelen, but as young as I was I did not go. I knew it was not for "Arbeit"...' Like so many of the prisoners she too had been handed over to the SS by Jacques, the Jewish informer.

A few weeks later I was able to give her the addresses of two other survivors of the twentieth transport, who lived only an hour's drive away from her in California. Marie and Gunther Mendel were mentioned on a list held by the Düsseldorf Memorial to the Victims of National Socialism (Mahn- und Gedenkstätte Düsseldorf) of the addresses of former Jewish citizens who had been driven out of Düsseldorf. They had been deported with numbers 1018 and 1082, but like Lily Schwartz they too were able to escape from the train. Almost sixty years after their flight from the twentieth convoy these three people made contact once again. They are now waiting with great excitement for this English-language edition, so that their children and grandchildren can read the story of the 'silent rebels', and gain a better understanding of a time that had such a crucial influence on their grandparents' lives.

Marion Schreiber
Brussels, December 2002

Acknowledgements

I should like to thank the deportees of the twentieth transport for their boundless willingness to tell me their stories: Willy Berler, Simon Gronowski and Régine Krochmal in Brussels; Ernst Landau, and Claire and Philippe Szyper-Prowizur in Tel Aviv; Jacques Grauwels in Ostende and Samuel Perl in Antwerp. I was able to ask Abela Crousel-Goldsteinas about her parents, who were freed by Robert Maistriau in the attack on the twentieth transport. It is to Maistriau himself, who spent forty-five years as a rancher and farmer in the Congo, and who now lives in Brussels again, that I owe the detailed description of this unique Resistance mission. The interviews with Inès De Castro-Lewin, David Lachman, Paul Halter and Yvonne Jospa have given me connections and background details for the Resistance that were not to be found in any book. Lily Coulon-Allègre, Marcel Hastir, Kaya Kengen, Henriette Vander Hecht and Jacqueline Opdenberg-Mondo brought me close to the character of Youra Livchitz. I learned the story of his family from his niece Maria Henninot in Paris, and from the Stolnikoffs of Genval. To Philippe Franklemon and Agnes Lecarte I am grateful for important information about their father, the musician Jean Franklemon, who died in 1977 in the GDR.

The basis for this reconstruction of the attack on the twentieth transport was provided by the Belgian historian Maxime Steinberg, who has documented the persecution, annihilation and resistance of the Jews in Belgium with scientific thoroughness. Ward Adriaens of the Joods Museum van Deportatie en Verzet was always a helpful and knowledgeable provider of information. The partisan Robert Korten from Boortmeerbeek, now sadly deceased, on whose initiative a memorial plaque was erected at the site of the event, opened up his private archive to me. Claire Barette and Sophie Vanderpontseele of the Service des Victimes de la Guerre, searched for files, reports and minutes from the time of the German occupation. In the regional court in Kiel I was able to look at the many files from the trial of Kurt Asche, who was condemned to seven years' imprisonment, and who died in 1997 in Hamburg.

I thank Christiane Kohl, who helped me – a journalist – overcome the initial difficulties I had in writing a book. Erika Dahners helped me read through the manuscript, and showed great commitment in transcribing the deportation lists. Thanks also to my editor, Maria Matschuk, who gave me strength and kept me going with her great fund of knowledge.

Bibliography

Adriaens, Ward. *Partizaan Frans Storms*, Antwerp, Nioba Uitgevers, 1988

Améry, Jean. *Jenseits von Schuld und Sühne*, Stuttgart, Klett-Cotta, 1997

Améry, Jean. *Örtlichkeiten*, Stuttgart, Klett-Cotta, 1980

Les Archives de l'ULB. *Des Hommes et des Pierres: Les Amis de la Liberté*, Bruxelles, 1997

Bodson, Herman. *Agent for Resistance*, Texas, A & M University Press, 1994

Bosquet, Alain. *Ma Mère Russe*, Paris, Grasset, 1994

Broder, Pierre. *Les Juifs Debout Contre le Nazisme*, Editions EPO, undated

Charles, Jean-Léon and Dasnoy, Philippe. *Les Dossiers Secrets de la Police Allemande*, Bruxelles, Editions Arts & Voyages, 1972

Depaene, Marc and Martin, Dirk (eds). *La Seconde Guerre Mondiale: Une Étape Dans l'Histoire de l'Enseignement*, Bruxelles, CREHSGEM, 1997

Despy-Meyer, Andrée. 'Une page importante dans notre histoire' in *Des Hommes et Des Pierres*, Bruxelles, Archives de l'ULB, 1997

Falkenhausen, Alexander von. *Mémoires d'Outre-Guerre*, Bruxelles, Editions Arts & Voyages, 1974

Garfinkels, Betty and Gottschalk, Max. *Les Belges Face à la Persecution Raciale 1940–1944*, Bruxelles, Edition de l'Institut des Sociologies, ULB

Gérard, Hervé. *La Résistance Belge Face au Nazisme*, Braine-L'Aleud, Editions J.-M. Collet, 1994

Gotovitch, José. *Du Rouge au Tricolore: Les Communistes Belges de 1939 à 1944*, Bruxelles, 1992

Gotovitch, José. 'Enkele aspecten van het dagelijkse leven van een klandestien' in *Het Dagelijkse Leven in Belgie*, Bruxelles, CGER, 1997

Gotovitch, José. 'L'engagement des intellectuals dans la résistance' in *Des Hommes et des Pierres*, Bruxelles, Archives de l'ULB, 1997

Gruman, Massia. 'L'Athénée d'Uccle' in Dupaene, Marc and Martin, Dirk, *La Seconde Guerre Mondiale*, Bruxelles, CREHSGEM, 1997

Hillberg, Raul. *Die Vernichtung der Europäischen Juden*, Vols 1–3, Frankfurt a. M., Fischer Taschenbuch Verlag, 1990

Han Suyin. *Une Fleur Mortelle*, Paris, Editions Stock, 1967

Klarsfeld, Serge and Steinberg, Maxime (eds.). *Die Endlösung der Judenfrage in Belgien*, Beate Klarsfeld Foundation

Klarsfeld, Serge and Steinberg, Maxime. *Mémorial de la Deportation des Juifs de Belgique*, Union des déportés juifs et fils et filles de la déportation, Avenue Ducpétiaux 68, 1060 Bruxelles

de Launay, Jacques. *La Belgique à l'Heure Allemande*, Brussels, Paul Legrain Editeur, undated

de Launay, Jacques. *La Drôle d'Occupation*, Bruxelles, Didier Hatier, 1990

Lauwaert, Dirk. 'Van publiek naar toeschouwer: Duitse films in belgische zalen' in *Het Dagelijkse Leven in Belgie*, Bruxelles, CGER, 1984

Liebman, Marcel. *Né Juif*, Paris-Gembloux, Editions Duculot, 1977

Lokker, Claude. *Les Batons Dans les Roués*, Bruxelles/Anvers, Editions MIM

Longerich, Peter. *Politik der Vernichtung*, Munich, Piper, 1998

Micheels, Louis J. *Doctor 117641: A Holocaust Memoir*, New Haven and London, Yale University Press, 1996

Michman, Dan (ed.). *Belgium and the Holocaust*, Jerusalem, Yad Vashem, 1998

Neuman, Henri. *Avant Qu'il Soit Trop Tard*, Bruxelles, Editions Duculot

Partisans Armés Juifs: 38 témoignages, édité par les enfants des partisans juifs de Belgique, Bruxelles, 1991

Prowizur-Szyper, Claire. *Conte à Rebours*, Bruxelles, Louis Musin Editeurs, 1997

Schreiber, Jean-Philippe (ed.). *Hertz Jospa – Juif, Resistant, Communiste*, textes réunis par Jean-Philippe Schreiber, Bruxelles, Editions Vie Ouvrière, 1997

Sommerhausen, Anne. *Journal d'une Femme Occupée*, Bruxelles, Didier Hatier, 1988

Steinberg, Maxime. *1942: Les Cent Jours de la Deportation*. Bruxelles, Editions Vie Ouvrière, 1984

Steinberg, Maxime. *La Question Juive 1940–1942*. Bruxelles, Editions Vie Ouvrière, 1983

Steinberg, Maxime. *La Traque des Juifs 1942–1944*, Vol I, Bruxelles, Editions Vie Ouvrière, 1986

Ugeux, William. *Histoires des Résistants*, Paris-Gembloux, Editions Duculot, 1979

Ugeux, William. *Le 'Groupe G' (1942–1944)*, Bruxelles, De Boeck-Wesmael, 1994

Wagner, Wilfried. *Belgien in der Deutschen Politik während des Zweiten Weltkrieges*, Wehrwissenschaftliche Forschungen, Ed. Militärgeschichtliches Forschungsamt, Boldt Verlag, 1974

Weber, Wolfram. *Die innere Sicherheit im besetzten Belgien und Nordfrankreich 1940–1944*, Düsseldorf, Droste Verlag

Weinzierl, Ulrich. *Dokumentationsarchiv des Österreichischen Widerstandes* (ed.); *Österreicher im Exil Belgien 1938–1945*, Vienna, Bundesverlag Wien, 1984

Welsch, Marc. *La Belgique Sous l'Oeil Nazi*, Ottignies LLN, Editions Quorum, 1998

UNPUBLISHED DOCUMENTS AND SOURCES

Bundesarchiv Berlin, Abteilung Reich: Personalakten Kurt Asche et al.

Centre des Recherches et d'Études Historiques de la Seconde Guerre Mondiale

(CREHSGM) Bruxelles: Reports of the military administration, newspaper articles, underground press

Gronowski, Simon: L'Enfant du Vingtième Convoi. Manuscript

Joods Museum van Deporatie en Verzet, Mechelen: Dokumente zur Verfolgung der Juden und zum Widerstand in Belgien

Landgericht Kiel: Kurt Asche trial files

Militärarchiv Freiburg: effects of General Alexander von Falkenhausen

Political archive of the German Foreign Office, Bonn: telegrams, reports to the Foreign Office

Private archive of Robert Korten, Boortmeerbeek

Service des Victimes de Guerre in the Ministère de Santé Publique, Bruxelles: Protokolle des Juderats, transcript of the diary of Salomon Vanden Berg, personal files of Resistance fighters and political prisoners, Security Service files, Mechelen–Auschwitz transport lists

Université Libre de Bruxelles: archive on 'Groupe G'

Zentrale Stelle der Landesjustizverwaltungen, Ludwigsburg: charges and judgment in the trial of Kurt Asche

APPENDIX: THE DEPORTEES

The names listed below comprise the deportees who boarded the twentieth transport from Mechelen to Auschwitz on 19 April 1943. Spelling of names is inconsistent since many deportees did not hold ID cards and often preferred to use the Belgian versions of their Jewish names. The list, compiled by Nazi officials at Mechelen, notes the name, date of birth, place of birth and occupation of each deportee. Numbers were assigned in order of arrival. There was also a category for nationality under which all deportees born outside Belgium were described as stateless. Belgian nationals appeared on a separate list.

The special list, which prefaces the main list, includes camp members such as Samuel Perl who had tried to escape the nineteenth transport but had been returned to Mechelen. Those on the special list had to wear their numbers crossed through with a red line to mark themselves out to the Germans as security-risks.

Some deportees on the general list for the twentieth transport were actually sent on to Auschwitz at a later date. Their final transport numbers are displayed in brackets.

LISTE SPÉCIALE

1. Feigin, Jacob	04. 05. 92	Odessa
2. Turko, David Lejbus	15. 05. 06	Konskie
3. Perl, Samuel	16. 10. 20	Ruscova
4. Schmitz, Rudolf Salomon	02. 12. 04	Kaisersesch
5. Zweig, Benjamin	16. 09. 02	Krakow
6. Ejzyn, Jojne	13. 08. 03	Lodz
7. Kuczynski, Jacob	13. 04. 11	Bia—
8. Melman, Uszer Berck	21. 07. 23	Ozarov
9. Blitz, Chaskel Feiwel	03. 05. 99	Tarnov
10. Posesorski, Lejb (XXIII-6)	18. 07. 18	Warsaw

11.	Dab recta Fleischman, Adolf	28. 11. 09	Jaslo	
12.	Kuczynski, Max	11. 03. 21	Plauen	
13.	Abramowicz, Salomon (xxiii-1)	23. 07. 16	Vienna	
14.	Fritz, Hans	13. 01. 12	Vienna	
15.	Tran-Rotholz, Fajga	01. 05. 98	Warsaw	
16.	Icek, Majer	01. 09. 19	Kusmia Grabowska	
17.	Icek, Kopel	23. 08. 13	Klanowa	
18.	Holzer, Arthur Israel (xxi-40)	26. 01. 05	Vienna	
19.	Paskusz, Moriz	23. 08. 01	Wartberg	

16. 01. 43

1.	Meyer, Julius	01. 03. 73	Berlin	lawyer
2.	Meyer-Tauber, Charlotte	21. 05. 87	Würzburg	housewife
3.	Deutsch, Fanny Marie	12. 07. 29	Vienna	schoolgirl
4.	Kapelner-Pardes, Esther	03. 12. 00	Zarki	seamstress
5.	De Vriend-Kromme, Rebecca	21. 02. 71	Amsterdam	none
6.	De Ceulaer-Margulies, Jenta	05. 07. 01	Strusow	nurse
7.	Bau, Georg	02. 04. 37	Vienna	none
8.	Weininger, Erich	23. 08. 20	Vienna	furrier
9.	Grynberg, Szlama	13. 12. 98	Tomaszow	furrier
10.	Grynberg, Fajga-Ruchla	07. 05. 26	Tomaszow	schoolgirl
11.	Grynberg, Chana	1929	Tomaszow	schoolgirl
12.	Nejman-Blachman, Temer	14. 02. 09	Lodz	tailor
13.	Kellermann-Isler, Pessel Rachel	11. 08. 08	Hanover	seamstress
14.	Kellermann, Hilde	13. 12. 36	Duisburg	schoolgirl
15.	Kanarek, Chaim	01. 05. 95	Hesko	furworker
16.	Kanarek-Bombach, Rywka Elke	20. 02. 98	Dobromil	housewife
17.	Kanarek, Herz	29. 10. 34	Leipzig	schoolboy
18.	Rothmann-Flaumenhaft, Chana	01. 04. 86	Zarnova	none
19.	Schächter-Tieger, Reizel	11. 10. 04	Koslov	housewife
20.	Schächter, Peppa	28. 06. 34	Lomberg	schoolgirl
21.	Schächter, Maurice	14. 04. 41	Antwerp	none
22.	Brand, Jacob	01. 12. 94	Tarnobrzog	businessman
23.	Brad-Atlas, Perla	04. 09. 94	Przeworski	housewife
24.	Brand, Feiwel Chaskiel	16. 11. 26	Leipzig	furrier
25.	Nejman, Michel	19. 11. 05	Sulejow	tailor
26.	Zylberszac, Hélène	31. 03. 27	Anderlecht	schoolgirl
27.	Wechselberg, Fani Sarah	17. 08. 35	Etterbeek	schoolgirl
28.	Szyf, Klemmens	31. 03. 02	Warsaw	trouser-maker
29.	Singer, Rosalia	26. 05. 33	Antwerp	schoolgirl
30.	Singer, Rachel	14. 08. 39	Antwerp	none

15. 01. 43

31.	Wajsman, Max Richard	25. 10. 96	Sokolow	fitter
32.	Gottfried, Charles	18. 04. 36	Brussels	none
33.	Micheels, Louis Josef	06. 06. 17	Amsterdam	medical assistant

34. Micheels-van, Esso	09. 10. 20	Amsterdam	dental assistant
35. Zwang, Helmuth Herbert	30. 10. 12	Adelsheim	decorator
36. Helman, Samuel (xxiii-15)	21. 09. 97	Warsaw	hotelier
37. Hanauer, Herman	04. 07. 88	Lingen	furrier

19. 01. 43

38. Schein, Samuel	18. 03. 91	Jurkow	tailor
39. Schein, Mendel Emmanuel (xxi)	04. 04. 26	Dobra	schoolboy
40. Leffmann, Albert Israel	11. 10. 07	Wanne i.W.	driver
41. Leffmann-Koffler, Berta-Sara	31. 05. 16	Viersen	saleswoman
42. Schmerler-Koffler, Paula	04. 02. 94	Rosulna	housewife
43. Gaenger, Eljaz	16. 12. 91	Oswierin	lawyer
44. Goldfarb, Hilel	30. 09. 04	Paskrjine	carpenter
45. Goldstein, Hetel David	05. 03. 01	Opocano	furrier
46. Goldstein-Lavendel, Liba	24. 04. 04	Zwrzoviczki	furrier
47. Goldstein, Isidoor Isaac	28. 06. 32	Brussels	schoolboy
48. Jakubowicz, Hilel	18. 09. 02	Noworadowak	carpenter
49. Fajnholc, Icek	1883	Siedlec	glove-maker
50. Fajnholc-Alterwahn, Chawa	1890	Warsaw	housewife
51. Eskenazy-Kalderon, Dora	15.12. 11	Monastir	none
52. Opoczynski, Szlama Zalma	11.08. 05	Kamiensk.	tailor
53. Nisenbaum-Wejntraub.	27. 09. 01	Budaljnzowska	tailor
54. Nisenbaum-Wejntraub, Laja	12. 03. 32	Brussels	seamstress
55. Nisenbaum, Juliette	12. 03. 32	Brussels	schoolgirl
56. Schein, Sanal	15. 10. 87	Jurkow	tailor
57. Schein-Kornbluth, Esther	21. 04. 92	Tarnopol	housewife
58. Schein, Moritz	15. 05. 13	Vienna	tailor
59. Schein, Magdalena	29. 03. 21	Szombathely	tailor
60. Schein, Erich	25. 08. 25	Oberwart	schoolboy
61. Gertner-Szperber, Rebecca	21. 01. 99	Warsaw	tailor
62. Michelewitz-Cygler, Ruchla	08. 02. 09	Tomaszow	tailor
63. Teitelbaum-Weber, Hildegard	14. 12. 98	Berlin	shorthand-typist
64. Moczydlinski-Fuks, Noma	1885	Warsaw	housewife
65. Kreindler, Josef Mordko	01. 02. 02	Kolomea	teacher
66. Lewkowitz, Walter (xxi-1)	10. 06. 01	Kempen	miner
67. Borenchole, Abraham Josek	16. 04. 94	Czyste	leather-worker
68. Borenchole-Landsberg, Fejga	23. 09. 94	Warsaw	tailor
69. Borenchole, Thérèse	09. 04. 26	Brussels	tailor
70. Cudykier, Mordka (xxiv-10)	02. 05. 03	Zakoczyn	schoolgirl
71. Cudykier-Drobiarz, Estera	24. 04. 07	Dzaloszyra	tailor
72. Cudykier, Leon	04. 12. 34	Brussels	schoolboy
73. Kwint-ova, Hendrik	27. 04. 40	Antwerp	none

21. 01. 43

74. Prowizur, Chaskel (Oscar)	28. 02. 99	Tarnow	furrier
75. Krik-Schwarz, Olga (widow Fischer)	03. 10. 85	Vienna	housewife

76. Spetter, Jacques	29. 08. 97	Rotterdam	businessman
77. Blum, Maurice	08. 04. 74	Galatz	tailor
78. Wald, Moritz	17. 12. 09	Munich	clerk
79. Preisz, Arthur	14. 05. 06	Vienna	none
80. Skornicki, Szmul	1898	Wodzialaw	tailor
81. Kaufman, Frajndla	10. 05. 04	Wodzialaw	tailor
82. Skornicki, Herman	07. 05. 32	Antw. Borgerhout	schoolboy
83. Lempert, Ovchie	20. 01. 08	Kichineff	engineer
84. Grünebaum, Heinrich	05. 11. 99	Rendel	businessman
85. Grünebaum-Strauss, Rosa	05. 02. 98	Frankf. a. M.	tailor
86. Grünebaum, Berthold	26. 07. 31	Gross-Koben	schoolboy
87. Grünebaum, Alice	27. 04. 38	Frankf. a. M.	none
88. Ajsenberg, Rywen	15. 03. 98	Zvolun-Radom	tailor
89. Ajsenberg-Szpilman, Malla (IX-210)	28. 03. 03	Ostrowice	seamstress
90. Ajsenberg, Peretz	02. 10. 31	Etterbeek	schoolboy
91. Ehrlich, Fritz	04. 9. 24	Dortmund	packer
92. Reinstein-Dörmer, Mina	21. 02. 80	Ruti	housewife
93. Kalfus-Reinstein, Anna	16. 06. 06	Cernauti	—
94. Czapnik-Knopmacher, Szaindla	1899	Miedzyczcie	housewife
95. Czapnik, Moizesz	20. 10. 26	Miedzyczcie	none
96. Freifeld, Josef Benjamin	03. 12. 92	—	businessman
97. Freifeld-Schifter, Augusta	14. 10. 95	Porschapper	none
98. Zylberberg, Chil	26. 11. 96	Miedzyczcie	—
99. Zylberberg, Jacob	06. 03. 21	Warsaw	tailor
100. Zylberberg, Nathan (XXI)	14. 12. 24	Warsaw	electrician
101. Pitermann, Abraham Alex	14. 08. 01	Lukow	tailor
102. Pitermann-Strauss, Reuti	04. 03. 09	Frankf. a. M.	tailor
103. Braschkin, Rafael	15. 11. 68	Kiev	electrical technician
104. Sametz-Wasser, Sali Leona	09. 11. 92	Lemberg	shorthand-typist
105. Bornstein, Bernhard	24. 12. 02	Vienna	accountant
106. Bornstein-Strauss, Lina	17. 8. 01	Frankf. a. M.	office-worker
107. Bornstein, Miriam	26. 09. 35	Frankf. a. M.	schoolgirl
108. Riedermann, Icek Lazar	04. 09. 66	Bylky	none
109. Potasz, Chaia Cywla	18. 12. 24	Sulejow	tailor
110. Bosel, Marlene	10. 10. 31	Vienna	schoolgirl
111. Markowicz-Goldsztaijn, Bina Nacha	13. 05. 96	Warta	housewife
112. Bikszenspan, Sena Marie	04. 06. 09	Apen-Vizni	housekeeper
113. Hartstein-Weisz, Julienne	15. 09. 98	Leliez	cook
114. Catzaf, Pinkus	16. 04. 71	Palesti	none
115. Catzaf, Leib	15. 02. 96	Rseanie	metal-worker
116. Herz, Hans Jakob Israel	13. 11. 05	Aachen	tailor
117. Kwaczkowski-Schocken, Gertrud	09. 07. 99	Czarnikau	seamstress
118. Wajdenfeld, Isucker Ber	20. 02. 97	Warsaw	leather-worker

119.	Holender, Chaim Abraham	24. 03. 13	Warsaw	glove-maker
120.	Baecher, Arthur Israel	21. 07. 96	Breslau	painter/decorator
121.	Jakubowicz, Maya	10. 01. 20	Predborg	seamstress
122.	Marx, Kurt	16. 02. 93	Krefeld	estate agent
123.	Nikolajewitch, Hermann	11. 05. 01	Tarnow	seamstress
124.	Weinwurm, Ernst	05. 07. 21	Vienna	baker

22. 01. 43

125.	Bernstein, Schmul	12. 05. 89	Odessa	mechanic
126.	Reens, Elisabeth	28. 10. 09	Antwerp	businesswoman
127.	Bucholc, Aron	10. 07. 10	Warsaw	photographer
128.	Metzger, Fischel	07. 11. 05	Starunia	hotelier
129.	Metzger-Ickovic, Estera	16. 01. 04	Tacevo	cook
130.	Bloemhof-Rodriguez, Femmetje	28. 03. 70	Amsterdam	none
131.	Kanner-Reissfeld, Klärl	20. 03. 70	Brody	none
132.	Schiffer, Armand	10. 02. 82	Kapovar	engineer
133.	Montezinos-Kooker, Jetta	31. 01. 95	Amsterdam	businesswoman
134.	Witteboon-Ziekenoppasser, Rozette	04. 11. 75	Amsterdam	none
135.	Safier Löw, Feiga	18. 05. 84	Blagowa	none
136.	Kernkraut, Tauchen	24. 08. 76	Neu-Sandez	none
137.	Kernkraut-Berggrün, Esther	20. 06. 85	Neu-Sandez	housewife
138.	Kalter-Mechel, Marjem	30. 06. 78	Jaliska	none
139.	Schwartz, Maximilian	23. 03. 09	Vienna	diamond-cutter
140.	Levy, Sophia	11. 01. 03	Amsterdam	office-clerk
141.	Luksenberg, David Laizer	15. 04. 74	Bendzin	none
142.	Luksenberg, Ella	24. 06. 06	Chrzanow	none
143.	Luksenberg, Hirsch	11. 05. 99	Chrzanow	businessman
144.	Luksenberg-Szönmann, Dwojra T.	30. 06. 18	Lagerow	cook
145.	Luksenberg, Marcel	19. 04. 39	Antwerp	none
146.	Luksenberg, Aron	09. 06. 97	Dobrowa	diamond-cleaver
147.	Luksenberg-Najmark, Malka	14. 05. 09	Bendzin	housewife
148.	Luksenberg, Annie	04. 03. 34	Antwerp	schoolgirl
149.	Luksenberg, Regina-Leia	11. 10. 39	Antwerp	schoolgirl
150.	Luksenberg-Herceberg, Machela	29. 12. 06	Bendzin	housewife
151.	Luksenberg, Samuel Isaac	05. 05. 35	Antwerp	schoolboy
152.	Luksenberg, Aron	13. 06. 36	Antwerp	schoolboy
153.	Luksenberg, Rebecca Reine	01. 03. 39	Antwerp	none
154.	da Silva Abenator, Abraham	10. 07. 76	Amsterdam	none
155.	da Silva Abenator-Mntanhes, Branca	02. 01. 69	Amsterdam	none
156.	Fink, Jakob	30. 12. 96	Radziechow	tripe-sorter
157.	Gottlieb, Moses Leib	15. 11. 75	Karajow	none
158.	Gottlieb-Feldberg, Frima	10. 11. 75	Planoza Mala	housewife
159.	Krajcman-Przewoznik, Ruchla L.	15. 01. 04	Plonsk	housewife
160.	Krajcman, Daniel	23. 11. 28	Antwerp	schoolboy

161. Krajcman, Anna-Stena	09. 10. 30	Antwerp	schoolgirl
162. Krajcman, Sara Margaret	30. 10. 38	Antwerp	none
163. Hacker-Tuchler, Hermine	11. 01. 68	Wilhelmburg	none
164. Mamber-Hacker, Malvine	25. 10. 93	Ramsan	housewife
165. Zuker, Josef	14. 12. 92	Borodylow	clockmaker
166. Zuker-Hacker, Margarethe	02. 07. 97	Vienna	housewife
167. Zuker, Berthold	13. 11. 28	Antwerp	schoolboy
168. Zuker, Jacques	14. 07. 30	Antwerp	schoolboy
169. Pasternak, Abraham Chaim	28. 07. 78	Zal—	none
170. Pasternak-Schmutz, Ryfka	03. 1. 79	Dukla	housewife
171. Pekel, Frederika	14. 03. 99	Amsterdam	masseuse
172. Haber, Sender	02. 09. 90	Zabno	businessman
173. Haber-Löw, Frimet	11. 01. 95	Sedpiszow	housewife
174. Haber, Sonja	17. 01. 26	Vienna	none
175. Low-Bakenroth, Cirla	15. 12. 80	Schodnica	none
176. Hochberger-Löw, Berta	17. 04. 04	Schodnica	housewife
177. Hochberger, Dwora Debora Dolly	10. 02. 39	Vienna	none
178. Berliner, Szmul	26. 01. 08	Warsaw	tailor
179. Wolf, Valk	26. 01. 97	Amsterdam	diamond grinder
180. Weinstein, Charles	28. 05. 99	Czernowitz	businessman
181. Grinberg, Hertz	25. 06. 10	Lodz	tailor
182. Montezinos, Rosamunde Luciana	30. 03. 26	Antwerp	none
183. Aron-Dolfman, Rebecca	26. 10. 80	Bucharest	none
184. Auster, David	15. 11. 08	Rawaruska	furrier
185. Eisenstark-Aron, Lisa	02. 04. 12	Bucharest	hairdresser
186. Eisenstark, Abraham Albert	31. 07. 32	Charleroi	schoolboy
187. Eisenstark, Esther	14. 06. 37	Charleroi	none
188. Weishaus, Leo	18. 07. 93	Leipzig	salesman
189. Weishaus-Piestreich, Bronislawa	15. 01. 04	Stanislau	housewife
190. Blocherman-Borzykowska, Chana	31. 05. 04	Radomsk	tailor
191. David, Arthur	29. 06. 01	Rheidt	fitter
192. Fiajgenblat, Estera	10. 04. 96	Podlasic	cook
193. Kirszenbaum, Chil	28. 09. 94	Kovartchoff	leather-worker
194. Kirszenbaum-Lajcher, Perla	03. 11. 95	Czestochowa	seamstress
195. Wyman, Aaron	24. 01. 90	The Hague	porter
196. Wyman-de Vrede, Rica	13. 09. 88	Anderlecht	housewife
197. Gompertz, Max	28. 01. 19	Amsterdam	boatman
198. Eisner, Joseph	06. 12. 04	Sambor	tailor
199. Eisner-Siegel, Marjem	05. 03. 02	Smolnice	tailor
200. Urstein-Brandriss, Marie	06. 01. 92	Grzymalow	seamstress
201. Mileband, Majer Brajs	26. 05. 94	Warsaw	bootmaker
202. Mileband-Rottesman, Ester	14. 02. 03	Neu Sandez	leather-worker
203. Wahl-Wachtel, Rachel	28. 02. 73	Rohatyn	none
204. Weizmann-Levkowitch, Baila	16. 06. 96	Lodz	housewife
205. Weizmann, Charlotte Blanche	01. 10. 26	Strasbourg	kindergarten teacher

206. Guterman, Sender	09. 06. 97	Piotrkow	tailor
207. Guterman-Cymring, Hena	10. 04. 04	Warsaw	tailor
208. Gutermann, Rosette	15. 11. 33	Paris	schoolgirl
209. Gutermann, Leon	14. 05. 35	Paris	schoolboy
210. Peretz, Mosez Gertzl	14. 02. 87	Krcetsburg	docker
211. Peretz-Leba, Gitla (Ketty)	28. 07. 90	Falticien	housewife
212. Peretz, Marietta	10. 08. 29	Antwerp	schoolgirl
213. Worms, Hyman	14. 04. 82	Amsterdam	businessman
214. Kaminski-Schütz, Joséphine	22. 11. 15	Anderlecht	tailor
215. Kaminski, Suzanne	11. 03. 43	Brussels	none
216. Schutz, Lea	02. 02. 19	Auderghem	none
217. [blank]			
218. Kropveld, Samuel	11. 03. 94	Amsterdam	butcher
219. Kropveld, David	03. 01. 18	Amsterdam	tailor
220. Goldman, Celli	02. 05. 16	Esch s. Alz.	saleswoman
221. Landau, Ernst	02. 01. 16	Vienna	editor

26. 01. 43

222. Reich, Bernard	22. 07. 06	Neu Sandes	butcher
223. Verheden-von Tuassic, Alice	16. 09. 74	Vienna	none
224. Welward, Wilhelm	22. 12. 21	Vienna	cook
225. Kostelaniec, Morduch	03. 04. 02	Molozadz	knitter
226. Grubner, Juda	21. 10. 07	Chrzanow	tailor
227. Grubner-Steinitz, Helene	20. 02. 09	Munich	housewife
228. Schaffel-Veiszner, Paula	05. 07. 14	Sighet	housewife
229. Fiszban, Eljasz	23. 06. 05	Lublin	tailor
230. Gorski, David	23. 09. 04	Chmielnik	ironer
231. Husserl, Ernst	30. 09. 04	Vienna	technician
232. Majerowitz, Moses Isaak	11. 02. 00	Rudna	furrier
233. Hass, Jakob	15. 09. 81	Halicz	none
234. Hass-Goldberg, Luba	30. 08. 91	Odessa	housewife
235. Mendelssohn-Vajda, Bianca Sara	17. 06. 92	Berlin	shorthand-typist
236. Langermann-Brauner, Sara	27. 10. 11	Berlin	housewife
237. Berneman, Dydja	07. 05. 11	Kozienice	tailor
238. Isralowitz-Friedlander, Schichla	27. 03. 75	Riga	none
239. Pinskier, Szaja	16. 02. 00	Warsaw	storekeeper
240. Berisch-Richter, Sara	03. 04. 90	Sokola	none
241. Sass-Lewowocz, Sara	16. 11. 64	Stanislawczyk	none
242. Rose-Sass, Augusta	12. 10. 88	Stanislawczyk	housewife
243. Süsser, Alexandre	23. 11. 06	Saranow	travelling salesman
244. Süsser, Salli	09. 02. 16	Luxemburg	none
245. Birnberg, Baruch Szymon	04. 12. 99	Kolomsa	waiter
246. Kirszenzaft, Jacob	11. 05. 28	Warsaw	
(=) Witkowski, David	06. 06. 29	Etterbeek	schoolboy
247. Gutman, Szama	28. 03. 05	Lomasz	tailor

27. 01. 43

248. Ekstein, Jacob	12. 09. 85	Tarnobrzeg	businessman
249. Kahn, Herman	15. 07. 92	Kettenbach	farmer
250. Dubrowin, Szlama	20. 08. 75	Mirslaw	none
251. Dubrowin-Nachimson, Groja	1881	Szawlo	housewife
252. Dattnerm, Stefan	29. 08. 04	Osmiecin	furrier
253. Brawerman-Pupko, Lubow	16. 12. 05	Lida	housewife
254. Szyper, Frain Wolf	12. 12. 16	Josofow	tailor
255. Szyper-Prowisor, Klara	30. 05. 22	Altona	tailor
256. Stern, Jankel/Josef	10. 06. 79	Warsaw	baker
257. Stern-Wermus, Ryfka Rebecca	21. 6. 83	Warsaw	housewife
258. De Buyl-Peltz, Cyrla	22. 03. 18	Lodz	housewife
259. Benkosi, Jacob	25. 11. 24	Jette	hairdresser
260. Jakubowitz, Bertha	08. 06. 25	Brussels	seamstress
261. Nasielski-Wolf, Rana	14. 12. 88	Doore	housewife
262. Nasielski, Estera Vera	19. 06. 14	Vladslawec	clerk
263. Krochmal, Régine	28. 07. 20	The Hague	nurse
264. Kuczbart, Abraham	07. 04. 03	Kroluck	tailor
265. Szwarcbard-Najhaus, Rywka G.	20. 04. 03	Prysuchow	tailor
266. Gorin, Moise	03. 04. 88	Staraja	businessman
267. Gutweter, Icek	24. 07. 90	Warsaw	scissors-maker
268. Lewy-Nawratzki, Frieda	16. 08. 00	Thorn	tailor
269. Cymerman, Robert	28. 06. 00	Warsaw	tailor
(=) Brajtman, Ruben	14. 03. 00		
270. Kleinberg, Alexander	02. 05. 06	Brody	tailor
271. Katzman, David	27. 07. 91	Kalusch	hairdresser
272. Heiliczer, Bernhard	03. 08. 15	Vienna	clerk

28. 01. 43

273. Vidokle, Icek	08. 01. 75	Kedaina	none
274. Vleeschdrager-Cohen-Rodriguez, Bathsheba	27. 05. 79	Amsterdam	none
275. Zelt, Nachim	26. 02. 07	Tarnow	tailor
276. Souritz, Abraham Ezchiel	22. 03. 94	Pskow	businessman
277. Souritz, Pauline	16. 04. 28	Antwerp	schoolgirl
278. Hollander, Siegmund Süsskind Süssel	02. 02. 94	Blazowa	restaurateur
279. Freifeld, Abraham	25. 01. 83	Pomaratz	none
280. Stern-ova, Ida	06. 08. 14	Zavidovo	housekeeper
281. Stern, Leopold	08. 09. 42	Antwerpen	none
282. Van Gelder, Benjamin	04. 09. 70	Brussels	none
283. Van Gelder, Jozefina	16. 04. 96	Amsterdam	none
284. Freifeld, Chaim	29. 04. 95	Budolowice	businessman
285. Grosz-Osztreicher, Rosalia	03. 07. 07	Satu Mare	housewife
286. Szternfeld, Manes	11. 11. 14	Otwien	leather-worker
287. Spaanbroek, Salomon	27. 12. 67	Rotterdam	none

288. Spaanbroek-Swalf, Bertha	31. 01. 70	Rotterdam	none
289. Steinhart-Huttner, Fanny	04. 05. 79	Vienna	none
290. Kolm-Werner, Helene	03. 01. 88	Vienna	housewife
291. Szklo, Josek	24. 12. 12	Radoazyce	rabbi
292. Gajzt, Brajla Bojla Jenta	24. 03. 24	Ludovice	tailor
293. Szternfeld-Gutsznick, Dyna	02. 01. 74	Rozmiezer	none
294. Wolffberg-Blumenthal, Friedda	25. 04. 01	Berlin	shorthand-typist
295. Nejman, Paul	24. 10. 28	St Gilles	schoolboy
296. Auster, Rachela	14. 03. 16	Lubaczow	seamstress
297. Jakubowitz, Martha	12. 07. 15	Ahrweiler	seamstress
298. Hauser, Simon	16. 11. 88	Mokrzyazow	diamond-splitter
299. Hauser-Anisfeld, Chaja	23. 08. 88	Podgorze	tailor
300. Gold, Mordka	10. 07. 85	Odessa	none
301. Feder, Bajla-Jochad	21. 03. 05	Smolnik	none
302. Jakubowicz, Lajb	30. 10. 94	Kutno	tailor
303. Jakubowicz-Rosenberg, Marjam	1905	Kutno	housewife
304. Jakubowicz, Bernard-Symcha	18. 03. 28	Kutno	schoolboy
305. Jakubowicz, Dorothea	05. 07. 34	Antwerp	schoolgirl
306. Jakubowicz, Eduard	08. 06. 38	Antwerp	none
307. Flaster, Wolf	15. 03. 97	Biecz	machine fitter
308. Flaster-Moskovic, Serena	23. 02. 06	Rukacovo	seamstress
309. Plaster, Leizer Chaskel	20. 12. 00	Biecz	businessman
310. Lachmann-Ova, Hanny	05. 12. 12	Dusina	tailor
311. Reichmann, Ludwig	22. 04. 76	Halmen	none
312. Reichmann-Glatt, Feiga	28. 09. 80	Ulanowpol	housewife
313. Rub, Lenca	07. 07. 06	Roa de Sus	waitress
314. Kains, Alfred Israel	10. 01. 15	Berlin	decorator
315. Goldstein, Elias Leo	29. 07. 10	Antwerp	diamond-splitter
316. Goldstein, Richard	07. 08. 13	Antwerp	diamond-cutter

29. 01. 43

317. Najberger, Moszek Icek	17. 12. 08	Tomaszow	furrier
318. Najberger-Flesik, Bajla	17. 09. 10	Warsaw	housewife
319. Najberger, Isidor Israel Marcel	01. 12. 34	Tomaszow	schoolboy
320. Najberger, Marcel Joseph Isidoor	14. 04. 37	Ixelles	none
321. Najberger, Haja Sura	1910	Tomraszowic	none
322. Minc, Jacob	28. 07. 97	Przedborg	tailor
323. Wainberger-Jakubowicz, Chaja Dwoja	1882	Przgry	seamstress
324. Resler, Mendel	22. 07. 94	Sulitsa Botosani	cutter
325. Resler-Gutmann, Rebecca	22. 07. 95	Jassy	tailor
326. Resler, Alexander	26. 12. 22	Bucharest	tailor
327. Resler, Mirace	06. 04. 26	Bucharest	accountant
328. Resler, Tauba	13. 06. 28	Bucharest	schoolgirl
329. Resler, Eva	02. 10. 29	Etterbeek	schoolgirl
330. Frydland, Israel-Majer	25. 01. 06	Grojze	tailor

331. Apfel-Frank, Clara Sara	17. 11. 66	Elsen-Grev.	none
332. Einmann, Adolf	30. 08. 97	Lukow	fitter
333. Einmann-Apfel, Ella (widow Leffmann)	19. 02. 95	Münstereifel	housewife
334. Tenenbaum, Szlajme Majer Salom	15. 12. 99	Tomaszow	tailor
335. Herschlikowitsch, Godel Israel	27. 11. 99	Zloezen	furrier
336. Neumann, Heinrich	03. 09. 09	Vienna	electrician
337. Isaak-Stein, Johanna Paula	25. 06. 82	Danzig	housewife
338. Silbersztejn, Henri Herz	15. 07. 23	Warsaw	tailor
339. Moskovic-Iczkovic-Ova, Ides	15. 11. 11	Nogovo	shirtmaker
340. Patron, Josef Majer	01. 11. 96	Warsaw	leather-worker
341. Patron-Bergerman, Szaindel	03. 11. 97	Warsaw	leather-worker
342. Majzel, Baruch	24. 06. 06	Leczyen	doctor
343. Majzel-Tabak, Sara	26. 08. 10	Stanislow	teacher
344. Ujlaki, Fritz (xxII-396)	12. 08. 09	Vienna	book printer
345. Tenenbaum, Ruwen (xxvI-1)	07. 05. 06	Warsaw	techn. text. mach.
346. Tenenbaum-Elsztajn, Hinda	15. 09. 12	Skiernicwice	tailor
347. Bloch-Loeb, Sofie	08. 02. 73	Boppard	housewife
348. Bunn, Feibisch	01. 06. 66	Bahin	none
349. Bunn-Seligmann, Johanna	22. 10. 78	Kettig	housewife
350. Kleinberg-false Zeisler, Beila Hinda	23. 03. 12	Brzeske	housekeeper
351. Ellbogen, Ludewig	23. 09. 01	Neutra	paint-maker
352. Hirsch, Moritz	30. 01. 74	Frankf. a. M.	businessman
353. Hirsch-Adler, Ida	08. 02. 77	Darmstadt	housewife
354. Baumann, Samuel	09. 07. 74	Illkirch	none
355. Dubrowin, David	15. 10. 11	—	leather-worker
356. Klein-Schimko, Edith	14. 06. 11	Vienna	tailor
357. Liber, Jacob	30. 01. 98	Czarnovice	tailor
358. Denkscherz-Ebenstein, Cäcilie	23. 05. 03	Vienna	shorthand-typist
359. Denkscherz, Paul	17. 12. 30	Vienna	schoolboy
360. de Groot, Abraham	21. 05. 07	Antwerp	diamond-grinder
361. de Groot, Louis	04. 11. 12	Amsterdam	diamond-grinder
362. Weisz, Sandor	18. 03. 11	Mendok	painter
363. Judkowic-Ova, Laja	01. 04. 10	Terebla	none
364. Immerglück, Chana Ittel	1907	Podgorze	diamond-cutter
365. Immerglück, Ruth Helena	03. 04. 40	Antwerp	none
366. Immerglück, Jeanne	29. 10. 42	Antwerp	none
367. Langerman, David Melech	07. 07. 88	Przenyel	none
368. Feldman, Ruchla Dwoira	15. 09. 86	Dobrzyce	housewife
369. Langerman, Chana	08. 01. 27	Berchem-Antw.	schoolgirl
370. Langerman, Lea	12. 02. 33	Antw. Borgerh.	schoolgirl
371. Smaragd, Szmul Zaisvell	24. 11. 82	Warsaw	businessman
372. Smaragd, Rose	30. 03. 24	Paris	seamstress
373. Beckering-Davids, Anna	15. 09. 71	Amsterdam	housewife

374. Metz-Cohen-Rodriguez, Sara	07. 10. 89	Amsterdam	saleswoman
375. Mintz-Gutterman, Helena	24. 12. 85	Warsaw	seamstress
376. Walzer, Bernard	30. 08. 02	Jaroslaw	businessman
377. Walzer-Brachfeld, Sprince	30. 01. 03	Jurkow	housewife
378. Walzer, Helene	14. 03. 40	Antwerp	none

02. 02. 43

379. Karpin, Motek	15. 11. 02	Warsaw	driver
380. Holzer-Schuster, Cäcilie	30. 12. 05	Vienna	tailor
381. Holzer, Erika	28. 11. 31	Vienna	schoolgirl
382. Fischer-Hart, Anna	10. 11. 02	Vienna	tailor
383. Kutnowski, Léon	18. 10. 19	Sidler	tailor
384. Falcman, Abram Fiszel	17. 02. 03	Strykow	leather-worker
385. Falcman-Wolf, Tauba Laja	28. 05. 06	Strykow	housewife
386. Wolf, Fiszel	11. 12. 02	Lodz	factory worker
387. Wolf-Lewik, Laja	10. 07. 01	Zarnowice	furrier
388. Wolf, Gela	04. 05. 22	Lodz	glove-maker
389. Korman, Uszer	24. 03. 99	Pietrkow	tailor
390. Korman-Dorfman, Ilena	1903	Ostrelonka	tailor
391. Fisch, Filip	04. 10. 07	Lvov	fitter
392. Fisch-Jakubowicz, Liba	19. 09. 00	Brzedborg	shoe-sewer
393. Fisch, Leon	25. 08. 92	Strusow	tailor
394. Fisch, Anna	23. 04. 37	Brussels	none
395. Goldsztajn, Israel	14. 01. 02	Pajengwo	cobbler
396. Goldsztajn-Szczupak, Sura	07. 05. 02	Dzialoszyn	seamstress
397. Brandt-Cymerman, Krasla	1889	Dzialoszyn	housewife
398. Leichtman, Fani	15. 10. 04	Sazbor	tailor
399. Urbach, Juda Arje	24. 03. 05	Czestochowa	tailor
400. Urbach-Poringer, Estera	03. 05. 10	Czestochowa	tailor
401. Urbach, Puk Rita	03. 04. 24	Czestochowa	schoolgirl
402. Morgenstern, Roza	25. 08. 92	Strusow	tailor
403. Schönfeld, Simon	13. 03. 84	Kolomea	bookbinder
404. Schönfeld-Spalter, Debora	15. 02. 92	Stojasnow	cook
405. Buchler-Sperber, Sprynca Gitla	25. 09. 99	Hinsko	tailor
406. Buchler, Bernard	09. 01. 29	Vienna	schoolboy
407. Gordin, Maurice	30. 10. 86	Polotzla	lawyer
408. Gordin-Churin, Ita	01. 07. 89	Kraslazel	none
409. Gordin, Frieda	26. 09. 15	Nizhni Novg.	teacher
410. Spektor, Saul (XXI-33)	07. 05. 15	Samba	tailor
411. Retman-Goldstein, Ryfka	14. 11. 95	Warsaw	none
412. Archinoff, Alexandre	07. 08. 99	Alexandrowsky	language teacher
413. Archinoff-Smorgonski, Frieda	14. 11. 94	Wilna	masseuse

03. 02. 43

414. Haberman, Soucher	07. 07. 13	Warsaw	furrier
415. Gutman, Abraham	10. 05. 69	Warsaw	leather-cutter

416. Handsman, Tauba Rywka	27. 08. 03	Warsaw	factory worker
417. Handsman, Cywja Julia	07. 11. 30	Brussels	schoolgirl
418. Feit, Leo	23. 03. 97	Sanok	textile worker
419. Eichel, Maks	07. 07. 07	Bosnowice	tailor
420. Heilbronn-Huhn, Klara	18. 07. 95	Staitlingsfeld	nurse
421. Lammfromm-Thorner, Johanna S.	03. 10. 80	Berlin	none
422. Zylberstajn, Zalma	14. 01. 09	Szezekociny	fitter
423. Frajman, Israel Jakob	15. 05. 02	Bralobzeg	carpenter
424. Lehrer, Markus	25. 03. 10	Limanow	rubber coat manufacturer
425. Lehrer, Chaim	11. 12. 81	Podgorze	businessman
426. Lehrer-Landau, Debora	14. 07. 80	Limanowa	housewife
427. Bandel, Benjamin	07. 03. 08	Sanok	driver
428. Berges, Marianne Rosa	08. 01. 20	Hamburg	none
429. Friend, Julius (xxv-2)	17. 12. 19	Belz	carpentry apprentice
430. Tabak, Chaim	06. 02. 13	Krzesjow	tailor
431. Littman, Herman Armand	03. 04. 84	Puesti	businessman
432. Kauf, Bernard	05. 06. 23	Berlin	furrier
433. Eisner-Lebensohn, Gitel	26. 12. 94	Podowola-Cz.	shirt-maker
434. Lewin, Heinz-Hermann Israel	23. 10. 11	Berlin	driver
435. Reissmann-Hecht, Liselotte	13. 05. 10	Berlin	seamstress
436. Atyas, Samuel (xxI-1058)	14. 04. 09	S—	salesman
437. Wachsman, Hirsch	12. 07. 95	Krakow	businessman
438. Wachsman, Julien (xxI-27)	18. 05. 16	Vienna	salesman
439. Wiesner, Kurt (xxI-27)	18. 05. 16	Vienna	clerk
440. Rosler-Werner, Sara	28. 08. 15	Vienna	housewife
441. Rosler, Helene	27. 04. 40	Antwerp	none
442. Rosler, Tulla	01. 04. 42	Antwerp	none
443. Langrock, Szyron	01. 03. 98	Krakow	furrier
444. Langrock-Landau, Dresel	02. 07. 04	Neu Sandez	housewife
445. Langrock, Salomon-Alexander	19. 01. 30	Antwerp	schoolboy
446. Langrock, Joel	01. 10. 34	Antwerp	schoolboy
447. Beer, Robert	02. 12. 94	Grodek	French polisher
448. Beer-Stapelfeldt, Solka Sora	10. 11. 97	Kolomsa	housewife
449. Beer, Hella Sara	16. 09. 23	Hamburg	tailor
450. Gutwein-Reinhald, Hudes-Helena	26. 02. 82	Reglice	housewife
451. Gutwein, Meilech	06. 07. 91	Neu Sandez	businessman
452. Gutwein-Beldengrun, Helena	15. 06. 95	Mszana	housewife
453. Richter-Kornfeld, Rosa	02. 06. 66	Seidziszow	none
454. Grosz-Reichman, Maria	18. 11. 02	Satu Mare	housewife
455. Grosz, Paula	16. 01. 26	Antwerp	schoolgirl
456. Grosz, Alexander	03. 07. 28	Antwerp	schoolboy
457. Grosz, Anni	26. 10. 29	Antwerp	schoolgirl
458. Fuss-Laufer, Malia	01. 11. 04	Tarnow	housewife

459. Fuss, Silvain	01. 11. 29	Antwerp	schoolgirl
460. Fuss, Arnold	09. 03. 34	Antwerp	schoolboy

04. 02. 43

461. Woythaler, Conrad	29. 02. 72	Bordzichow	none
462. Mayer-Woythaler, Erika	23. 03. 02	Danzig	seamstress
463. Dr Van Thyn, Branko	26. 12. 97	Zaandam	chemist/pharmacist
464. De Leeuwe, Louis	28. 03. 03	Enschede	electrician
465. De Leeuwe-Velleman, Klaartje	30. 12. 03	Gröningen	office worker
466. De Leeuwe, Abraham (xxi-4)	06. 06. 25	Enschede	electrical apprentice
467. De Leeuwe, Marion	27. 02. 40	Enschede	schoolgirl
468. Kesing-De Vos, Betty	16. 05. 07	Amsterdam	housewife
469. Kesing, Roosje Yvonne	08. 03. 34	Amsterdam	schoolgirl
470. Kesing, Ingrid Marietta	26. 10. 35	Amsterdam	schoolgirl
471. Kesing, Kees	16. 10. 36	Amsterdam	schoolboy

05. 02. 43

472. Giller, Srul	05. 03. 07	Ostrow	leather-worker
473. Spiro-Pastein, Esther Beila	25. 12. 85	Warsaw	housewife
474. Spiro, Chaja Scheindel	28. 05. 08	Warsaw	tie-maker
475. Czyzyk-Farkasova, Silvina	18. 10. 15	Sevlus	housewife
476. Czysyk, Myriam	05. 07. 42	Antwerp	none
477. Schnitzer-Lemberger, Hinda Beila	16. 07. 98	Krakow	housewife
478. Schnitzer, Henriette	03. 05. 40	Antwerp	none
479. Fuks, Berek Rolf	16. 08. 98	Turobin	diamond-splitter
480. Fuks-Mahler, Rosa Elke	23. 07. 06	Przeworsk	housewife
481. Fuks, Salomea	13. 10. 36	Antwerp	schoolgirl
482. Fuks, Moses	05. 02. 38	Antwerp	none
483. Casoetto-Querido, Reine	08. 09. 72	Amsterdam	none
484. Novosedzas, Naftelis	05. 09. 00	Pasvalys	clerk
485. Novosedzas-Goldsztaub, Marjem	28. 06. 00	Warsaw	housewife
486. Novosedzas, Esther Augusta	02. 07. 30	Antwerp	schoolgirl
487. Novosedzas, Charlotte Frieda	26. 11. 33	Antwerp	schoolgirl
488. Berliner-Reinhard, Meta	03. 07. 05	Holsen	tailor
489. Berliner, Isaak	10. 04. 39	Cologne	none
490. Berliner, Felix	13. 08. 40	Antwerp	none
491. Weinberger-Haferling, Rywa	06. 09. 01	Krosno	housewife
492. Weinberger, Albertine Babine	23. 11. 35	Antwerp	schoolgirl
493. Weinburger, Abraham Chaim	18. 10. 38	Antwerp	none
494. Weinberger, Anna	07. 10. 42	Antwerp	none
495. Teff, Mordchay (xxi)	22. 05. 12	Bialystok	tailor
496. Turko-Frajfus, Chaja	23. 11. 11	Warsaw	housewife
497. Turko, Simon	13. 05. 36	Antwerp	schoolboy

06. 02. 43

498. Israels, Gustave	14. 11. 96	Molenbeek	clerk

499. Israels-Alexander, Suzanne H. L.	03. 05. 00	Antwerp	housewife
500. Israels, Alice Renée	18. 10. 30	Molenbeek	schoolgirl
501. Wozniak, Julia	30. 10. 99	Barzenia	trouser-maker
502. Herschensohn, Abram	29. 04. 96	Lublin	cap-maker
503. Herschensohn-Schneider, Beile Bline	31. 8. 08	Vinkovie	seamstress
504. Herschensohn, Margot	30. 10. 29	Cologne	schoolgirl
505. Hertzdahl, Sylvain	02. 09. 90	Sittard	factory director
506. Hertzdahl-Bloemgarten, Marie	22. 06. 97	Heerlen	housewife
507. Bonem, Rudolf	01. 01. 90	Trèves	hide-sorter
508. Goldgicht-Kac, Marjem	1905	Radzymin	tailor
509. Teichberg, Chaim Meyer	30. 10. 78	Saborow	businessman
510. van Bienen, Jules	28. 01. 77	Amsterdam	none
511. Landay, David	26. 07. 23	Zarebki	diamond-worker
512. Marcus, Alfred	26. 09. 86	Luneburg	dental technician
513. Kisner, David (xxi)	11. 04. 17	Baar	painter
514. Hobenwarten, Golda (xxi)	23. 10. 18	Wartenau	none
515. Rozen, Dawid	03. 09. 10	Blonse	tailor
516. Rozen-Rozencwajg, Syma Simonne	26. 05. 15	Lodz	tailor
517. Rafalowicz, Fanna Joseph	27. 05. 12	Radom	leather-worker
518. Rafalowicz-Stajnbaum, Rojza Etla	20. 04. 13	Radom	leather-worker
519. Solberg, Aron	28. 04. 93	Warsaw	businessman
520. Solberg-Lazarescu, Maria	25. 12. 04	Tannieu	tailor
521. Solberg, Frajda Myska	16. 06. 27	Roux	schoolgirl
522. Wallach, Fritz Israel	23. 03. 74	Berlin	none
523. Storm, Elias	13. 12. 11	Tarnow	tailor
524. Naftaniel, Hersch	09. 09. 14	Berlin	hairdresser
525. Schmidt, Paul	12. 07. 91	Tarnow	businessman
526. Besser, Isidor	13. 09. 96	Tarnow	businessman
527. Heimann, Fritz	01. 06. 87	Berlin	businessman
528. Roter-Tenenbaum, Haja	09. 05. 06	Walbran	tailor
529. Hertz, Walter Israel	04. 05. 15	Eschweiler	gardener
530. Oehlenberg, Paul	23. 08. 18	Vienna	car mechanic
531. Kirschenbaum, Feiwel	05. 05. 91 (93)	Tarnobrzeg	businessman
532. Steppel, Jacques	15. 10. 25	Antwerp	schoolboy
533. Steppel, Helene	30. 03. 28	Antwerp	schoolgirl
534. Steppel, Renée	03. 03. 33	Antwerp	schoolgirl
535. Steppel, Liliane	18. 08. 37	Antwerp	schoolgirl
536. Steppel, Bernardus	08. 02. 22	Antwerp	leather-worker

09. 02. 43

537. Kruk, Jacob (xxi)	12. 06. 11	Zelinea	businessman
538. Masznik, Izrael Katma	29. 10. 13	Novy Korczyn	joiner
539. Masznik-Zyngier, Chaja Hinda	10. 07. 17	Lodz	needlewoman
540. Masznik, Monique Clairette	31. 01. 34	Liège	none

541. Polaczek, Natan	24. 12. 84	Geniedz	businessman
542. Abrahams, Joseph	01. 11. 92	Arnhem	travelling salesman
543. Ungierowicz-Sochaczewska, Liba	20. 12. 91	Linczyck	seamstress

10. 02. 43

544. Wachsberger-Schneid, Gusta	12. 12. 97	Lemberg	tailor
545. Schneid, Max	03. 01. 08	Vienna	shoemaker
546. Schneid-Altmann, Grete	01. 04. 13	Vienna	tailor
547. Zybel, Salomon	31. 12. 98	Vilna	accountant
548. Zybel-Mioduszewska, Dwojra N.	06. 01. 08	Ostrow	seamstress
549. Mioduszewski, Froim Tauchim	12. 04. 06	Ostrow	wool-worker
550. Mioduszewski-Strauber, Chana Sara	04. 01. 13	Glasgow	seamstress
551. Bahr, Saly	16. 10. 98	Brühl	saddler
552. Mendlewicz-Iglinski, Szajna Golda	18. 01. 11	Wloclawek	tailor
553. Luftman-Iglinski, Frania	10. 02. 12	Wloclawek	tailor
554. Drummerova, Eugenie Jenny	18. 12. 22	Rostoka	housekeeper
555. Berberich, Abraham Israel	14. 09. 69	Gross Krotzenburg	none
556. Engelsztajn, Daniel	22. 01. 08	Tomaszow	tailor
557. Engelsztajn-Lefler, Estera	25. 02. 09	Krasnobrod	tailor
558. Fuks-Bach, Ruchla	15. 04. 04	Przynicka	tailor
559. Ajdler, Wolf Lajb	02. 01. 06	Warsaw	clockmaker
560. Pinatycki, Socher	24. 11. 95	Priesk	ironer
561. Pinatycki-Rozenberg, Ester	30. 03. 97	Tomaszow	leather-worker
562. Korn, Akiwa	15. 11. 96	Warsaw	furrier
563. Kaufmann, Heinz Israel	19. 07. 07	Wiesbaden	designer
564. Farber, Max	23. 03. 99	Wikowice	businessman
565. Rodriguez-Lopez, Leopold Mozes	30. 08. 03	Amsterdam	businessman
566. Slodzina, David Abram	26. 05. 74	Kalisz	weaver
567. Kaplan, Martha	20. 02. 04	Kalisz	housewife
568. Grün, Moses David	30. 03. 00	Brzesko	salesman
569. Grün-Hellfeld, Necha Nelly	02. 03. 04	Stanislawow	office worker
570. Heigmans, Eliazer	11. 11. 64	Amsterdam	none
571. Agsterribbe-Heigmans,	26. 10. 93	Amsterdam	housewife
572. Wijnschenk, Maurits	10. 11. 04	Amsterdam	storekeeper
573. Wijnschenk-Da Silva Abenator, Rachel	27. 09. 01	Amsterdam	company secretary
574. Stolowicz, David	14. 09. 12	Warsaw	diamond-grinder
575. Stolowicz-Halbzaijd, Rosa	14. 02. 10	Odessa	saleswoman/ seamstress
576. Stolowicz, Abraham Robert	08. 06. 36	Antwerp	schoolboy
577. Wijnschenk, David	27. 04. 08	Amsterdam	mechanic
578. Wijnschenk-Da Silva Abenator, Elisab.	07. 11. 05	Amsterdam	housewife
579. Goldmann, Baruch	01. 02. 83	Kanczugs	businessman

580.	Goldman-Karniol, Rikel	30. 12. 11	Sokal	housewife
581.	Goldman, Oscar Maurits	25. 06. 41	Antw. Berchem	none
582.	Hamburger, Jesaia	04. 03. 83	Amsterdam	none
583.	Hamburger-Blom, Esther	21. 05. 80	Uithoorn	housewife
584.	Blom, Jacob	07. 08. 52	Mijdrecht	none
585.	Velleman, Salomon	26. 10. 77	Antwerp	none
586.	Velleman-Van Been, Bertha	10. 09. 83	Rotterdam	housewife
587.	Gompers-Velleman, Roosje	03. 10. 72	Rotterdam	none
588.	Treff, Mozes	14. 01. 87	Dukla	businessman
589.	Treff-Lderberger, Esther	18. 03. 97	Wisnicz	housewife
590.	Treff, Fanny	15. 08. 30	Berlin	schoolgirl
591.	Weinreb-Weinreb, Rosa	1893	Baranow	housewife
592.	Weinreb, Scheindla	29. 11. 21	Baranow	milliner
593.	Hamburger, Simon	18. 01. 72	Amsterdam	none
594.	Hamburger-Helmstadt, Jeannette	22. 08. 75	Amsterdam	housewife
595.	Losner, Josef	06. 02. 81	Radautz	travelling salesman

11. 02. 43

596.	Rosenfeld-Franck, Germaine Esther	21. 09. 88	Bayonne	leather-worker
597.	Porges, Erwin	16. 07. 91	Prague	office worker
598.	Wachsman-Jakubowicz, Chaja Hel.	25. 09. 98	Wodisislaw	seamstress
599.	Szpajer, David Albert	22. 04. 10	Darmstadt	decorator
600.	Goldmann, Maria	20. 10. 19	Cologne	milliner
601.	Bienstock-Wolf, Chana Feigel	07. 08. 97	Wischnitz	housewife
602.	Bienstock, Emmanuela	08. 06. 29	Dortmund	schoolgirl
603.	Glazman, Moszek	15. 10. 82	Staszow	tailor
604.	Caron-Gefner, Gusti	23. 01. 20	Vienna	housewife
605.	Sieradszki-Krys, Liba	03. 02. 00	Lodz	seamstress
606.	Sieradski, Jankiel Jules	20. 03. 27	Wierzow	schoolboy
607.	Greidinger, Hermann (xxiii-16)	03. 03. 00	Dobromil	tailor
608.	Goldstein, Abraham	16. 12. 79	Garsolin	none
609.	Farkas, Saja Matya	06. 12. 90	Ruske	shoemaker
610.	Stein, Max	28. 05. 89	Vienna	accountant
611.	Stein-Aufrichter, Karoline	01. 07. 94	Boskowitz	housewife
612.	Krasucki, Moszek	30. 09. 87	Warsaw	leather-worker
613.	Markovics, Meyer	07. 06. 05	Tomaszow	tailor
614.	Mittelbach, Icek Izaak	04. 04. 95	Noury-Awor	poissonier
615.	Singer-Kupfer, Pessil	09. 05. 06	Przeworsk	nurse
616.	Medman-Vacman, Szprinca	1869	Gorzkoma	none
617.	Herszkowicz-Medman, Sury	1911	Opoczne	tailor
618.	Siedner, Felix Karl	25. 06. 05	Breslau	electrical mechanic
619.	Lewin, Moszko	10. 04. 21	Biala	tailor
620.	Sztaynberg, Szaja	02. 02. 99	Tomaszow	tailor
621.	Sztaynberg-Jacobowicz, Paula M.	15. 10. 06	Piotrkow	tailor

12. 02. 43

622. Blicher, David Laib	18. 01. 97	Radymmo	hotel employee
623. Blicher-Stockhamer recta Garfunkel, Chana	17. 12. 04	Radymmo	seamstress
624. Rozenstein, Helene	16. 04. 11	Lodz	nurse
625. Jakubowicz, Salomon	12. 12. 72	Kamyk	cobbler
626. Sainderichin-Brodsky, Maria	04. 06. 81	Kischineff	housewife
627. Mühlrad-Schick, Blanka	28. 07. 99	Radocfcofcs	housewife
628. Mühlrad, Erich	25. 02. 34	Vienna	schoolboy
629. Neuberger-Mahler, Liba	15. 12. 87	Krakow	housewife
630. Siedlecki, Wolf	31. 12. 07	Kolbiel	knitter
631. Siedlecki-Rosen, Curtla	15. 05. 05	Warsaw	seamstress
632. Siedlecki, Sara	10. 10. 31	Antwerp	schoolgirl
633. Siedlecki, Bernard	30. 10. 32	Antwerp	schoolboy
634. Siedlecki, Stella	13. 06. 38	Antwerp	none
635. Zonszajn, Eljezar	23. 07. 08	Warsaw	mechanic
636. Zonszajn-Siedlecka, Estera Laja	20. 07. 08	Warsaw	seamstress
637. Zonszajn, Fajga Dina	12. 02. 29	Warsaw	schoolgirl
638. Zonszajn, Dora	26. 07. 36	Antw. Borgerhout	schoolgirl
639. De Vries-Kleinberger, Lea	31. 03. 75	Krakow	none
640. Komkommer, Joseph	31. 12. 81	Amsterdam	none
641. Preso-De Groot, Esther	14. 05. 87	Amsterdam	none
642. Hoffmann, Rudolf	03. 04. 75	Neuss a. Rh.	none
643. Blauner, Szymon	12. 03. 08	Tarnow	businessman
644. Hoffmann-Seligmann, Clara	28. 08. 79	Darmstadt	housewife
645. Hermann, Mendel	01. 08. 91	Stanislaw	fruit preserve manufacturer
646. Landau-Krupel, Krawel	15. 11. 97	Berchy	furrier
647. Berman, Hil	1878	Jurburg	none
648. Getreider, Chaskel	09. 11. 99	Cswiescin	diamond-grinder
649. Monitz, Charles	04. 10. 93	Crewa	goldsmith/tinsmith
650. Schabes-Teichner, Gizela	21. 06. 04	Tarnow	housewife

13. 02. 43

651. Miller-Sprenger, Gertrud	21. 06. 94	Stettin	housewife
652. Mayer, Karl	16. 11. 09	Vienna	company director shoe factory
653. Fogelsen, Sebastian	23. 01. 79	Krievija	factory director
654. Kandel, Jakob Israel	24. 02. 06	Vienna	travelling salesman
655. Kandel-Getzl, Martha	17. 12. 13	Vienna	tailor
656. Kandel, Renée	17. 10. 38	Brussels	none
~~657. Kandel, Henri~~	~~10. 01. 40~~	~~Brussels~~	
658. Kandel, Camilla	07. 05. 42	Brussels	none
659. Kandel-Krausz, Gertrude	27. 06. 21	Vienna	housewife

660. Kandel, Henri	29. 04. 41	Hasselt	none
661. Klein-Thalheim, Elisabeth	29. 05. 01	Vienna	housewife
662. Lüfschütz, Bela	06. 11. 01	Budapest	electrician
663. Louis-Rakowsky-Glancz, Malvinel	08. 07. 84	Wartberg	model designer
664. Rambam, Moses	15. 11. 96	Combien	accountant
665. Rambam-Frenkel, Ester	07. 06. 00	Lodz	housewife

15. 02. 43

666. Glaser, Simon	07. 04. 92	Boryslaw	tailor
667. Glaser, Karl	10. 08. 27	Vienna	schoolboy

16. 02. 43

668. Desau, Juda Ber	20. 06. 95	Belchatow	tailor
669. Desau-Bogdanska, Sara Rywka	1902	Tuszyn	tailor
670. Desau, Rafael	29. 06. 27	Tuszyn	tailor
671. Silberstern, Moritz	15. 03. 66	Goltsch-Fenikau	none
672. Szpiro-Jakubowitsch, Ita	1886	Sulejow	housewife
673. Szpiro-Bornszejn, Raca	18. 08. 09	Lask	leather-worker
674. Gutman, Szulem Moszke	10. 07. 00	Ruda	leather-worker
675. Gardyn-Rozenbaum, Ita Gitla	1893	Reuspol	housewife
676. Bleiberg-Hefter, Gitel	17. 03. 80	Bohorodezany	housewife
677. Bleiberg, Meschulim-Chaim	01. 03. 07	Mikuliczyn	travelling salesman
678. Bleiberg-Giniewski, Ruchel	07. 03. 14	Stanislaw	tailor
679. Bleiberg, Anna	06. 03. 41	Zottegem	none
680. Ajzenfisz-Desau, Blima Rajga	12. 06. 22	Tuszow	tailor
681. Rozenfeld-Weberman, Chaja	1869	Lukow	none
682. Gutman-Rosenfeld, Reisla	1894	Lukow	housewife
683. Gutman, Ester	12. 10. 33	Anderlecht	schoolgirl
684. Jellinek, Leopold	21. 09. 62	Znaim	none
685. Jellinek-Hollitscher, Therese	08. 12. 66	Nikolsburg	housewife
686. Passman-Vogelsang, Jeannette	28. 01. 78	Gelsenkirchen	none
687. Hechtkopf, Max	30. 05. 94	Culin	baker
688. Hechtkopf-Scholna, Thea	08. 10. 02	Berlin	housewife
690. Scholna-Reihsner, Gertrud	12. 09. 66	Sochow	none
691. Ackerhalt-Fried, Reisel	19. 08. 97	Krakow	none
692. Hausner, Mendel Lei	29. 12. 09	Ropica	linen-cutter
693. Hausner-Kalter, Frieda	08. 10. 12	Düsseldorf	housewife
694. Hausner, Max	25. 06. 36	Düsseldorf	schoolboy
695. Goldstein, Bernard	12. 03. 14	Teuste	tailor
696. Goldstein-Buchsbaum, Pessel	15. 12. 12	Wisnicz	storekeeper
697. Goldstein, Jacob	03. 07. 41	Alken	none
698. Lubolski-Bornstein, Laja	19. 07. 82	Kowal	none
699. Grunbaum-Bornstein, Fella Feiga	07. 10. 88	Kowal	none
700. Stark, Hugo	06. 12. 09	Vienna	clockmaker
701. Stark-Engel, Hildegarde	30. 10. 09	Vienna	housewife
702. Stark alias Engel, Pierre René	29. 11. 39	Brussels	none

703. Kohn-Pollak, Bertha	02. 10. 94	Vienna	tailor
704. Bueno de Mesquita-Edelstein, Toni	05. 01. 23	Warsaw	furworker
705. Edelstein, Adela	05. 01 23	Warsaw	machine seamstress
706. Hahn, Herbert (xxi)	01. 01. 13	Cologne	baker
707. Hahn-Domb, Blima (xxi)	17. 01. 18	Zurich	off-the-peg clothes manufacturer
708. Dalicz, Ignaz (xxi)	18. 11. 94	Brody	tailor
709. Keinigsmann, Chaim	15. 08. 02	Warsaw	off-the-peg clothes manufacturer
710. Adler-Brauner, Louisa B.	24. 08. 73	Odessa	none
711. Kleinrock-Adler, Cornelia	10. 03. 02	Vienna	bank official
712. Kleinrock, Suzanne	02. 12. 30	Vienna	schoolgirl
713. Lederer-Guttmann, Marie	12. 10. 01	Vienna	housewife
714. Schick-Sax, Cornelia	19. 03. 99	Vienna	tailor
715. Goldwasser, Abram	01. 04. 98	Odessa	tailor
716. Goldwasser-Lubelski (Grojnowksi), Fale	18. 07. 08	Radjiejow	tailor
717. Eisner, Juda (xxi)	10. 10. 94	Husokow	businessman
718. Klein, Joseph	08. 03. 98	Trumbowla	waiter
719. Cahen, Irma	07. 10. 78	Arlon	needlewoman
720. Cahen, Camille	18. 08. 82	Arlon	needlewoman
721. Hausner-Goldberg, Pesia Gina	21. 07. 05	Tarnobzeg	housewife and seamstress
722. Rottenberg, Elias David	02. 02. 06	Stanislaw	farm worker
723. Rottenberg-Berkelhammer, Bertha	25. 09. 09	Vienna	housewife
724. Rottenberg, Robert	31. 12. 28	Vienna	schoolboy

18. 02. 43

725. Jablonsky-Dykierman, Ruchla	30. 11. 78	Wiernzow	none
726. Goldszteyn-Kaplan, Masze	13. 12. 00	Zelschow	housewife
727. Goldsztein, Regina	16. 12. 29	Brussels	schoolgirl
728. Goldsztein, Rosa Frieda	19. 12. 31	Antwerp	schoolgirl
729. Goldsztein, Maria	29. 01. 37	Antwerp	none
730. Rychter, Szlama Mordechay (xxi)	01. 01. 07	Biala	tailor
731. Grünblatt, Moses	20. 10. 88	Riga	diamond-worker
732. Aron-Finkelstein, Salomea	18. 08. 77	Tarnopol	none
733. Epstein-Weisz, Ester	26. 06. 95	Szylaes (Romania)	none
734. Goldstein, Dina	24. 01. 33	Etterbeek	schoolgirl
735. Stein, Ester	19. 01. 28	Antwerp	schoolgirl
736. Tzwern-Wasyng, Hena	01. 01. 13	Warsaw	housewife
737. Zanger-Frand, Feige Ruchel	30. 04. 61	Dubiecko	none
738. Grinberg, Joseph	18. 10. 05	Warsaw	baker
739. Greizerstein-Zingher, Zilda	05. 03. 07	Vetcani	housewife

740.	Greizerstein, Ruth	03. 08. 29	Leipzig	schoolgirl
741.	Greizerstein, Jacob	16. 06. 31	Leipzig	schoolboy
742.	Greizerstein, Manfred	14. 01. 36	Antwerp	schoolboy
743.	Gründland-Gradus, Elka	1861	Warsaw	none
744.	Gründland, Marjem	1887	Warsaw	none
745.	Gehl-Joachimsmann, Frieda	08. 10. 03	Trappau	office worker
746.	Hoffmann-Loew, Sara Hilda	17. 03. 79	Mogendorf	none
747.	Breso, Willem (xxi)	04. 06. 24	Antwerp	tailor's apprentice

19. 02. 43

748.	Mogielnicki, Lejbus	22. 06. 09	Uszczanow	tailor
749.	Birn, Moritz (xxii-1)	15. 09. 12	Chemnitz	furrier
750.	Ames, Lejzor (xxiiA)	10. 03. 98	Dubiecko	tailor
751.	Biglajzen, Henri	01. 03. 35	Etterbeek	schoolboy
752.	Werner, Leon (xxiii-10)	07. 05. 04	Stanislau	mechanic
753.	Brzustowski-Hoffman, Rywka	14. 10. 04	Dobrowice	tailor
754.	Brzustowski, Hersch	04. 02. 06	Lodz	tailor
755.	Borenstein-Cwajman, Fajga	27. 03. 99	Warsaw	housewife
756.	Berger, Samuel	19. 01. 96	Przemysl	manual worker
757.	Berger-Stahl, Anna	13. 10. 11	Lemberg	housewife
758.	Sisslé, Salomon Marcusoff	20. 09. 90	Lithanew	bookbinder
759.	Steinwolf, Moses (xxii)	07. 07. 01	Podwolodziska	businessman
760.	Zylberszac, Szmul Szulem (xxvi-58)	13. 05. 94	Ozorkow	leather-worker
761.	Blum-Beglajzer, Chawa	10. 07. 97	Tomaszow	tailor
762.	Lindner, Hubert	12. 04. 25	Vienna	dental technician
763.	Schäfler, Penäler Saul (xxiii-13)	06. 12. 01	Kolomea	teacher
764.	Cleffmann, Alex Israel	06. 12. 78	Wesel a. Rh.	businessman
765.	Liebeskind-Sztark, Golda	1897	Ozorkow	tailor
766.	Liebeskind, Sophia	12. 07. 27	Lodz	schoolgirl
767.	Liebeskind, Cecilia	18. 06. 30	Brussels	schoolgirl
768.	Pytel, Benejon Noach	1903	Lodz	businessman
769.	Pytel-Szulman, Zelda	21. 05. 01	Lodz	housewife
770.	Gutman-Rosenberg, Frieda	18. 02. 96	Bendzin	cook
771.	Piekerz, Wolf	25. 09. 98	Nosgobody	tailor
772.	Piekerz, Faga Ryfka	20. 07. 24	Etterbeek	tailor
773.	Piekerz, Paula Madeleine	05. 11. 29	Etterbeek	schoolgirl
774.	Martchouk, Chaim Bozuk	15. 03. 71	Mechelmotte	musician
775.	Ajzenfisz, Joseph	04. 04. 22	Warsaw	leather-worker
776.	Desau, Brana	02. 02. 24	Tuszyn	corset-maker
777.	Löw, Walter Max	01. 10. 96	Hamburg	director of dipl. Archives
778.	Löw-Flatow, Edith Vera	27. 01. 02	Berlin	housewife
779.	Goldsteinas, Mendelis Judelis	05. 10. 01	Maryampolis	chemist
780.	Goldsteinas-Vistinezki, Henda	17. 12. 05	Maryampolis	office worker
781.	Bornsztejn-Lajtmann, Szajndla	28. 09. 08	Warsaw	seamstress

782. Liberman, Szylam	23. 03. 03	Warsaw	cook and waiter
783. Herszaft-Fuchs, Pessa	June 66	Warsaw	none
784. Herszaft, Joseph	24. 03. 91	Warsaw	leather-worker
785. Herszaft-Blech, Judith	16. 06. 01	Gerzd	door-to-door saleswoman
786. Gorowicz-Kawa, Sara Zysa	1864	Racinz	none
787. Matzner-Klug, Margarethe	03. 07. 90	Szered	housewife
788. Pardes-Goldwasser, Braune	15. 11. 03	Czwiecin	housewife
789. Litwer, Karel	20. 02. 89	Amsterdam	diamond-grinder
790. Van Rijn-Elsas, Johanne	18. 11. 19	Amsterdam	housewife
791. Van Rijn, Jaak	08. 05. 41	Antw. Deurne	none
792. Weitz, Nachmann	25. 06. 93	Laak	electrician
793. Weitz-Hampel, Chaja	10. 06. 94	Nowo Radomsk	tailor
794. Weitz, Szymon Israel	07. 11. 27	Konin	tailor
795. Schops-Drucker, Seraphina	08. 03. 04	Cernowitz	milliner
796. Schops, Eveline Paula	20. 08. 27	Antwerp	milliner
797. Schops, Annie	31. 10. 30	Antwerp	schoolgirl
798. Landau, Maurice	17. 11. 97	Vizny Svidnik	pharmacist
799. Schreiber-Anisfeld, Chaja	14. 11. 90	Krakow	housewife
800. Hirsch, Maurice	14. 03. 70	Galatz	none
801. Gottfried-Kupfer, Chaja	03. 06. 08	Irgevorsk	tailor
802. Worms-Gans, Esther	16. 06. 76	Amsterdam	none
803. Thaler recta Wedner, Estera	20. 02. 02	Ustrzyki-Dolna	housekeeper
804. Woloski, Abraham	20. 01. 30	Antw. Borgerh.	schoolboy
805. Woloski, Anna	07. 10. 31	Antw. Borgerh.	schoolgirl
806. Woloski, Isaak	26. 05. 35	Antwerp	schoolboy
807. Woloski, Israel	19. 10. 38	Antwerp	none
808. Wizen-Wedner, Mirla	June 1905	Ustrzyki-Dolna	housewife
809. Wizen, Anna	01. 09. 36	Antwerp	schoolgirl
810. Wizen, Eva	15. 02. 39	Antwerp	none
811. Wizen, Nathan	19. 02. 41	Antwerp	none
812. Fischmann-Izrael, Esther	29. 01. 01	Turulung	housewife
813. Fischmann, Joseph	24. 05. 29	Antwerp	schoolboy
814. Blasz, Serena Sarah	16. 08. 13	Peten	diamond-grinder
815. Blasz, Bertha (Eva)	06. 10. 33	Antwerp	schoolgirl
816. Schuldenfrei-Goldstein, Esther	16. 07. 11	Lopan	tailor
817. Schuldenfrei, Heinz Adolf	14. 05. 33	Leipzig	schoolboy
818. Schuldenfrei, Manfred Moritz	07. 08. 35	Leipzig	schoolboy

20. 02. 43

819. Frenkiel, Dawid	23. 04. 11	Warsaw	travelling salesman
820. Fefer, Leo Siegfried	08. 02. 09	Offenbach a. M.	barber
821. Fefer-Binder, Estera Bracka	15. 09. 02	Corlice	housewife
822. Fefer, Hilda	29. 08. 34	Antwerp	schoolgirl
823. Jungst, Herke	14. 06. 05	Ozorkow	travelling salesman
824. Kaufmann, Max	07. 02. 77	Kornelimünster	none

825.	Bonn, Fanni	01. 01. 57	Malbach	none
826.	Bleiberg, Herman (XXIII-8)	15. 12. 08	Borchow	tailor
827.	Beff, Samuel	20. 08. 83	The Hague	musician
828.	Schwalb, Moritz	25. 04. 27	Smetkovice	businessman
829.	Jurysta-Fink, Sofia	09. 11. 00	Dzialoszyce	seamstress
830.	Jurysta, Berta	02. 02. 26	Antwerp	fur-maker
831.	Jurgskta-Apelbaum, Idessa	1872	Koroczyn	none
832.	Herschlikovitsch-Jurgskta, Rywka	30. 11. 98	Rendzin	cardboard worker
833.	Rosenzweig-Diamant, Golda	12. 07. 98	Strumiowa	tailor

23. 02. 43

834.	Sprecher, Eljasz	06. 08. 99	Sanok	diamond-cleaver
835.	Neuman, Abraham	06. 04. 19	Krakow	diamond-cutter
836.	Seelenfreund, Jonas	20. 01. 99	Ueszew	furrier
837.	Seelenfreund-Trieger, Mathilda	10. 10. 00	Noerisch-Ostro	housewife
838.	Adler, Klara	08. 11. 05	Gebweiler	kindergarten teacher
839.	Swaab, Samuel	10. 01. 21	Amsterdam	furrier
840.	Lewkowicz, Josef	14. 01. 08	Wieckewicz	tailor
841.	Lewkowicz-Freund, Ingeborg	04. 11. 21	M. Gladbach	tailor
842.	Goldschmidt, Hermann	12. 09. 23	Bonn a. Rh.	tailor
843.	Nudel, Moses	04. 08. 10	Warsaw	salesman
844.	Nudel-Fuswerk, Chaja	28. 03. 14	Warsaw	seamstress
845.	[blank]			
846.	Sochezcawski, Taube Marie (XXI)	04. 03. 15	Alexandrof	saleswoman
847.	Grün, Leon Lejzer	03. 08. 08	Brzesko	furrier
848.	Silber, Josef	14. 07. 08	Picnicza	businessman
849.	Südwerts-Knispel, Salome	15. 10. 02	Rzezow	tailor
850.	Südwerts, Adolf	09. 10. 28	Berlin	schoolboy
851.	Seiden-Altberger, Rosa	12. 02. 11	Frankf. a. M.	housewife
852.	Seiden, Leon	11. 12. 31	Cologne	schoolboy
853.	Seiden, Moritz Jakob	03. 06. 33	Cologne	schoolboy
854.	Eisenstark, Selda	28. 08. 16	Wtasyowa	tailor
855.	Haas, Emile	31. 05. 80	Kirschseifen	butcher
856.	Frogel, Nathan	04. 01. 00	Sceranow	joiner
857.	Frogel-Kaufmann, Hilde	15. 08. 01	Blumenthal	shorthand-typist
858.	Ingwer, Bernhard	03. 11. 07	Zloczow	tailor
859.	Ingwer-Salomon, Jeanne	14. 09. 12	Voelklange	correspondent
860.	Ingwer, Wilhelm	04. 08. 12	Voelklange	tailor
861.	Kimelfed-Rosenzweig, Dora	15. 04. 92	Tornazow	seamstress

25. 02. 45

862.	Markowicz-Rosental, Laja	19. 04. 07	Czestochowa	tailor
863.	Markowicz, Rudolf	12. 12. 31	Antwerp	schoolboy
864.	Jakab, Maria	14. 04. 08	Asualjul	cook
865.	Klapholz, Mayer	11. 06. 69	Nowy-Saez	none
866.	Stokler-Willdorff, Else	30. 03. 91	Danzig	housewife

867. Stockler, Anna Lise	25. 10. 26	Berlin	tailor
868. Man, Froim	23. 03. 05	Pradz	tailor
869. Kitaj, Estera Rena	11. 08. 96	Mlawa	tailor
870. Weiss aka Süsswein, Mayer	19. 10. 11	Neu-Sanez	—?
871. Dab recta Fleischman, Saul	30. 12. 11	Jaslo	installer
872. Dab, Blima	22. 10. 22	Jaslo	furworker
873. Kalter-Zimmermann, Chaja	March 65	Sekuren	none
874. Kohn-Stein, Filomena	15. 06. 73	Neu-Rosnitz	none
875. Kadinsky-Kabalkin, Marthe	1861	Doubrowno	none
876. Goldblat-Kadinsky, Polina	01. 12. 83	Dangoupils	none

26. 02. 43

877. Seiden, Markus Meyer	07. 03. 05	Bochnia	clockmaker
878. Finchelstein, Aizic	15. 01. 08	Tighine Kzarnanic	teacher
879. Westheimer, Julius	13. 06. 01	Canstatt	butcher
880. Westheimer-Borg, Meta (xxi)	09. 11. 04	Berlin	seamstress
881. Jaskiel, Abraham Jacob (xxv-9)	14. 11. 02	Czestochowa	travelling salesman
882. Finkelkraut, Isaak	July 91	Warsaw	tailor
883. Kruszel, Icek	21. 07. 02	Pawsinck-Wilance	tailor
884. Kruszel-Calka, Gela	1901	Kolbig	housewife
885. Kruszel, Maria Laja	14. 01. 29	Brussels	schoolboy
886. Lapman, Abram (xxi)	02. 08. 11	Warsaw	traveller
887. Goldring, Marie (xxi-18)	13. 08. 19	Leipzig	cinema artiste
888. Meyer, Johanna Sara	18. 07. 11	Euskirchen	hotel clerk
889. Glotzer-Molnar, Magdalena	07. 02. 13	Vienna	clerk
890. Fajngold, Moise Szyk	15. 07. 66	Janow	businessman
891. Fajngold-Fitrin, Liba	10. 10. 66	Janow	housewife
892. Rozentraub-Fajngold, Braimscha	25. 08. 07	Basle	none
893. Weisz, Miksa (xxv-4)	26. 08. 95	Budapest	plumber
894. Lebovic, Chaja	30. 01. 05	Sulchovce	tailor
895. Gottfeld, Ernst	14. 08. 03	Wuppertal	manufacturer
896. Brunner-Weindling, Anna Mina	25. 04. 61	Mako	none
897. Gutter-Brünner, Malvina	28. 07. 95	Sastoraljanglely	housewife
898. Gutter, Sylvia	18. 07. 25	Antwerp	schoolgirl
899. Gutter, Fernande	06. 05. 30	Antwerp	schoolgirl
900. Gutter, Marguerite Helene	03. 09. 33	Antwerp	schoolgirl
901. Blonder-Binnenstock, Tauba Ettel	01. 12. 80	Kolbuszowa	housewife
902. Czarna, Cyja	17. 05. 06	Wilma	masseuse
903. Czarna, Anna	04. 06. 40	Antwerp	none
904. Witteboon, Aron	25. 07. 77	Amsterdam	none
905. Witteboon-Swaab, Fenima	27. 12. 75	Hilversum	housewife
906. Rabinovitch-Garber, Beila	15. 03. 82	Novograd	housewife
907. Majbruch, Izak Lazar	05. 09. 13	Krakow	engineer/auditor
908. Majbruch-Rabinovitch, Laura	08. 07. 11	Novograd	housewife

909. Majbruch, Jacob	03. 04. 37	Antwerp	none

28. 02. 43

910. Gasman, Iechok Ajrijk	28. 08. 06	Lodz	cook
911. Karolinski, Jules	21. 12. 14	Warsaw	glove-maker
912. Sad, Michael	16. 03. 83	Kalisz	teacher
913. Weingarten, Frankisch	10. 10. 07	Volowa	tailor
914. Weingarten-Sad, Rana	10. 09. 05	Kalisz	tailor
915. Sad, Blima	28. 10. 17	Kalisz	glove-maker
916. Backer, Jakob	18. 11. 91	Wieszcourt	leather-cutter
917. Backer-Kainer, Rosa	21. 12. 88	Tarnow	housewife
918. Backer, Irène	02. 3. 23	Berlin	tailor
919. Backer, Adolf	09. 12. 24	Berlin	upholsterer
920. Borensztejn, Joseph	18. 04. 93	Warsaw	tailor
921. Borensztejn-Szklawer, Blina	15. 03. 94	Warsaw	none
922. Borensztejn, Mozek Aron	21. 07. 26	Warsaw	tailor
923. Borensztejn, Rachel	25. 10. 28	Warsaw	schoolgirl
924. Icek, Abraham	02. 07. 90	Bolsalawice	pastry-cook
925. Icek-Bulke, Gucia	16. 11. 87	Zlozen	housewife
926. Friedman, Nati	17. 09. 24	Vienna	mechanic
927. Mandel, Moses Leib	25. 04. 08	Loszensk	businessman
928. Icek, Szmul Heisz	20. 09. 27	Lututow	pastry-cook
929. Gliksman, Chaim Wolf	02. 01. 00	Zdunska Wola	off-the-peg tailor
930. Gliksman, Izak Mordka	09. 03. 24	Lodz	tailor
931. Leybtschik, Jefin	15. 10. 88	Bowrowak	clockmaker
932. Leybtschik-Kempler, Lea	20. 03. 05	Krakow	seamstress
933. Ghelmann-Pila, Masza	17. 06. 97	Zniamenka	hand seamstress
934. Grosman, Jacob Sechok	04. 07. 22	Warsaw	furrier
935. Pinkus, David Josef	01. 09. 02	Bendzin	furrier
936. Pinkus-Pinkus, Estera	29. 10. 99	Bendzin	furworker
937. Pinkus, Heinrich	02. 02. 30	Düsseldorf	schoolboy
938. Redlich-Lenkawicka, Maria Tila	16. 10. 01	Warsaw	housewife
939. Reinman, Laser	03. 06. 14	Lemberg	furrier
940. Reinman-Klein-Ova, Frida	03. 12. 19	Viliki	housewife
941. Reinman, Felicien	17. 12. 42	Ixelles	none
942. Glasz, Max	18. 04. 15	Vienna	furrier
943. Birnbaum, Abraham	13. 02. 07	Sazajah	quilt-maker
944. Birnbaum-Karmazyn, Tauba	23. 02. 11	Lodz	quilt-maker
945. Gross, Siegried	26. 09. 99	Kroznska	decorator
946. Gross-Gumpert, Liesbeth	14. 06. 02	Berlin	shorthand-typist
947. Rotschild, Wilhelm Israel	30. 12. 11	Gross-Armstadt	furworker
948. Dankewitz, Mojzesz Salomon	04. 04. 03	Krakow	businessman
949. Altbregin, Michel	May 1885	Polaska	carpenter
950. Altbregin, Wolf Vulp	04. 09. 13	Gangavspuls	leather-worker
951. Weinberger, Gustav (XXI)	06. 01. 06	Vienna	butcher
952. Reichgott, Rita (XXI-11)	07. 11. 11	Zurich	secretary

02. 03. 43

953. Szpiro, Bruchla	03. 05. 04	Warsaw	furworker
954. Stökl, Friedel	31. 07. 21	Vienna	furrier
955. Schimanowicz, Adolphe	22. 10. 99	Lodz	fitter
956. Schimanowicz-Kiper, Chana Gitla	21. 11. 00	Tomaszow	tailor
957. Schimanowicz, Bertha	08. 04. 38	Marcinelle	none
958. Kranz-Gerstel, Dessa	14. 09. 77	Mrelecz	none
959. Storch-Kranz, Marie	23. 02. 05	Rzeszow	housewife
960. Storch, Ernestine	14. 09. 36	Vienna	schoolboy
961. Blacherman, Abraham	20. 11. 95	Yanow	tailor
962. Blacherman-Sapenck, Ruchla	25. 04. 95	Lomarcz	tailor
963. Blacherman, Fradlia	03. 11. 27	Etterbeek	tailor
964. Rath, Adolf Leon	16. 11. 79	Kolowice	businessman
965. Lewkowicz, Philip	14. 01. 08	Lodz	furworker
966. Lewkowicz, Albert	27. 05. 30	Antwerp	schoolboy
967. Lewkowicz, Isidore	14. 04. 36	Antwerp	schoolboy
968. Lipschutz-Kalischer, Szajndel Anna	11. 09. 56	Krakow	none
969. Freudenfeld, Aron	28. 08. 97	Tarnow	ironer
970. Freudenfeld-Gastwirth, Fania	03. 02. 07	Pilzno	housewife
971. Freudenfeld, Axel	03. 10. 40	Bevel	none
972. Flam, Icek	19. 04. 94	Piotrkow	baker
973. Flam-Roth, Adela	30. 05. 98	Ouaryckow	housewife
974. Flam, Amalie	28. 03. 23	Cologne	schoolgirl
975. Blioger, Sura-Marianne	06. 02. 02	Czestochowa	tailor
976. Rozenblum, Zelman Joseph	08. 04. 96	Warsaw	clockmaker
977. Eckert, Osias	23. 03. 93	Vienna	linen-sewer
978. Herz-Wachtel, Dina Perl	06. 11. 90	Tarnow	housewife
979. Scharf-Wachtel, Helene Chaja	18. 10. 98	Tarnow	housewife
980. Proner-Roth-Knohl, Adela	14. 12. 07	Toporow	linen-sewer
981. Schiller, Julius	08. 09. 98	Frankf. a. M.	butcher
982. Löwenwirth, Samuel	19. 05. 13	Loze	tailor
983. Löwenwirth-Dronzek, Eva	01. 05. 14	Antwerp	tailor
984. Löwenwirth, Ruth	30. 12. 41	Brussels	none
985. Gutman-Gerstl, Rosa	13. 04. 99	Zurich	housewife
986. Gutman, Anenka Adelaide	17. 02. 24	Würzburg	artist
987. Gutman, Charlotte Sonia	26. 05. 30	Brussels	schoolgirl
988. Gurtman, Josefina	26. 08. 40	Brussels	none
989. Kudisch, Abraham	26. 10. 05	Wolance	knitter
990. Kudisch-Wenig, Bindla	12. 05. 11	Dobromil	knitter
991. Kudisch, Philip	29. 10. 42	Brussels	none
992. Steinberger, Aurel	24. 11. 01	Satu Mare	field-worker
993. Steinberger-Holldener, Rosalia	14. 12. 05	Kivyadz	housewife
994. Steinberger, Jacques	20. 10. 31	La Louvière	schoolboy
995. Steinberger, Maurice	31. 05. 33	Etterbeek	schoolboy

#	Name	Date	Place	Occupation
996.	Steinberger, Robert	02. 07. 36	Laeken	schoolboy
997.	Steinberger, Henriette	19. 05. 40	Brussels	none
998.	Rapaport, Franz	01. 11. 95	Bern	ironer
999.	Wolff-Baum, Elvira	02. 04. 10	Bausendorf	housewife
1000.	Wolff, Jacqueline	15. 03. 33	Luxembourg	schoolgirl
1001.	Leiberg, Konrad	24. 06. 94	Warsaw	nurse
1002.	Leiberg-Hoffmann, Anna	02. 03. 91	Caernowitsch	milliner
1003.	Silberstein, Jecheskel (xxv-5)	03. 06. 12	Krakow	furrier
1004.	Brauner, Simon (xxiii-5)	25. 04. 86	Sandomitz	cap-maker
1005.	Neumann, Zita	15. 02. 22	Berlin	milliner
1006.	Schüller, Meyer	15. 03. 10	Cologne	—maker
1007.	Pawloicz, Szaja	20. 12. 16	Warta	food technician
1008.	Raichert-Strang, Reizla	Aug. 97	Zdunska Vola	needlewoman
1009.	Russek, Zalman	08. 02. 92	Kalisz	furworker
1010.	Russek-Bielinska, Brana	1894	Turok	tailor
1011.	Russek, Lejb	23. 06. 22	Kalisz	furworker
1012.	Russek, Henoch David Henri	17. 03. 25	Kalisz	fur-sewer
1013.	Russek, Priwa	19. 11. 32	Kalisz	schoolboy
1014.	Wajngart, Aron	11. 07. 16	Warsaw	cardboard worker
1015.	Wajngart-Liberman, Estera	10. 10. 12	Warsaw	housewife
1016.	Katz, Arno	10. 02. 99	Bunda	natural healer
1017.	Katz-Ransenberg, Jenny	10. 06. 92	Holxer	housewife
1018.	Neufeld, Marie Mela	23. 11. 19	Berlin	saleswoman
1019.	Siekierska-Bihman, Sara	07. 01. 99	Cetatoa-Alba	tailor
1020.	Gerstl-Neumann, Rosa	04. 01. 89	Vienna	housewife
1021.	Gerstl, Adolf	03. 06. 26	Vienna	barber
1022.	Markus, Egon Israel	05. 03. 22	Berlin	glazier
1023.	Weiss, Karl	18. 11. 04	Berlin	clerk
1024.	Weiss-Lipschütz, Bertha	06. 08. 99	Frankf. a. M.	housewife
1025.	Fischer, Moritz	13. 03. 81	Gemet Szolgyen	businessman
1026	Fischer-Herzka, Ella	12. 03. 88	Vienna	housewife
1027.	Hammer, Schaye Hersch (xxvi-2)	04. 04. 97	Lodz	accountant
1028.	Hammer-Glücksmann, Lina Charl.	03. 11. 03	Berlin	housewife
1029.	Kurgan, Samuel	13. 09. 03	Wilna	engineer
1030.	Wiesenfeld, Marken	04. 11. 19	Berlin	furrier

05. 03. 43

#	Name	Date	Place	Occupation
1031.	Strauss, Paul Israel	09. 08. 79	Nuremberg	businessman
1032.	Urstein, Leibusch	30. 05. 79	Petrikau	none
1033.	Sternefeld-Van Kreveld, Rosa	18. 09. 63	Goude	none
1034.	Szwentarski, Israel Szmul	28. 11. 86	Lodz	travelling salesman
1035.	Gorlicki-Grinbaum, Chana Maya	03. 03. 03	Chnichnik	tailor
1036.	Nadel, Hersch	25. 04. 98	Neu Sandez	upholsterer
1037.	Daszkal-Weisz, Pepi	19.03. 97	Witko	housewife
1038.	Daszkal, Edith	19. 08. 23	Satu Mare	tailor
1039.	Brisk, Hermann	26. 03. 79	Poltsama	businessman

1040. Anysch, Samuel	29. 12. 11	Dresden	electrician
1041. Minder, Julius	30. 12. 93	Plugie	storekeeper
1042. Stolar-Rabinowitz, Sara Beila	28. 08. 77	Schtokmanshoff	none
1043. Cop-Radziwiller, Chaja	15. 12. 78	Brody	housewife
1044. Tessler-Briljantchik, Paulina	13. 05. 06	Brody	housewife
1045. Teszler, Rachel	19. 03. 31	Antwerp	schoolgirl
1046. Teszler, David	19. 05. 34	Antwerp	schoolboy
1047. Teszler, Silvia Gisela	26. 11 35	Antwerp	schoolgirl
1048. Blanes-de Vries, Saartje	15. 11. 80	Vianen	housewife
1049. Streep, Hartog	24. 11. 70	Amsterdam	none
1050. Streep, Jacob	16. 03. 75	Amsterdam	none
1051. Streep-Voorzanger, Roosje	19. 02. 68	Amsterdam	none
1052. Halmans, David	24. 09. 82	Amsterdam	diamond-sawer
1053. Weinreb, Israel	1874	Baranowo	none
1054. Weinreb-Rosenblith, Etla	1875	Kopki	none
1055. Melzer-Biegeleisen, Esther	20. 01. 68	Kolbuszowa	none
1056. Ryb, David	08. 02. 83	Krzyweza	none
1057. Ryb-Kraut, Blima	1888	Sokolow	none
1058. Berler, Wilhelm	18. 04. 18	Meselocanti	student

06. 03. 43

1059. Waldberg, Berthold (xxiv)	25. 02. 16	Vienna	tailor
1060. Klausner, Leopold (xxiv)	06. 05. 08	Vienna	cutter
1061. Blockerman, Benjamin	27. 11. 97	Jano Podlowska	tailor
1062. Goldberg-Szmulewicz, Cylka	12. 12. 07	Kalisz	tailor
1063. Prowizor, Chaim	31. 03. 95	Tarnow	tailor
1064. Frenkiel, David	23. 01. 08	Tomqozow	waiter
1065. Bresler, Kopel	04. 03. 71	Delatin	none
1066. Reischer, Eric	02. 04. 25	Vienna	mechanic
1067. [blank]			
1068. De Saegher-Neumann, Herta Sara	15. 07. 20	Frankf. a. M.	tailor
1069. Abramowicz, Hermann	08. 08. 13	Vienna	goldsmith
1070. Abramowicz-Steckel, Martha	04. 01. 18	Vienna	milliner
1071. Abramowicz, Freddy	23. 01. 38	Vienna	none
1072. Steckel, Betty	01. 02. 20	Vienna	housewife
1073. Steckel, Gitta	06. 02. 39	Vienna	none
1074. Brod-Lufer, Frida	03. 09. 21	Berlin	seamstress
1075. Schönheim, Rudolf	31. 10. 92	Bleicherode	businessman
1076. Feldman, Abraham	08. 06. 93	Przemyse	leather-worker
1077. Feldman-Rotman, Mariem	14. 05. 88	Usteryki	leather-worker
1078. Schussel-Grunhut-Kanfer, Mancia	28. 07. 97	Jazlowice	tailor
1079. Levi, Hananel Henri	24. 12. 10	Salonique	car mechanic

08. 03. 43

1080. Sapcaru, Jozef Herman	27. 04. 07	Galatz	building engineer

1081. Sapcaru-Ellmann, Similia	30. 08. 10	Galatz	tailor
1082. Mendel, Günther	02. 07. 19	Düsseldorf	furrier
1083. Bergman, Israel Jajne	16. 06. 03	Lodz	leather-worker
1084. Bergman-Fajerman, Sosza	31. 08. 05	Czestochowa	housewife
1085. Szafir, Joel (xxii)	29. 07. 89	Warsaw	electrician
1086. Podgorz, Pinkas	12. 04. 05	Baligrod	furrier
1087. Kurs, Markus Jozef	27. 04. 96	Sokal	tailor
1088. Kurs-Kaul, Sisel Jenty	03. 04. 94	Sokal	tailor
1089. Potasinski, Moszek Abraham	29. 08. 03	Kzias-Wielki	tailor
1090. Potasinski-Wajslic, Emilia	27. 03. 14	Warsaw	tailor
1091. Finkelszteijn, Israel David	23. 12. 04	Warsaw	furrier
1092. Reif, Chaim	09. 12. 03	Babin	travelling salesman
1093. Mikanovska, Mirla	21. 08. 91	Warsaw	tailor
1094. Wachsberg-Sobelmann, Renata	17. 01. 80	Leipzig	none

10. 03. 43

1095. Naparstek, Szymon	1879	Chjainy	tailor
1096. Naparstek-Sale, Rywka Rojza	1888	Sochaczow	cook
1097. Miller, Chil Jacob	30. 11. 95	Ghodisk	leather-worker
1098. Miller, Elsa	14. 04. 23	Lasgendresge	seamstress
1099. Korenberg, Dora	09. 04. 29	Zswierncie	leather-worker

11. 03. 43

1100. Szwiercewski, Szmul	22. 09. 08	Zelow	cobbler
1101. Jakubowicz, Chana Tauba	12. 05. 95	Lodz	housewife
1102. Markowicz, Paula Iska	02. 04. 09	Zdunska	furworker
1103. Markowicz, Maria Paula	05. 08. 26	Liège	schoolgirl
1104. Markowicz, Esther	1904	Zdunska Wola	furworker
1105. Friszman-Szrajber, Tauba	22. 02. 03	Edunaba	tailor
1106. Surovetchi, Meer	07. 08. 01	Crioms-Ozera	travelling salesman
1107. Dimidschstein, Michel	08. 04. 92	Ksenetz	tailor
1108. Damidschstein-Zylberman, Gienendla	21. 05. 95	Sandomierz	housewife
1109. Rotsztein-Wajcblum, Chaja	10. 05. 09	Opatow	seamstress
1110. Blumenfeld-Wajcblum, Chaja	10. 05. 09	Opatow	furworker
1111. Slezingher, Wolf	15. 03. 80	Aichinoff	pharmacist-chemist
1112. Slezingher-Reitich, Sofia	04. 05. 84	Aichineff	housewife
1113. Kheifetz-Moguilevitch, Dina	15. 03. 79	Tchimobyl	none
1114. Curvicius, Peisachas	19. 01. 01	Koshedary	teacher
1115. Curvicius-Kheifetz, Sara	27. 07. 03	Ekaterinaslaw	housewife
1116. Danziger, Theresia	23. 12. 08	Wajdacaka	tailor
1117. Flaschtaz-Aronsohn, Dichla	10. 3. 01	Sawolki	housewife
1118. Lachman, Aron	19. 11. 98	Sulejow	tailor
1119. Flaschtaz, Henri	18. 10. 27	Antwerp	student
1120. Flaschtaz, Suzanne	24. 06. 35	Antwerp	none
1121. Frankfort, Jonas	19. 04. 82	Amsterdam	none

1122. Frankfurt-Philips, Clara	27. 08. 84	Amsterdam	housewife
1123. Frankfort, Lehman	18. 11. 27	Amsterdam	schoolboy
1124. Jakubowicz-Rozencwajg, Liba-Golda	23. 03. 12	Stopnica	tailor
1125. Swaap, Abraham	23. 01. 03	Amsterdam	diamond-grinder
1126. Biederberg-Weissberg, Rywka	23. 05. 07	Ruda Breniecka	seamstress
1127. Biederberg, Anna	21. 07. 41	Antwerp	none
1128. Elsas, Emmanuel	25. 01. 31	Antwerp	schoolboy
1129. Wolf-Cassuto, Mirjam	02. 04. 73	Amsterdam	none
1130. Keizer, Isaac	15. 07. 97	Antwerp	none
1131. Hilsberg, Moszek Chil	15. 03. 95	Warsaw	tie—
1132. Hilsberg-Rotblat, Perla	05. 03. 92	Warsaw	housewife
1133. Altmann-Hofstaedter, Marjem	12. 04. 06	Wiesbaden	housewife
1134. Altmann, Heinz	13. 09. 33	Wiesbaden	schoolboy
1135. Mittelman, Louis	03. 06. 15	Lodz	building technician
1136. Rosenberg, Mendel (xxi)	01. 07. 20	Pelanzi	tailor
1137. Abraham, Abraham	15. 06. 96	Pilsno	businessman
1138. Abraham-Chamajdes, Adela	14. 11. 05	Drhobycz	housewife
1139. Abraham, Arthur	13. 05. 42	St Gilles	none

12. 03. 43

1140. Widawski, Jakob	13. 02. 01	Nowo Miasto	shirt-tailor
1141. Widawski-Zarzewski, Sura	18. 09. 00	Lodz	shirt seamstress
1142. Widawski, Dina	27. 08. 27	Lodz	shorthand-typist
1143. Marbach-Halm, Perl Rosa	21. 01. 95	Wijnita	cook
1144. Friedmann, Régine div. Heimann	23. 11. 03	Podroloczyska	assistant
1145. Glotzer, Kiwe	15. 01. 14	Bursztijn	—maker
1146. Gnazik, Elias	25. 04. 95	Kalisz	tailor
1147. Reig, Leib	28. 05. 10	Kalisz	furworker
1148. Reig-Landskroner, Berta	04. 03. 22	Vienna	tailor
1149. Szmulewicz, Ajzyk	05. 05. 10	Kalisz	tailor
1150. Szmulewicz-Trajman, Perla	04. 01. 15	Bletzin	tailor
1151. Kraus, Rudolf	03. 08. 97	Berlin	bank official
1152. Wolkenfeld, Lily	27. 08. 22	Mor Ostrawa	tailor
1153. Castegnier-Weinreb, Isabella	02. 11. 19	Frankf. a. M.	housewife
1154. Dym, Schabse	15. 05. 99	Liska	businessman
1155. Perkal, Wigdor Henoch (xxv-1)	23. 01. 06	Nowo Minsk	insurance agent
1156. Sann, Chaja	09. 01. 98	Rzeszow	none
1157. Fuchs, Kurt (xxi)	07. 05. 23	Vienna	cobbler
1158. Fuchs, Johanna	28. 05. 26	Vienna	needlewoman
1159. Dutke, Arnold (xx11a)	21. 10. 21	Vienna	radio technician
1160. Judelowitz-Feuermann, Ester	04. 05. 94	Kolomea	needlewoman
1161. Judelowitz, Helene	16. 08. 32	Berlin	schoolboy
1162. Ochs-Preiss, Debora	15. 06. 80	Barbosow	housewife
1163. Roth, Elias Samuel	07. 12. 06	Tyrowa Wolaska	temple singer
1164. Roth-Ochs, Bina	14. 07. 11	Zbarow	accountant

1165. Roth, Sarah	04. 12. 37	Vienna	none
1166. Roth, Josef	08. 04. 40	Antw.-Berchem	none
1167. Roth, Rebekka	21. 08. 42	Antw.-Borgerhout	none
1168. Steinreich-Henig, Ruchel	16. 02. 09	Bochnis	housewife
1169. Steinreich, Ruth	10. 07. 34	Antwerp	schoolgirl
1170. Steinreich, Sophie	06. 08. 37	Antwerp	none
1171. Steinreich, Marc	15. 03. 40	Antwerp	none
1172. Lerner-Steinreich, Marie	21. 07. 99	Wisniczby Bochnis	seamstress
1173. Lerner, Sophie	07. 05. 28	Frankf. a. M.	schoolboy
1174. Lerner, Gusti	21. 07. 30	Frankf. a. M.	schoolgirl
1175. Wynberg-Lessing, Esther	26. 03. 80	Amsterdam	seamstress
1176. Henig-Lewy, Chaja	10. 07. 76	Bochnis	housewife
1177. Laub-Henig, Brucha	01. 09. 04	Bochnis	office clerk
1178. Laub, Marcel	07. 06. 31	Antwerp	schoolboy
1179. Laub, Noemie	14. 09. 36	Antwerp	none
1180. Kichelmacher, Szymon	02. 02. 01	Osmolica	diamond-worker
1181. Kichelmacher-Sobel, Laja Dwora	15. 01. 01	Lublin	housewife
1182. Kichelmacher, Jehuda-Lejb	11. 10. 26	Warsaw	student
1183. Kichelmacher, David	15. 12. 32	Antwerp	schoolboy
1184. Stern-Brotman, Majer	06. 09. 79	Krakow	housewife
1185. Stern, Sali	09. 02. 11	Vienna	tailor

13. 03. 42

1186. Jelen, Chil Mayer	25. 05. 90	Bdonie	businessman
1187. Jelen-Goldberg, Perla	12. 11. 91	Grodsisk	housewife
1188. Klajnzynger-Jelen, Gitla	11. 05. 20	Warsaw	shorthand-typist
1189. Jelen, Mala	10. 10. 26	Warsaw	tailor
1190. Wald-Mansklajd, Ruchla	28. 05. 18	Warsaw	hairdresser
1191. Kryksman, Gedelja Szlama	29. 05. 18	Ruda Guswoska	tailor

16. 03. 43

1192. Mayer, Jakob (xxi)	31. 07. 05	Frankf. a. M.	businessman
1193. Mayer-Fischbein, Frieda	12. 01. 11	Kiev	bank clerk
1194. Heuberg, Samuel	06. 03. 02	Nielec	furrier
1195. Heuberg-Dobschütz, Laura	20. 09. 03	Juroslaw	tailor
1196. Heuberg, Sylvia	24. 01. 32	Brussels	schoolgirl
1197. Haber, Anna	12. 12. 23	Altona	tailor
1198. Eisenstab, Louis	15. 03. 30	Brussels	schoolboy
1199. Ryback-Sylberberg, Elka	Oct. 84	Warsaw	housewife
1200. Birnbaum, Itta	1898	Czestochowa	tailor
1201. Seiler-Pensel, Sara Rebecca	16. 09. 77	Sochaczew	housewife
1202. Teitel, Abraham (xxiii-6)	15. 09. 19	Berlin	tailor
1203. von Wassermann, Robert Siegfried	08. 01. 97	Berlin	businessman
1204. Johr, Sally	16. 04. 82	Lopsens	none

1205. Johr-Krakauer, Margarethe	22. 02. 91	Thorn	housewife
1206. Körnacker-Sobotki, Ruth	12. 04. 04	Elberfeld	saleswoman
1207. Lehrer, Michael	19. 04. 98	Jassy	businessman
1208. Rubin, Leon Robert (XXIII-21)	13. 02. 06	Lille	driver
1209. Beiline, Alfred (XXI)	08. 02. 24	Neufchâtel	manual worker

17. 03. 43

1210. Steinberg, Israel	14. 07. 90	Wilno	tailor
1211. Rosenstraub, Eisig (XXIV-20)	21. 12. 90	Belatyn	tailor
1212. Steiner-Kolbuszowar, Hermine	04. 03. 08	Vienna	milliner
1213. Raychman, Michael (XXIIA)	22. 07. 93	Warsaw	sales representative
1214. Raychman-Spitz, Rence (XXIIA)	27. 07. 01	Vienna	housewife
1215. Keller, Moses	03. 09. 93	Rzeszow	diamond-cleaver
1216. Keller, Rachel	20. 06. 28	Antwerp	schoolgirl
1217. Lachin, Michel	01. 09. 80	St Petersburg	none
1218. Loszynski-Abraham, Hansshen	02. 09. 87	Posen	housewife
1219. Sztabzyb, Ajzyk David	22. 02. 12	Warsaw	travelling salesman
1220. Sztabzyb-Szklarowicz, Freyda	01. 04. 11	Wilno	tailor
1221. Sztabzyb, Isidore-Isaac	15. 01. 39	Brussels	none
1222. Siederer-Wachheiser, Stella (XXI)	19. 11. 08	Vienna	housewife
1223. Stawicki, Ichel Wolf	01. 05. 96	Leczyca	tailor
1224. Tawicki-Szopp, Regina	12. 07. 91	Radzmaco	tailor
1225. Igalson, Itta	29. 01. 96	Warsaw	none
1226. Igalson, Maurice	30. 10. 30	Brussels	schoolboy
1227. Keisman, Jankiel (XXIII-11)	23. 07. 99	Lowicz	businessman
1228. Jakobowicz, Josef	05. 08. 76	Zdunska-Wola	none
1229. Doxtorczyk-Igalson, Machla	25. 02. 99	Warsaw	slipper-maker
1230. Doxtorczyk, Basia	06. 10. 30	Etterbeek	schoolgirl
1231. Rosenbaum, Max	11. 06. 82	Schlehtern	businessman
1232. Rosenbaum-Plaut, Dina	03. 03. 78	Lutter	none
1233. Gronowsky-Kaplan, Chana	10. 12. 02	Jurbarkas	tailor
1234. Gronowsky, Simon	12. 10. 31	Uccle	schoolboy

19. 03. 43

1235. Polak, Jonas	12. 01. 18	Amsterdam	textile factory director
1236. Bremer-Bremer, Sofia	27. 06. 19	Amsterdam	doctor's assistant
1237. Bremer, Karin Bianca Irène	06. 01. 41	Amsterdam	none
1238. Thaler, Samuel	15. 06. 66	Mielce	none
1239. Kaiser, Sally	18. 07. 72	Priekhofen	none
1240. Kaiser-Sternberg, Elise	12. 09. 66	Westerberg	none
1241. Spinner, Salomon	26. 07. 61	Talbow	none
1242. Spinner-Peczenik, Henriette	10. 05. 65	Tarnopol	none
1243. Linhart, Eliasz	01. 04. 03	Sambor	hatter
1244. Linhart-Meisel, Cyla	20. 11. 10	Botromil	housewife
1245. Linhart, Rosa	07. 05. 39	Antwerp	none

1246. Meisel-Blauer, Marie	26. 01. 03	Vienna	housewife
1247. Freund-Frechter, Ruchla	1903	Bokacz	housewife
1248. Freund, Helene Regine	16. 10. 33	Antwerp	schoolgirl
1249. Hartog, Josephine	22. 05. 90	Moorsel	saleswoman
1250. Engel, Mojzes	23. 12. 04	—	shoemaker
1251. Engel-Grunberger, Helena	30. 12. 04	Zapson	housewife
1252. Engel, Armin	29. 01. 40	Antwerp	none
1253. Engel, Samuel	17. 01. 42	Antwerp	none
1254. Mandel recta Kwadrat, Jacques	26. 11. 24	Antwerp	carpenter
1255. Rozenfeld, Esthera	05. 04. 04	Dunska Wola	housewife
1256. Bok, Rachel	27. 08. 30	Blankenberghe	schoolgirl
1257. Schneider, Helene	27. 10. 00	Krakow	diamond-cleaver
1258. Schneider, Elsa Eva	01. 03. 15	Caya	none
1259. Thaler-Sztejnfeld, Esther	20. 07. 95	Warsaw	housewife
1260. Kaminski, Chaskiel (XXIII-13)	23. 05. 18	Rensin	businessman
1261. Steigler-Monassohn, Manscia	20. 09. 86	Petrograd	housewife
1262. Steigler, Rachel	12. 09. 20	Berlin	teacher
1263. Böhm, Max (XXI)	10. 07. 22	Cologne	electrician
1264. Weichselbaum, Nachman	20. 12. 71	Rubaczow	none
1265. Gross, Israel	04. 04. 97	Padworno	furrier
1266. Kneppel-Taub, Basche	18. 07. 97	—	tailor

20. 03. 43

1267. Osterreicher, Robert	21. 01. 12	—	cook
1268. Behr, Lucien	04. 10. 69	Neuviller	rabbi
1269. Behr-Hoenel, Julie	24. 06. 71	Minversheim	housewife
1270. Edelstein, Szlama	20. 04. 91	Warsaw	businessman
1271. Gans-Heissfeld, Margarete Sara	24. 06. 87	Sassin	piano teacher
1272. Goldner-Klein, Risa	15. 07. 90	Vienna	housewife
1273. Ehrlich, Berek	20. 04. 98	Radoszyck	leather-worker
1274. Ehrlich-Lipski, Laja	27. 01. 04	Lodz	leather-worker
1275. Erlich, Wolf Willy	12. 07. 29	Anderlecht	schoolboy
1276. Heffner, Naftali (XXIV-15)	27. 04. 11	Dubiecko	tailor
1277. Srebnik, Lejzor Icek (XXI)	20. 06. 10	Biedlice	cobbler
1278. Braun, Adolf (XXI)	26. 05. 94	Klingenthal	businessman
1279. Marjenberg, Refuel	28. 11. 03	Warsaw	leather-worker
1280. Marjenberg-Mlodek, Ruchla (XXI)	10. 03. 03	Michon	tailor
1281. Marienberg, Moise (Maurice)	19. 06. 05	Warsaw	leather-worker
1282. Marienberg-Marienberg, Elba	28. 09. 03	Warsaw	leather-worker
1283. Korenberg, Jankiel	03. 09. 06	Zawiezce	butcher
1284. Keppich-Feldman, Rozalia	03. 08. 10	Satu Mare	tailor
1285. Bilsky, Max	09. 01. 80	Kilusov	tailor
1286. Bilsky-Kutner, Ella Marja	23. 07. 90	Lodz	tailor
1287. Devries, Georges	10. 01. 76	Roermond	none
1288. Da Costa da Fonseca, Jacobus	11. 07. 78	Amsterdam	diamond-grinder

1289. Da Costa da Fonseca-Kapper, Jantje	29. 06. 84	Amsterdam	housewife
1290. Kernadel-Falk, Simone	05. 01. 12	Warsaw	tailor
1291. Lindner-Kanner, Feiga	06. 12. 72	Lanout	none
1292. Mandel-Deutsch, Rosalia	08. 11. 00	Baia Mare	housewife
1293. Mandel, Bela	29. 03. 28	Baia Mare	schoolboy

24. 03. 43

1294. Mandel, Albert	23. 12. 29	Antwerp	schoolboy
1295. Mandel, Elisabeth	03. 08. 33	Antwerp	schoolgirl
1296. Katz-Deutsch, Regina	02. 07. 09	Carasca	housewife
1297. Katz, Lilly	20. 01. 32	Antwerp	schoolgirl
1298. Feldman, Maurice	02. 06. 76	Satu Mare	tailor
1299. Feldman-Grünfeld, Hanny	02. 07. 78	Satu Mare	housewife
1300. Feldman, Oscar	03. 04. 16	Satu Mare	tailor
1301. Brodtmann-Segal, Hanny	13. 05. 98	Spandau	shorthand-typist

27. 03. 43

1302. Regutkowicz, Berck Janiel	04. 01. 05	Ryki	shoemaker
1303. Regutkowicz-Majster, Dwojra	04. 12. 11	Rypin	shoe-worker
1304. Mytnowiecki-Skop, Sura	12. 12. 06	Dobrzyn	rubber coat gluer
1305. Riksenpan, Ruchela Rachel	15. 01. 05	Apsa-Vysni	rubber coat gluer
1306. Szriftgieser-Brill, Eva Hava	30. 09. 98	Kischinow	tailor
1307. Kornblum-Szwarcfuter, Rywfka	14. 01. 08	Konskie	housewife
1308. Sadokrzycki-Pik, Ilena	15. 12. 04	Zdunska Wola	seamstress
1309. Moos-Sondheimer, Therese	18. 08. 74	Zell a. Mosel	none
1310. Sondheimer, Amalia	19. 11. 75	Zell a. Mosel	none

30. 03. 43

1311. Koschminski, Erwin Martin	09. 12. 14	Berlin	teacher
1312. Koschminski-Gensaite, Frieda	18. 08. 11	Kolotek	housewife
1313. Zonszajn, Abraham (xxi)	02. 11. 24	Warsaw	tailor
1314. Grauwels, Jakob	25. 12. 24	Warsaw	student
1315. Belfer, Lejb	29. 12. 96	Pinczow	bootmaker
1316. Belfer-Belfer, Hina	13. 01. 89	Pinczow	housewife
1317. Ilzycer, Icchok	28. 03. 99	Warsaw	French polisher
1318. Ilzycer-Dembrowska, Pesa Chaja	28. 12. 05	Warsaw	housewife
1319. Ilzycer, Mina	30. 06. 28	Brussels	schoolgirl
1320. Gopenajk, Mindla	18. 01. 00	Konskowale	tailor
1321. Weleman, Zymel	27. 05. 02	Blatzki	leather-cutter
1322. Weleman-Ejdelman, Chaja	20. 05. 06	Tomascow	tailor
1323. Brenner, Leiser	04. 05. 89	Phiona	lace-maker
1324. Mangot-Halfgot, Ryfla Ruchla	1868	Nowy Dwor	none
1325. Jutkowic, Rosa	23. 12. 25	Bedwla	furrier
1326. Neubart, Joseph	22. 02. 83	Tarnow	businessman
1327. Neubart-Puretz, Henna	06. 01. 87	Przeczow	housewife
1328. Pisk, Paul	25. 12. 91	Vienna	businessman

1329. Finkelstein, Friedrich	04. 07. 83	Stanislau	businessman
1330. Finkelstein-Finkelstein, Amalie	13. 07. 90	Stanislau	housewife
1331. Fischer-Finkelstein, Klara	09. 09. 12	Stanislau	housewife

02. 04. 43

1332. Rosenbaum-Lichtenstein, Margaretha	13. 01. 92	Frankf. a. M.	none
1333. Werkendam-Leeda, Bertha	10. 01. 74	Amsterdam	none
1334. Blimbaum, Sacha	27. 12. 24	Leipzig	furrier
1335. Bos, Marcel	04. 11. 85	Amsterdam	diamond-cleaver
1336. Bos-Werkendam, Judith	21. 06. 91	Amsterdam	housewife
1337. Bos, Mary	12. 01. 28	Antwerp	schoolgirl
1338. Kesner, Salomon	20. 05. 77	Amsterdam	diamond-grinder
1339. Schaap-Schaap, Keetje	21. 09. 68	Amsterdam	none
1340. Metzelaar, Jacob	10. 01. 88	Amsterdam	diamond-grinder
1341. Metzelaar-Schaap, Evelina	26. 08. 93	Amsterdam	housewife
1342. Gruber, Abraham	09. 12. 78	Mastrywielki	sales representative
1343. Frederikstadt-De Vries, Rachel	25. 01. 93	Amsterdam	tailor
1344. Frederikstadt, Rebecca	18. 04. 30	Amsterdam	none
1345. Schaap, Lea	07. 05. 89	Amsterdam	none
1346. de Smit-de Wolf, Heintje	17. 10. 56	Amsterdam	none
1347. Melchior, René (xxiiA)	20. 01. 89	Brussels	—
1348. Molnar-Singer, Paula	28. 08. 04	Vienna	housewife
1349. Singer, Ernst	30. 03. 15	Vienna	salesman
1350. Grosman, Leyer (xxiv)	02. 03. 07	Warsaw	diamond-cutter
1351. Konarski-Frankfrski, Malka	02. 04. 05	Szestochowa	tailor
1352. Konarski, Severin	10. 05. 31	Antwerp	schoolboy
1353. Kummer-Götzler, Else	25. 01. 00	Frankf. a. M.	housewife
1354. Berger-Perlman-ova, Frieda	08. 11. 04	Mukscevo	tailor
1355. Berger, Jacques	28. 12. 32	Antwerp	schoolboy
1356. Rosenvaser-Rozenberg, Hermina	14. 11. 11	Fuciumi	seamstress
1357. Rosenvaser, Willy	24. 07. 41	Antwerp	none
1358. Rosevaser, Renée	26. 11. 42	Antwerp	none
1359. Rucker, Mina	29. 12. 89	Wionisca	none

03. 04. 43

1360. Fischel, Abraham	04. 08. 21	Antwerp	pastry-cook
1361. Zylberberg, Szoel Haim	14. 12. 96	Radom	door-to-door salesman
1362. Mitelsbach, Nuchim Nathan	15. 01. 07	Warsaw	businessman
1363. Mitelsbach-Berry,	14. 06. 09	Bedzin	housewife
1364. Fink, Hirsch Moses (xxvi-8)	09. 04. 03	Pikelovka	ironer
1365. Winter, Naftali	28. 10. 86	Tarnow	goldsmith
1366. Cyngiser, Israel Jacob	24. 08. 04	Krasnick	shoemaker
1367. Zloto-Szterenlicht, Necha	01. 08. 11	Warsaw	housewife
1368. Lewenkron-Anuszewicz, Sura Fajga	05. 07. 95	Warsaw	housewife

1369.	Wolman, Icek Moszek	28. 04. 06	Wyczogrod	cutter
1370.	Lokcinski-Rotenberg, Anna	23. 07. 01	Lodz	tailor
1371.	Kriksman, Szrul	21. 12. 04	Grodzak	tailor
1372.	Schaffman, Chaim	12. 03. 94	Kichineff	tailor
1373.	Jablonski-Rosenstein, Dyna (XXIIA)	20. 05. 20	Lask	nurse
1374.	Lieder-Keller, Breindel	11. 09. 83	Krakow	housewife
1375.	Belfer, Ruth	30. 10. 30	(Poland)	schoolgirl
1376.	Ryfenholc, Icek	04. 06. 95	Warsaw	leather-worker
1377.	Ryfenholc-Kleniec, Ruchla	11. 11. 95	Warsaw	seamstress
1378.	Ryfenholc, Albert	27. 11. 30	Brussels	schoolboy
1379.	Weberman, Symche	05. 01. 09	Lyszyce	knitter
1380.	Bloder, Abraham	19. 12. 12	Warsaw	tailor
1381.	Tabakman, Meher (XXIII-17)	03. 09. 12	Siedlec	shoe-cutter
1382.	Swiercs, Maurice	17. 11. 99	Brataczowice	carpenter
1383.	Swiercs-Galeck, Rachel Ruchla	10. 05. 97	Warsaw	housewife
1384.	Bainvol, Leibus	15. 01. 87	Surkowice	leather-worker
1385.	Bainvol-Schwartzberg, Esther	1888	Plotzk	housewife
1386.	Isaac-Plotke, Ida	15. 08. 97	Berlin	milliner

07. 04. 43

1387.	Sztokman, Paltyl	13. 10. 05	Bututow	hatter
1388.	Sztokman-Mydlek, Estera	06. 06. 04	Kutno	housewife
1389.	Sztokman, Aron	03. 01. 42	Schaerbeek	none
1390.	Apteker-Rotter, Anna	26. 11. 68	Ottynia	none
1391.	Apteker, Nathan	03. 01. 95	Kolomen	cook
1392.	Apteker-Goldmann, Editha-Helena	23. 11. 02	Harburg	tailor
1393.	Apteker, Lisette	16. 09. 30	Harburg	schoolgirl
1394.	Apteker, Suzanne	06. 11. 34	Antwerp	schoolgirl
1395.	Apteker, Charles	13. 10. 41	Brussels	none
1396.	Millet, Isidor	24. 12. 85	Lemberg	paperer
1397.	Millet-Buk, Sali	09. 03. 98	Liwowve	housewife
1398.	Finger-Cohen, Ida	24. 05. 88	Oberhausen	tailor
1399.	Finger, Ignaz	25. 05. 14	Gladbach	tailor
1400.	Meyer-Cahn, Rosa	04. 02. 89	Mühlheim	seamstress
1401.	Silbermann, Max Israel	01. 04. 06	Wilhelmshafen	decorator
1402.	Silbermann-Walter, Liselotte	24. 05. 16	Bonn	tailor
1403.	Weiss, Oscar	15. 08. 97	Baden b. Wien	cook
1404.	Weiss-Wilner, Bertha	07. 05. 99	Vienna	shorthand-typist
1405.	Rzepkowicz, Szmul	23. 08. 17	Lodz	interpreter
1406.	Mühlbauer, Isidor (XXI)	23. 04. 09	Lvov	furworker
1407.	Kahn, Rudolf	07. 11. 00	Warsaw	sales representative
1408.	Ultmann, Hilda	04. 10. 20	Vienna	tailor
1409.	Eisler-Strausz, Fanny	01. 01. 79	Lopasso	none
1410.	Weiserbs-Rozenbaum, Marie	03. 06. 96	Warsaw	seamstress
1411.	Neumann-Fuchs, Rosa	08. 05. 00	Vienna	housewife

1412. Grünbaum, Ester	29. 08. 16	Warsaw	corset seamstress
1413. Grynbaum, Udla	14. 07. 04	Przedborg	housekeeper
1414. Kupferminc, Lajbus	04. 08. 89	Przedborg	tailor
1415. Kupferminc-Kupferminc, Sara	15. 07. 89	Przedborg	seamstress
1416. Kutnowski-Kupferminc, Anna	10. 08. 14	Przedborg	furworker
1417. Kupferminc, Aron Mordka	16. 07. 12	Przedborg	tailor
1418. Kupferminc-Ajzenfisz, Chawa	21. 09. 10	Minsk Mazowich	housewife
1419. Kupferminc, Hilda	05. 06. 39	Anderlecht	none
1420. Heller, Heinrich	07. 03. 12	Vienna	fitter
1421. Heller-Holländer, Marie	30. 09. 14	Vienna	housewife
1422. Blumenthal, Willi Josef	23. 03. 94	Berlin	fitter
1423. Posener, Ludwig	09. 04. 26	Berlin	none
1424. Ginsberg, Gerson	07. 05. 01	Wisnicz	sales representative

10. 04. 43

1425. Holländer, Regina	10. 05. 73	Pivniczna	none
1426. Aronsfrau, Leon (xxi)	08. 12. 87	Bochnia	businessman
1427. Aronsfrau-Hollander, Eva	28. 07. 93	Radomysl	housewife
1428. Aronsfrau, Leonore	08. 12. 87	Bochnia	businessman
— (xxi)	08. 09. 20	Dresden	none
1429. Kolski-Graneck, Esthera M.	04. 10. 01	Wielum	housewife
1430. Gothelf, Jakob Josef	05. 10. 04	Babjanice	cutter
1431. Gothelf-Erlich, Brandla	14. 02. 02	Grostechowa	seamstress
1432. Moddel, James (xxi-1279)	22. 05. 04	Berlin	furrier
1433. Moddel-Horowitz, Edith	10. 12. 05	Berlin	housewife
1434. Moddel, Evelina	10. 10. 32	Berlin	schoolgirl
1435. Wiegel, Anna	10. 08. 15	Berlin	seamstress
1436. Epstein, Joseph	03. 12. 01	Warsaw	ladies' tailor
1437. Epstein-Sturm, Marie Jonte	29. 08. 07	Kolbuszowa	craftswoman
1438. Glatt, Salomon	03. 11. 00	Prodzinko	milkman
1439. Glatt-Dancygier, Selda Fajgla	08. 03. 99	.awkorcie	housewife
1440. Glatt-Fliegelman, Anna	17. 12. 25	Duisburg	apprentice tailor
1441. Hercberg, Ruth	16. 05. 31	Duisburg	schoolgirl
1442. Loszyca-Klajman, Bina Mayem	10. 03. 14	Piotrkow	tailor
1443. Poznanski, Szmul Boruch	27. 06. 91	Warsaw	handbag worker
1444. Poznanski-Chlewner, Chaja M.	29. 08. 02	Warsaw	housewife
1445. Bomberg-Birentzveig, Sura L.	16. 07. 04	Warsaw	housewife
1446. Grosskop, Moses	11. 01. 94	Opatow	tailor
1447. Weinberg, Josef	12. 10. 09	Salzburg	teacher
1448. Jauze, Isaac	20. 02. 87	Warsaw	sales representative
1449. Jauze-Rosemberg, Laja	18. 10. 88	Warsaw	housewife
1450. Frydman-Cukier, Chaja (xxiii)	25. 09. 08	Vrzitik	tailor
1451. Dym-Gotzel, Ettel	07. 07. 97	Cieszanow	housewife
1452. Dym, Roza	11. 03. 28	Berlin	schoolgirl
1453. Lipszyc, Fiszel Abram (Felix)	15. 03. 23	Lodz	tailor

1454. Herskovic, Sachla (XXI)	29. 12. 07	Vulchova	tailor
1455. Goldine, Afchic	10. 03. 12	Anderlecht	cutter
1456. Olszyn, Mendel M.	03. 11. 00	Zubrazyn	tailor
1457. Korn, Ira	10. 08. 05	Stanislaw	businessman
1458. [duplication – see 895]			
1459. Bloemgarten-Wesly, Maria Anne	22. 08. 56	Maastricht	none
1460. Bloemgarten, Leonie	05. 04. 86	Maastricht	housewife
1461. Bloemgarten, Victor	23. 03. 92	Maastricht	businessman
1462. Rutgajzer, Israel	03. 02. 04	Uman	musician
1463. Vischraper, Simon	09. 05. 70	Amsterdam	businessman

12. 04. 43

1464. Blumsack, Josef	08. 10. 07	Frankfurt a. M.	lawyer
1465. Lustbader, Markus	11. 09. 05	Novy-Sagz.	tailor
1466. Kastner-Fenger, Mina	13. 08. 91	Berlin	housewife
1467. Fenger, Irmgard	09. 02. 09	Berlin	nurse
1468. Jellinek, Samuel	19. 02. 84	Eiwonitz	tailor
1469. Jellinek-Neubroch, Karla Charlotte	04. 8. 79	Vele	housewife
1470. Justman, Henoch	28. 09. 02	Lodz	leather-worker
1471. Justman-Albek, Chaja	29. 07. 26	Warsaw	seamstress
1472. Lachman, Berck	09. 10. 90	Lodz	tailor
1473. Lachman, Michel Ichok	25. 07. 26	Lodz	tailor
1474. Lajzerowicz, Jochene Luzer	10. 05. 97	Kowal	tailor
1475. Lajzerowicz-Charenzowska, Hendla	1895	Lodz	seamstress
1476. Lajzerowicz, Lejb	11. 12. 24	Lodz	tailor
1477. Magier, Schlama	15. 03. 96	Bendzin	tailor
1478. Magier-Abramovicz, Sura	20. 04. 94	Bendzin	housewife
1479. Majerowicz, Szlama	18. 04. 93	Konin	leather-worker
1480. Majerowicz-Lancman, Marie	26. 02. 99	Kolo	seamstress
1481. Masiewicki, Aron	25. 04. 05	Warsaw	butcher
1482. Masiewicki-Rotter, Chaja Fajda	14. 03. 04	Warsaw	tailor
1483. Masiewicki, Benjamin	15. 09. 31	Brussels	schoolboy
1484. Masiewicki, David	12. 11. 37	Brussels	schoolboy
1485. Mazelman, Mordka	05. 03. 89	Warsaw	leather-worker
1486. Mazelman, Mojsze Ichok	03. 11. 22	Warsaw	leather-worker
1487. Mazelman, Fanni Fajga	28. 03. 28	Warsaw	schoolboy
1488. Moskowicz, Tobias	30. 11. 91	Stawitzyn	tailor
1489. Moskowicz-Klieger, Regine	14. 03. 89	Warsaw	shorthand-typist
1490. Praszkewicz, Jankiel	30. 04. 04	Brzeznica	tailor
1491. Praszkiewicz-Zilberberg, Ita Laja	23. 01. 09	Minsk	housewife
1492. Praszkewicz, Charles	11. 09. 36	Brussels	schoolboy
1493. Schotland, Dina	05. 11. 16	Majdan	tailor
1494. Strauber-Ertenstreich, Schendel R.	26. 05. 98	Abertyn	seamstress
1495. Stern, Abraham	18. 12. 17	Hujcze	furrier

1496. Singer, Isaak	19. 08. 02	Chrzanow	tailor
1497. Singer-Rosenzweig, Rosale	15. 12. 06	Berlin	seamstress
1498. Wolkowicz, Herszel	13. 06. 02	Zdunska-Wola	tailor
1499. Wolkowics-Glucha, Liba Dwojra	17. 08. 01	Zdunska-Wola	tailor
1500. Bacman, David	15. 02. 77	Karlovla	none
1501. Bacman-Ghelfand, Haja	14. 07. 79	Lircova	none

16. 04. 43

1502. Weingast aka Erde, Joel	05. 05. 04	Biala	sales representative
1503. Weingast-Glattstein, Hinda	03. 10. 06	Odessa	tailor
1504. Weingast aka Erde, Georges	29. 05. 31	Antwerp	schoolboy
1505. Weingast aka Erde, Numa	11. 10. 34	Antwerp	schoolboy
1506. Weingast aka Erde, Ruth	10. 01. 39	Antwerp	none
1507. Levee, Hartog	04. 09. 77	Amsterdam	none
1508. Levee-Wolf, Anna	11. 05. 83	Amsterdam	housewife
1509. Halloy-Heidt, Eva (widow Höflich)	21. 12. 89	Frischenich	housewife
1510. Höflich, Jacob (Siegfried 09. 09. 16)	25. 07. 19	Aachen	technician
1511. Wajdenbaum-Fogelgarn, Chana Ita	14. 04. 05	Warsaw	housewife
1512. Wajdenbaum, Joseph	19. 04. 35	Etterbeek	schoolboy
1513. Wajdenbaum, Jacob Wolf	25. 07. 40	Schaerbeek	none
1514. Steinberg, Marjem	14. 07. 20	Tarnow	furworker
1515. Strosberg, Esther Edith	15. 04. 18	Kieler	furworker
1516. Zucker, Moses	13. 01. 71	Krakow	none
1517. Zucker-Hirschberg, Chana	05. 04. 71	Krakow	housewife
1518. Zucker, Hinda	21. 12. 98	Krakow	office clerk
1519. Elbaum-Berlinerblau, Chana	Nov. 85	Warsaw	housewife
1520. Elbaum, Fajwel Rafael	06. 03. 08	Warsaw	clerk
1521. Elbaum, Abram	12. 04. 15	Warsaw	businessman
1522. Rotenberg, Markus	19. 09. 10	Antwerp	diamond-cleaver
1523. Rotenberg-Strosberg, Laja Chana	06. 02. 13	Slupia Nova	fur seamstress
1524. Libersohn recta Klughaupt, Josef	30. 12. 92	Brody	clerk
1525. Liebersohn-r. Klugh.-Dominitz, Anna	08. 01. 91	Prajbatycza	housewife
1526. Krynek, Leon	20. 06. 90	Lodz	businessman
1527. Steil-Meiseles, Elisa	31. 03. 07	Lemberg	housewife
1528. Piepsz-Herschberg, Rifka	1885	Tomaszow	housewife
1529. Klein-Lesczczynski, Laja	13. 10. 98	Kleszow	tailor
1530. Klein, Alfons	08. 06. 32	Antwerp	schoolboy
1531. Cremer-Goldman, Cyrla	15. 07. 04	Chenow	housewife
1532. Cremer, Benni	30. 07. 42	Antwerp	none
1533. Jungst-Wrochawska, Chana	24. 09. 92	Osorkow	housewife
1534. Jungst, Abraham Samuel	17. 01. 24	Zagyrow	none
1535. Kornmehl-Ginzburg, Sipra Alte	07. 01. 84	Eyglice	none
1536. Tenzer, Chaja	11. 12. 12	Prechow	office worker

1537. Wins-Wagenaar, Sophia	24. 06. 56	Amsterdam	none
1538. Wins, Marianne	04. 04. 80	Amsterdam	none
1539. Tencer, Chana Mindel	19. 07. 10	Preclow	milliner
1540. De Coster-De Jong, Bertha	28. 06. 82	Amsterdam	none

17. 04. 43

1541. Trygier-Ber, Hinda	01. 05. 04	Sognawice	tailor
1542. Burak-Lewkowicz, Maria	02. 04. 02	Wielum	housewife
1543. Silberstein, Suzanna	24. 01. 20	Warsaw	shopworker
1544. Konstantinowsky, Samuel	10. 05. 74	Bechtere	businessman
1545. Dylewski, Anna (Rosa Ruda 28. 09. 28)	16. 03. 31	Charleroi	schoolgirl
1546. Dylewski-Grynszpan, Itta	10. 01. 01	Radoszek	housewife
1547. Rusek, Mordche Mendel	17. 02. 69	Lask	none
1548. Jakobs, Moritz	14. 01. 78	Dinslaken	none
1549. Jakobs-Freudenberg, Martha	16. 11. 81	Bochum	housewife
1550. Zechel, Moise	04. 01. 99	Kichineff	dentist
1551. Nozice, Noe	08. 10. 04	Techenz	furworker
1552. Nozice-Lasar, Marthe	01. 04. 07	Anderlecht	housewife
1553. Nozice, Gisèle	12. 02. 33	Chenée	schoolgirl
1554. Nozice, Robert	13. 06. 36	Chenée	schoolboy
1555. Glat-Kalinska, Chana Pera	1899	Lodz	housewife
1556. Glat, Maurice	15. 11. 28	Lodz	schoolboy
1557. Glat, Maier	10. 11. 29	Szomice	schoolboy
1558. Glat, Sara	13. 02. 40	Liège	none
1559. Pikowski, Israel	21. 12. 97	Nikolaief	plumber
1560. Pikowski-Nemarcq, Gabrielle	18. 05. 01	St Wiel	housewife
1561. Pikowski, Olga	11. 07. 23	Bochum	tailor
1562. Goldberg-Reich, Marien Esther	1885	Tarnoczeg	housewife
1563. Goldberg, Chaim	11. 01. 13	Tarnow	door-to-door salesman
1564. Goldberg-Oesterreicher, Ester Etelka	24. 12. 13	Kassa Kosice	tailor
1565. Ajzenstein, Nuchim Chaim	04. 11. 09	Pinsk	electrical engineer
1566. Popper, Otto	17. 08. 71	Prague	none
1567. Popper-Fried, Ida	20. 05. 82	Bondweis	housewife
1568. Kempner-Rozen, Marjam	28. 02. 91	Pabjanice	housewife
1569. Grub, Abram Josek (XXI-825)	18. 07. 11	Drobin	travelling salesman
1570. Grub-Kempner, Brandel	29. 09. 22	Düsseldorf	tailor
1571. Rozen, Alter Jacob	27. 08. 88	Pabjanice	photographer
1572. Gelbtrung, Israel Chaim	30. 11. 03	Warsaw	travelling salesman
1573. Gelbtrung-Rubinstein, Nechrima	13. 09. 02	Wloclawek	milliner
1574. Schwab-Slawkowska, Zlata Lotte	27. 01. 04	Lodz	housewife
1575. Schwab, Margit	10. 11. 27	Halle a. S.	schoolgirl
1576. Schwab, Liliane	22. 12. 29	Halle a. S.	schoolgirl

1577. Wachter, Abraham	01. 11. 83	Rotzmatow	businessman
1578. Wachter-Lichtenstein, Henny Sara	05. 07. 99	Halle a. Saale	housewife
1579. Lichtenstein, Gertrud	04. 05. 03	Halle a. Saale	businesswoman
1580. Goldstein-Davidmann, Regina	15. 04. 05	Vienna	seamstress
1581. Goldstein, Nelly	04. 07. 26	Vienna	fur seamstress
1582. Karminer Mojsek	1892	Kaskowele	none
1583. Karminer-Burej, Hudes	1892	Baranow	housewife
1584. Karminer, Chaja Cywja	24. 01. 25	Lublin	seamstress
1585. Karminer, Frida Fumez	22. 03. 27	Ixelles	schoolgirl
1586. Karminer, Jacques	29. 05. 31	Uccle	schoolboy
1587. Karminer, Maurice	12. 01. 33	St Gilles	schoolboy
1588. Muller-ova, Perl Paula	11. 01. 15	Ganice	none
1589. Markovic-ova, Helena	15. 04. 17	Sovlus	worker
1590. Spirn, Leib	07. 07. 96	Tarnobrzeg	none
1591. Spirn, Esther	04. 03. 29	Berlin	schoolgirl
1592. Spirn, Isaak	02. 02. 32	Berlin	schoolboy
1593. Müller, Marten	12. 01. 03	Ganice	none
1594. Polaczek/Polakow, David	1865	Berziankowice	none
1595. Appel, Juda	05. 05. 97	Toplitze	clerk
1596. Ruthen, Alois	31. 08. 10	Vienna	manual worker
1597. Ruthen-Binstok, Dwojra	11. 05. 08	Lovice	seamstress
1598. Clement-Goldgicht, Golda	10. 12. 23	Warsaw	mechanic
1599. Goldsztaub, Anszel Icek	06. 06. 83	Warsaw	leather-worker
1600. Berlinerblau-Krantz ,Berta Rosa	10. 05. 89	Warsaw	none
1601. Lichtman, Chaim	07. 12. 85	—	—
1602. Einhorn-Lipschütz, Erna	28. 08. 10	Krakow	office worker
1603. Einhorn, Renée	25. 06. 39	Antwerp	none
1604. Einhorn, Maurice	21. 08. 42	Antwerp	none
1605. Mond-Gross, Rosa	17. 12. 91	Zmigrod	housewife
1606. Mond, Aron	01. 10. 92	Zolynia	cutter
1607. Klein, Joseph	21. 05. 13	Pilky	agr. worker
1608. Klein-ova, Irena	16. 02. 18	Komnaty	seamstress
1609. Klein-Rosenberg-ova, Rosalie	29. 06. 10	Anck	housewife
1610. Klein, Lea	16. 10. 36	Antwerp	schoolgirl
1611. Klein, Josef	16. 03. 38	Antwerp	schoolboy
1612. Goldman, Szmul	07. 05. 14	Otwock	furworker
1613. Goldman-Jankelovic, Malka	30. 03. 13	Novoselie	housewife
1614. Goldman, Eva	21. 10. 40	Brussels	none
1615. Goldman, Adam	06. 09. 42	Brussels	none
1616. Beck-Herzig, Karolina	14. 03. 85	Krakow	none
1617. Einhorn-Beck, Sarolta-Sari	05. 07. 18	Eger	housewife
1618. Beck, Regina	29. 03. 06	Duhla	none
2601. Schive, Rakhniel	09. 12. 68	—	—